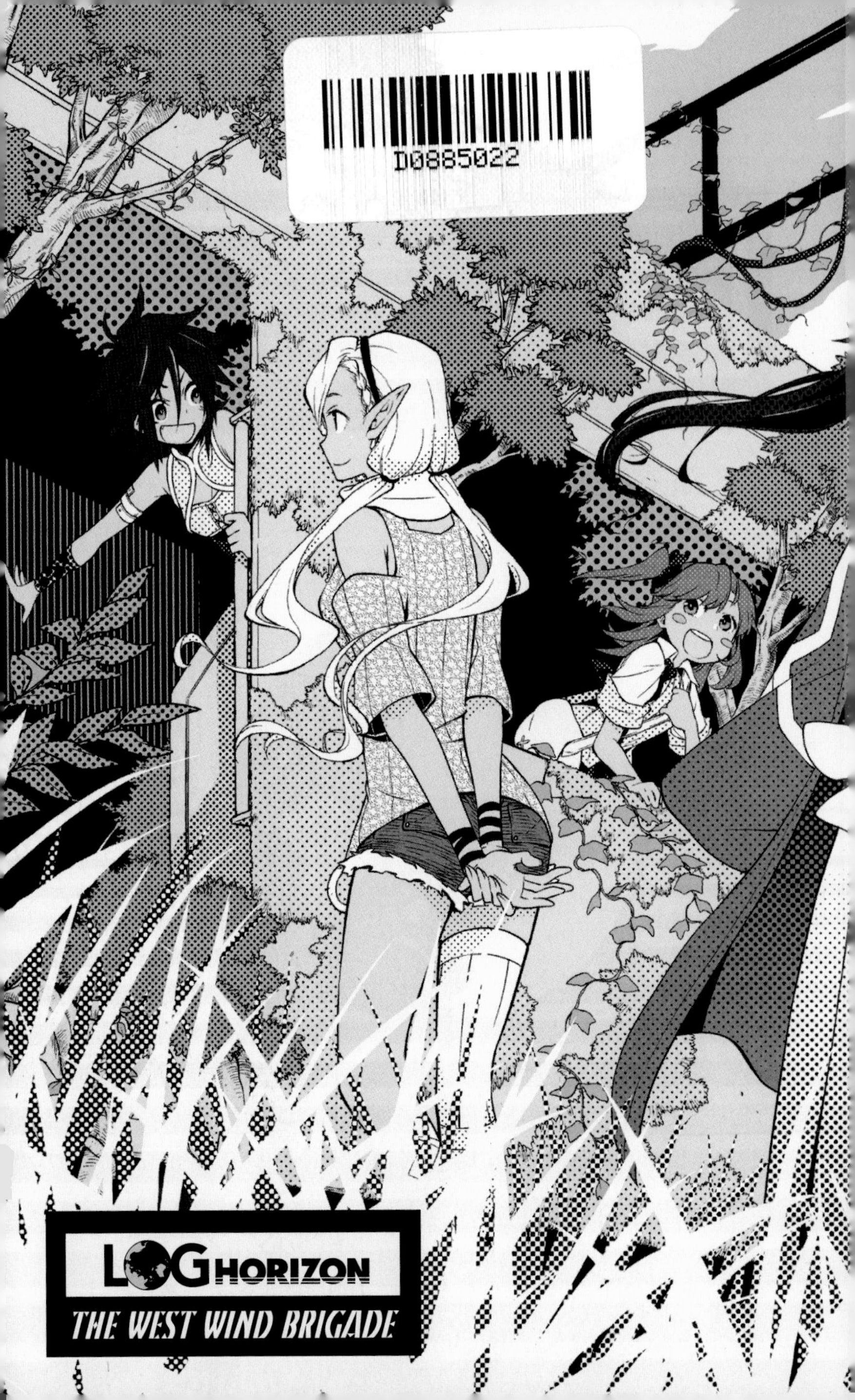
LOG HORIZON
THE WEST WIND BRIGADE

[CONTENTS]

LOG HORIZON **THE WEST WIND BRIGADE** ④

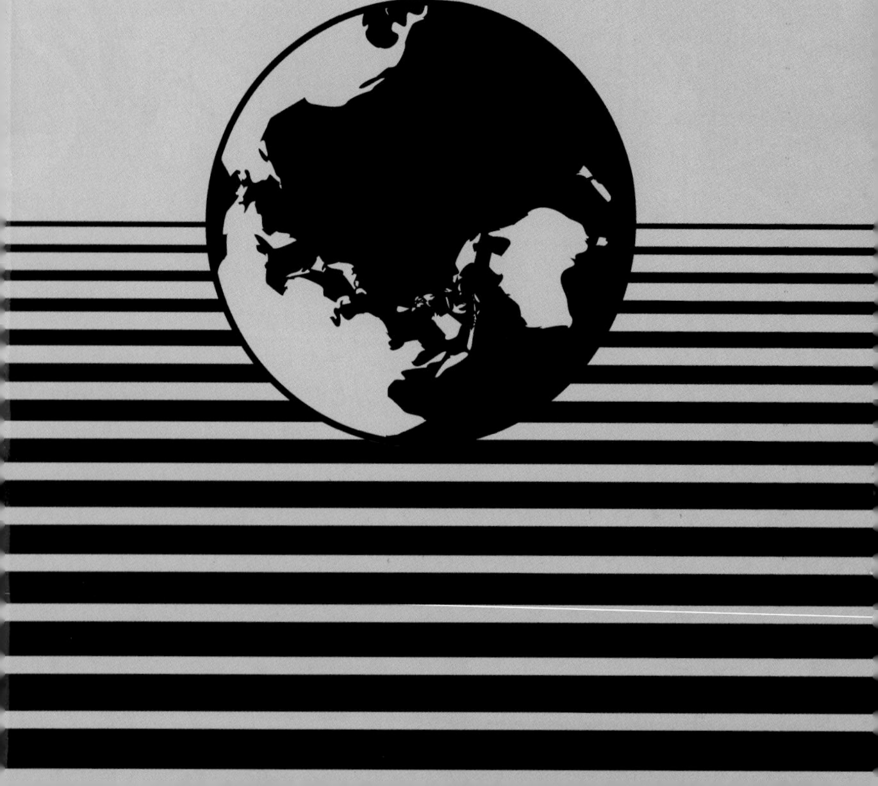

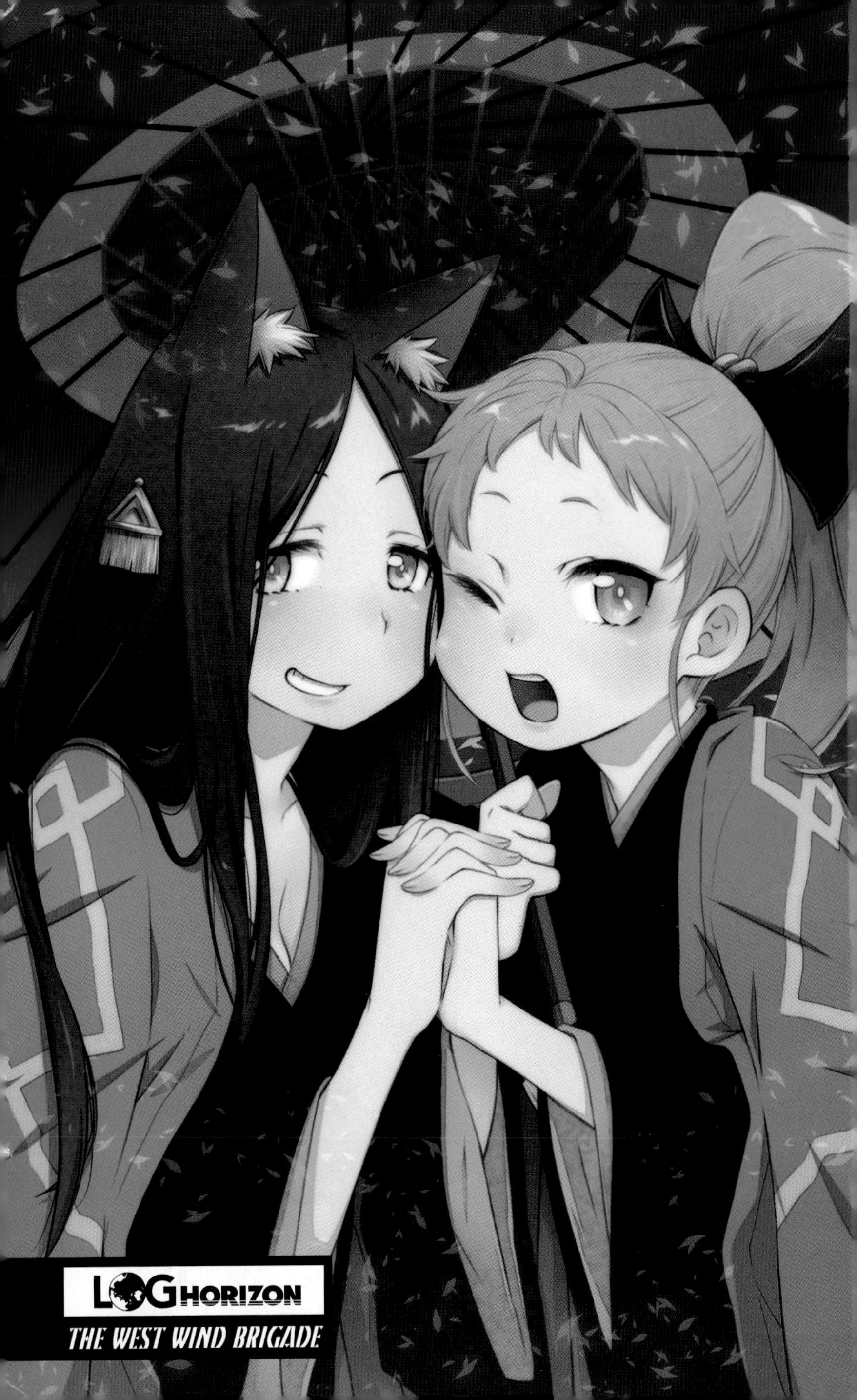
LOG HORIZON
THE WEST WIND BRIGADE

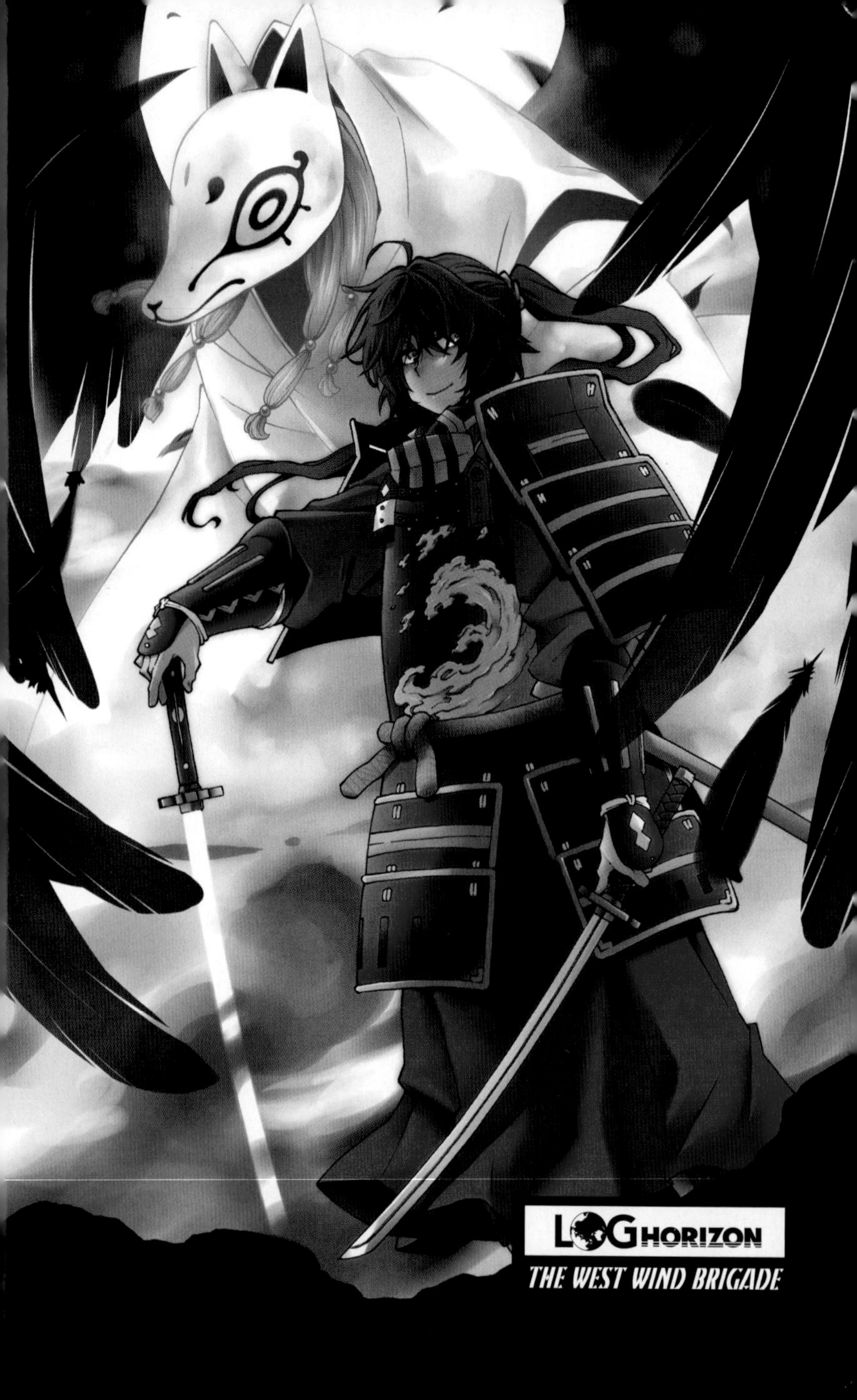
LOG HORIZON
THE WEST WIND BRIGADE

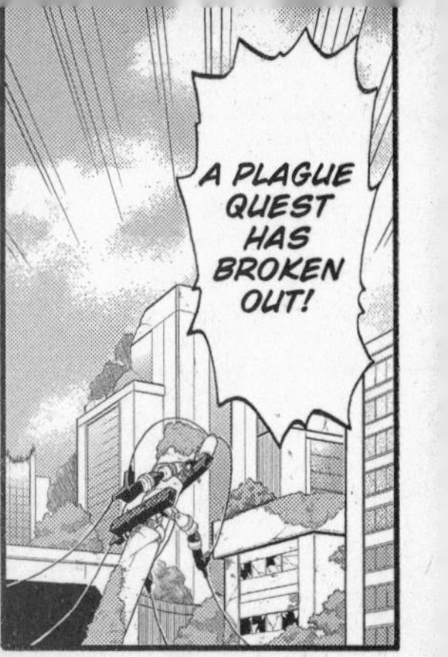
A PLAGUE QUEST HAS BROKEN OUT!

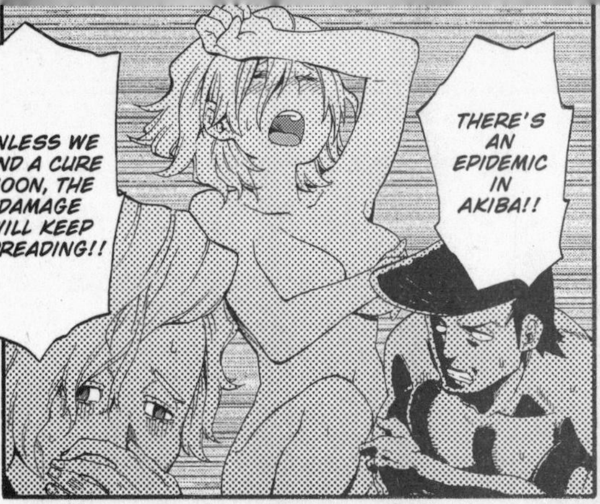
THERE'S AN EPIDEMIC IN AKIBA!!
UNLESS WE FIND A CURE SOON, THE DAMAGE WILL KEEP SPREADING!!

*PLAGUE QUEST
A QUEST THAT BREAKS OUT SUDDENLY. BEING AFFLICTED WITH THE ILLNESS RESULTS IN A VARIETY OF NEGATIVE EFFECTS, INCLUDING LOWERED STATUS. IT CAN'T BE CURED WITH ORDINARY RECOVERY ITEMS. A SPECIFIC REMEDY MUST BE FOUND.

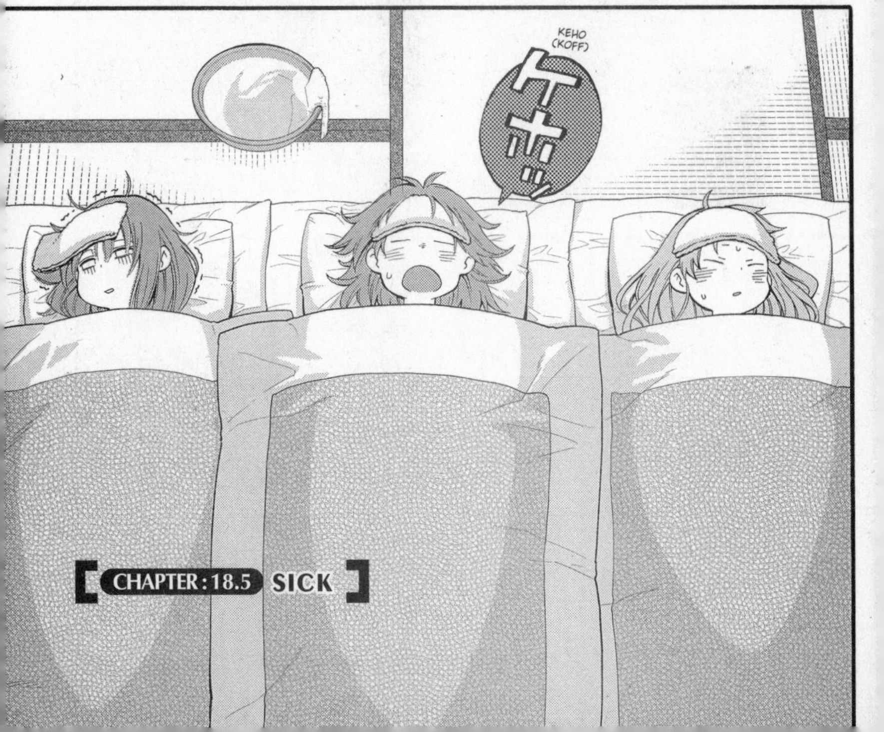
KEHO (KOFF)
[CHAPTER : 18.5 SICK]

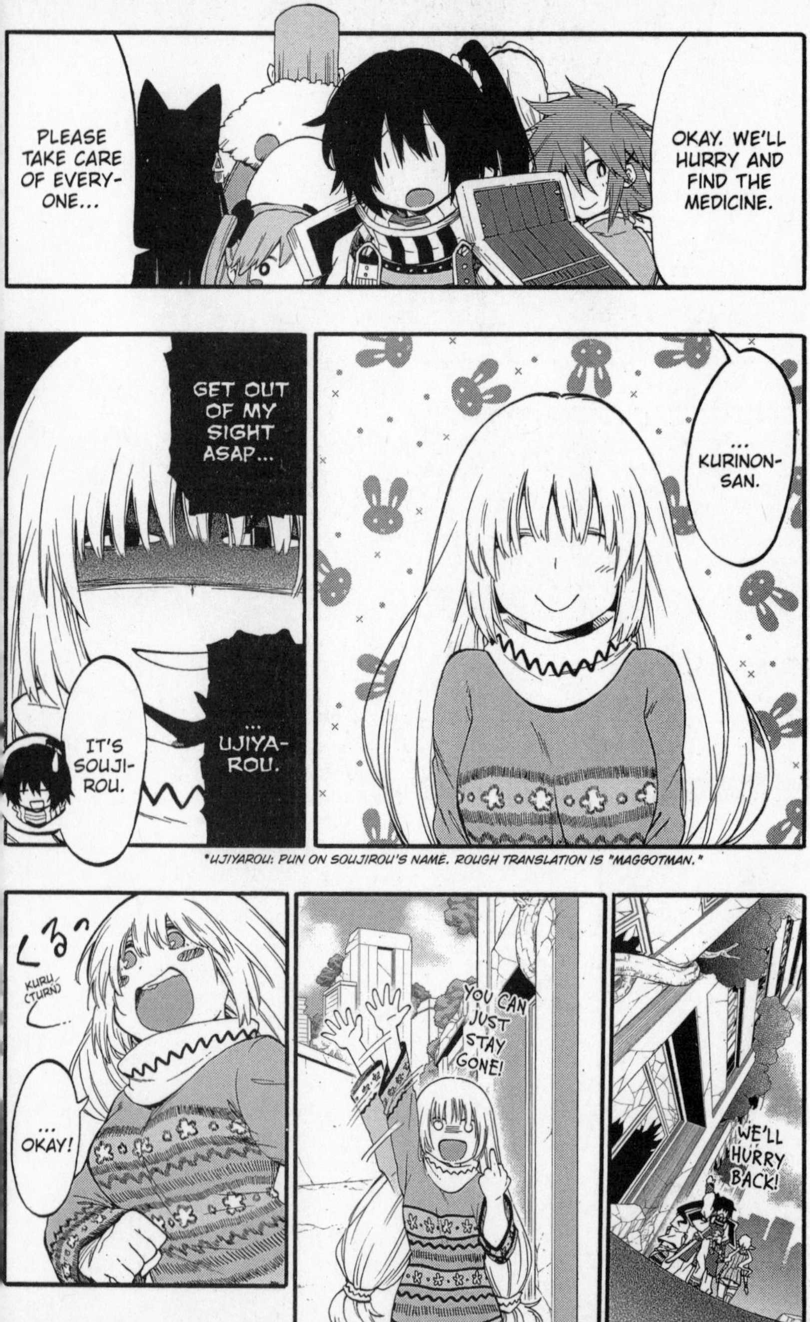
OKAY. WE'LL HURRY AND FIND THE MEDICINE.
PLEASE TAKE CARE OF EVERY-ONE...
... KURINON-SAN.
GET OUT OF MY SIGHT ASAP...
... UJIYA-ROU.
IT'S SOUJI-ROU.
WE'LL HURRY BACK!
YOU CAN JUST STAY GONE!
くるっ
KURU (TURN)
... OKAY!

*UJIYAROU: PUN ON SOUJIROU'S NAME. ROUGH TRANSLATION IS "MAGGOTMAN."

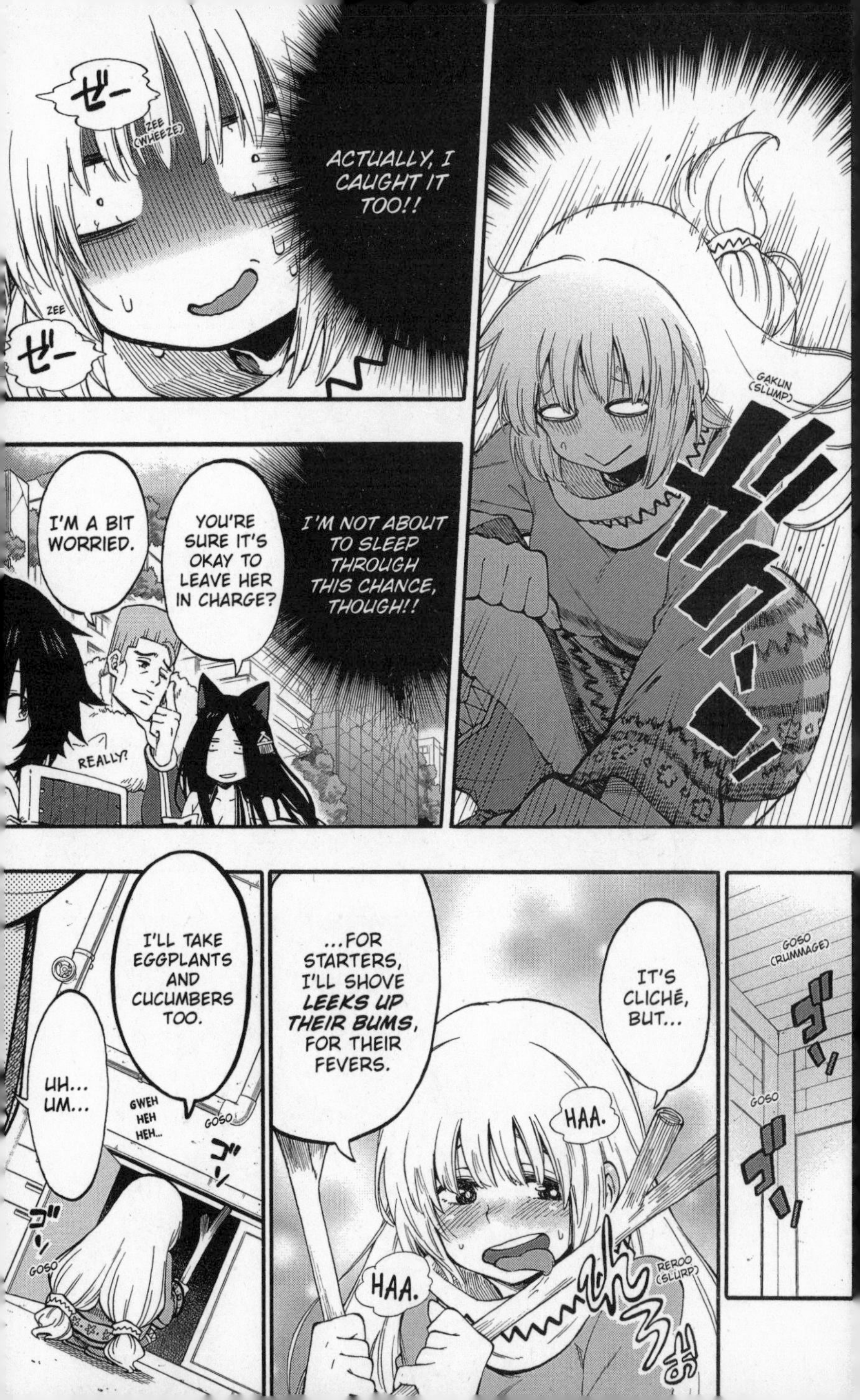
GAKUN (SLUMP)
ゼー
ZEE (WHEEZE)
ACTUALLY, I CAUGHT IT TOO!!
ZEE
ゼー
I'M NOT ABOUT TO SLEEP THROUGH THIS CHANCE, THOUGH!!
YOU'RE SURE IT'S OKAY TO LEAVE HER IN CHARGE?
I'M A BIT WORRIED.
REALLY?
GOSO (RUMMAGE)
GOSO
IT'S CLICHÉ, BUT...
HAA.
...FOR STARTERS, I'LL SHOVE ***LEEKS UP THEIR BUMS***, FOR THEIR FEVERS.
REROO (SLURP)
HAA.
I'LL TAKE EGGPLANTS AND CUCUMBERS TOO.
GWEH HEH HEH...
GOSO
UH... UM...
GOSO

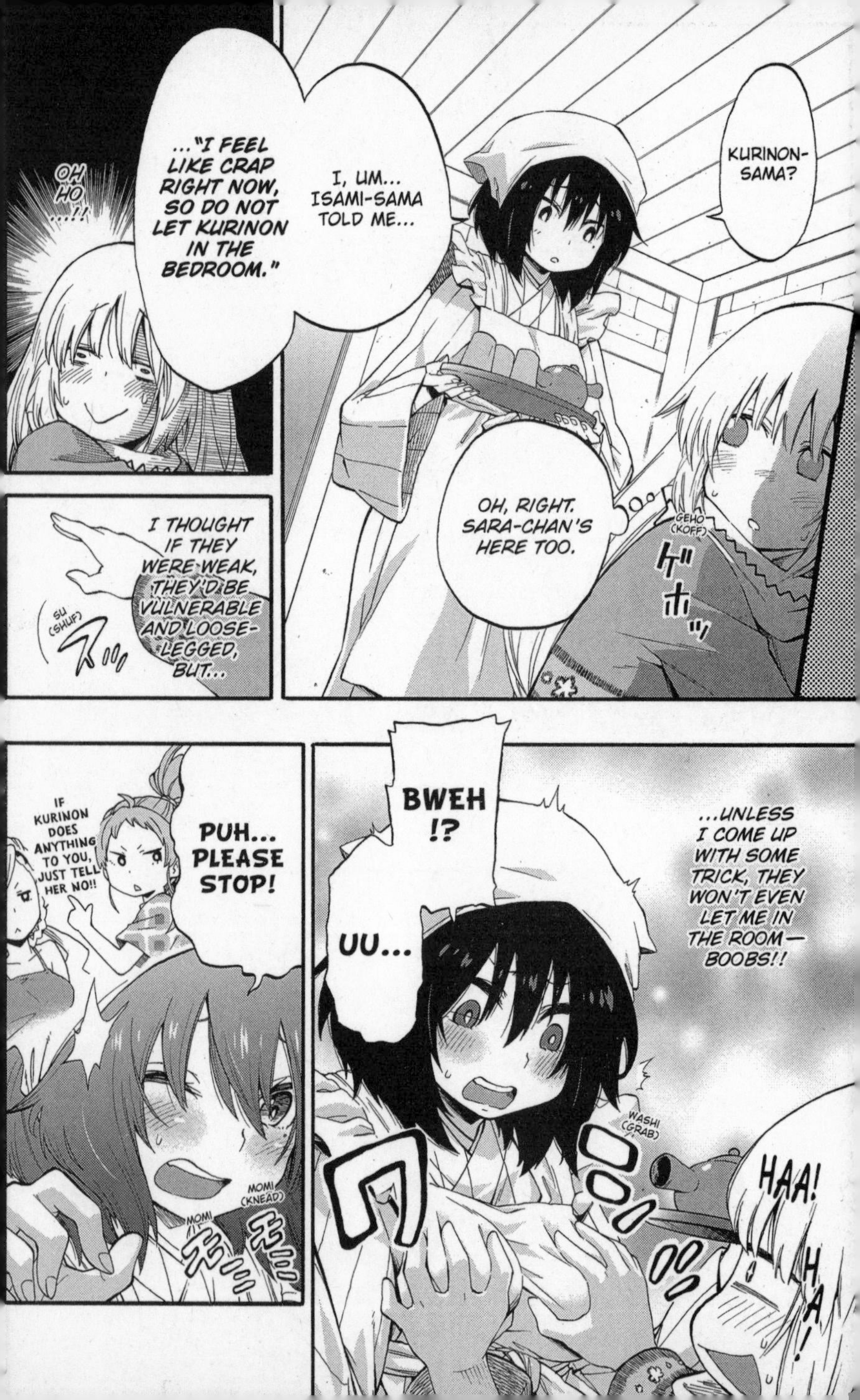
KURINON-SAMA?
I, UM... ISAMI-SAMA TOLD ME...
..."I FEEL LIKE CRAP RIGHT NOW, SO DO NOT LET KURINON IN THE BEDROOM."
OH, RIGHT. SARA-CHAN'S HERE TOO.
GEHO (KOFF)
OH HO...!!
I THOUGHT IF THEY WERE WEAK, THEY'D BE VULNERABLE AND LOOSE-LEGGED, BUT...
SU (SHUF)
...UNLESS I COME UP WITH SOME TRICK, THEY WON'T EVEN LET ME IN THE ROOM—BOOBS!!
BWEH !?
UU...
WASHI (GRAB)
HAA! HA! HA!
PUH... PLEASE STOP!
IF KURINON DOES ANYTHING TO YOU, JUST TELL HER NO!!
MOMI (KNEAD)
MOMI

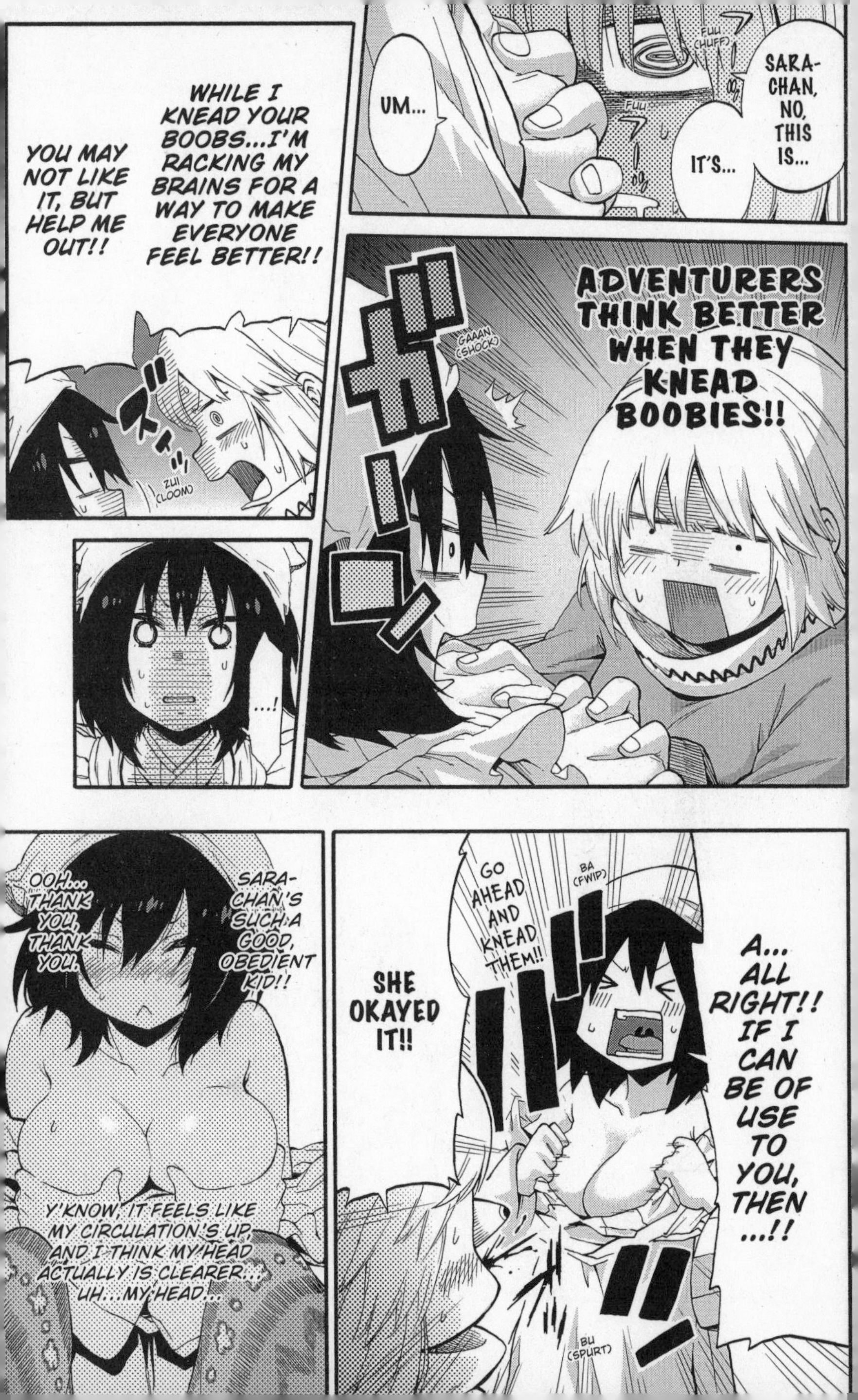
FUU (HUFF)
SARA-CHAN, NO, THIS IS...
IT'S...
FUU
UM...
WHILE I KNEAD YOUR BOOBS...I'M RACKING MY BRAINS FOR A WAY TO MAKE EVERYONE FEEL BETTER!!
YOU MAY NOT LIKE IT, BUT HELP ME OUT!!
ZUI (LOOM)
ADVENTURERS THINK BETTER WHEN THEY KNEAD BOOBIES!!
GAAAN (SHOCK)
...!
A... ALL RIGHT!! IF I CAN BE OF USE TO YOU, THEN ...!!
BA (FWIP)
GO AHEAD AND KNEAD THEM!!
SHE OKAYED IT!!
BU (SPURT)
SARA-CHAN'S SUCH A GOOD, OBEDIENT KID!!
OOH... THANK YOU, THANK YOU.
Y'KNOW, IT FEELS LIKE MY CIRCULATION'S UP, AND I THINK MY HEAD ACTUALLY IS CLEARER... UH...MY HEAD...

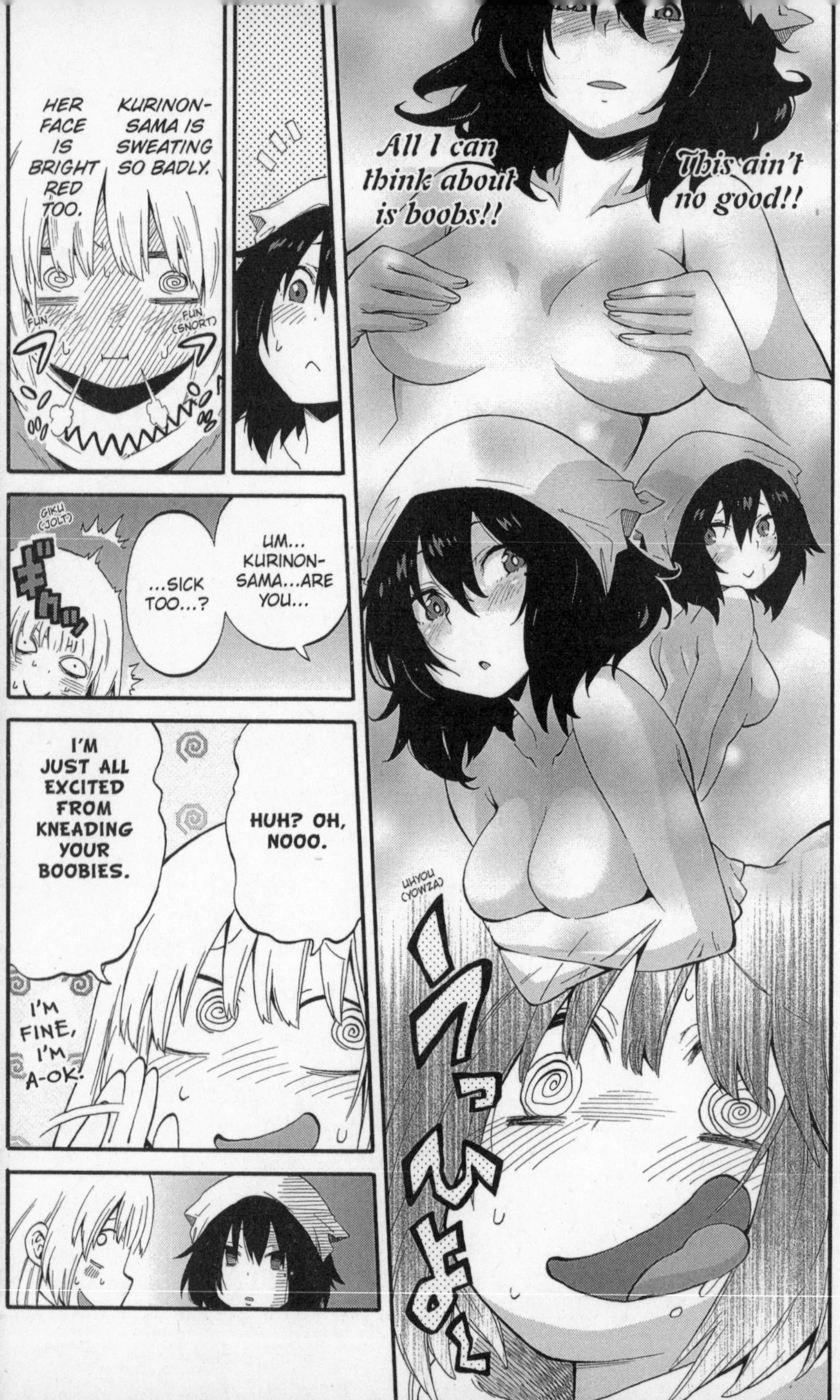
This ain't no good!!
All I can think about is boobs!!
UHYOU (YOWZA)
KURINON-SAMA IS SWEATING SO BADLY.
HER FACE IS BRIGHT RED TOO.
FUN
FUN (SNORT)
UM... KURINON-SAMA...ARE YOU...
...SICK TOO...?
GIKU (JOLT)
HUH? OH, NOOO.
I'M JUST ALL EXCITED FROM KNEADING YOUR BOOBIES.
I'M FINE, I'M A-OK.

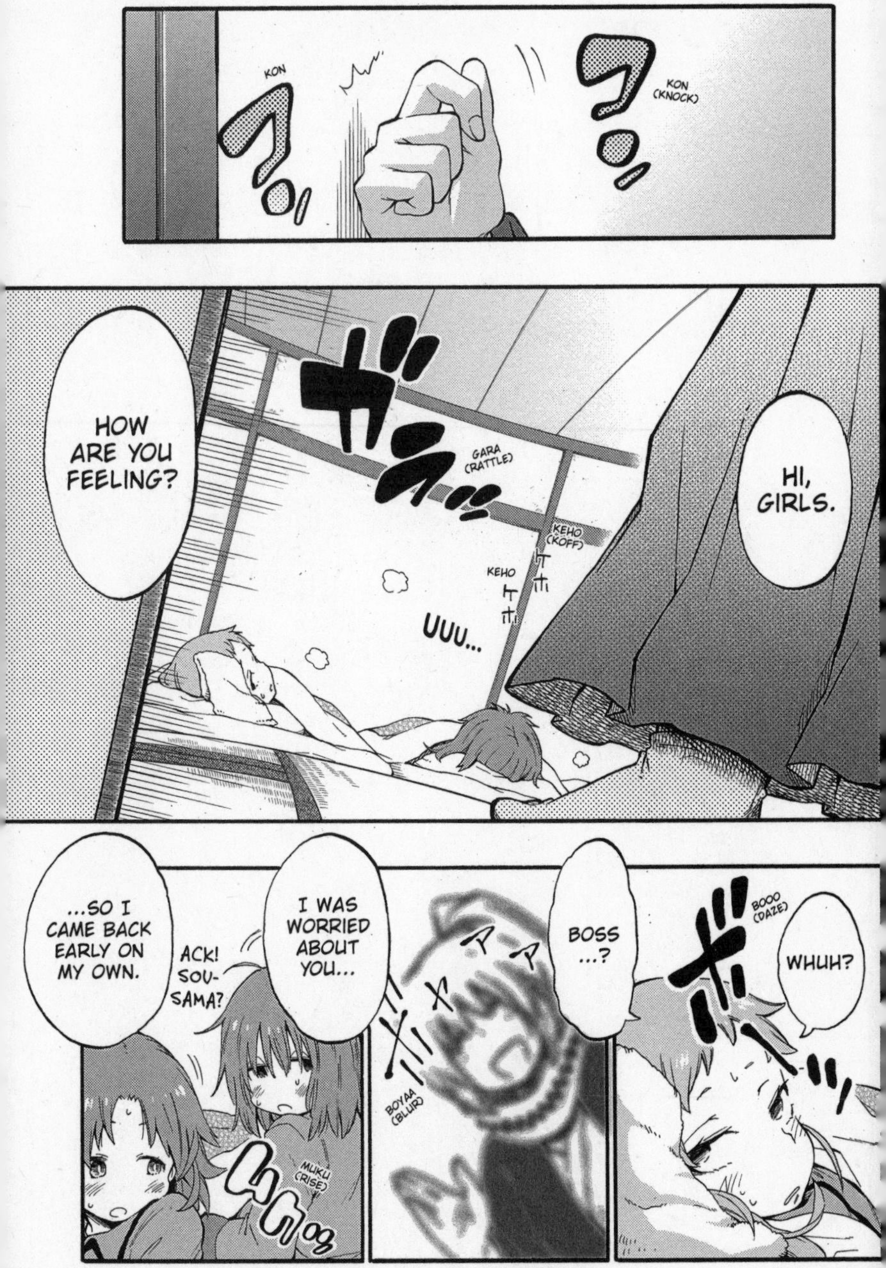
KON (KNOCK)
KON
HI, GIRLS.
GARA (RATTLE)
KEHO (KOFF)
KEHO
UUU...
HOW ARE YOU FEELING?
BOOO (DAZE)
WHUH?
BOSS ...?
BOYAA (BLUR)
I WAS WORRIED ABOUT YOU...
ACK! SOU-SAMA?
...SO I CAME BACK EARLY ON MY OWN.
MUKU (RISE)

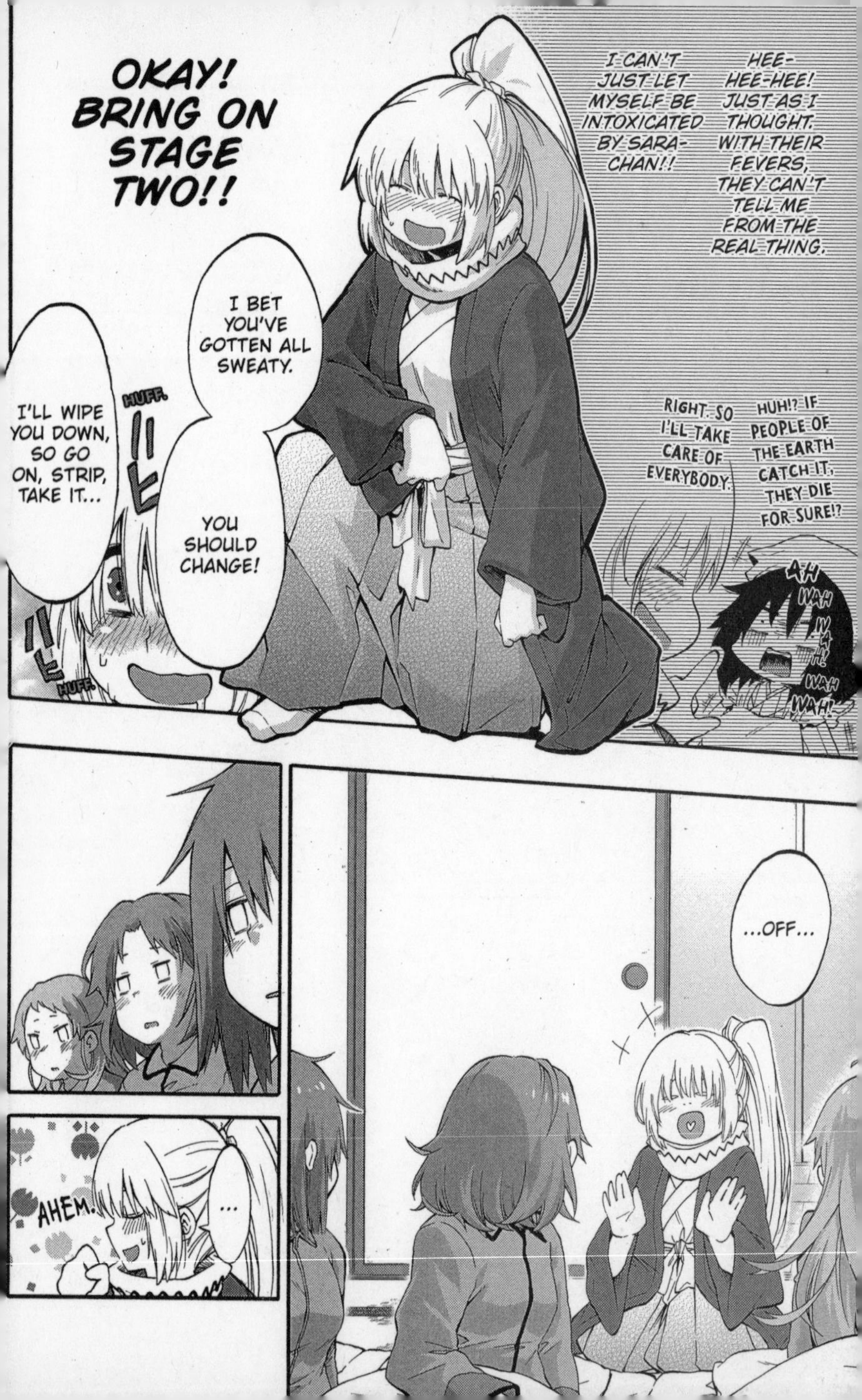
HEE-HEE-HEE! JUST AS I THOUGHT. WITH THEIR FEVERS, THEY CAN'T TELL ME FROM THE REAL THING.
I CAN'T JUST LET MYSELF BE INTOXICATED BY SARA-CHAN!!
OKAY! BRING ON STAGE TWO!!
HUH!? IF PEOPLE OF THE EARTH CATCH IT, THEY DIE FOR SURE!?
RIGHT. SO I'LL TAKE CARE OF EVERYBODY.
AH WAH WAH! WAH WAH!
I BET YOU'VE GOTTEN ALL SWEATY.
YOU SHOULD CHANGE!
HUFF.
I'LL WIPE YOU DOWN, SO GO ON, STRIP, TAKE IT...
HUFF.
...OFF...
...
AHEM.

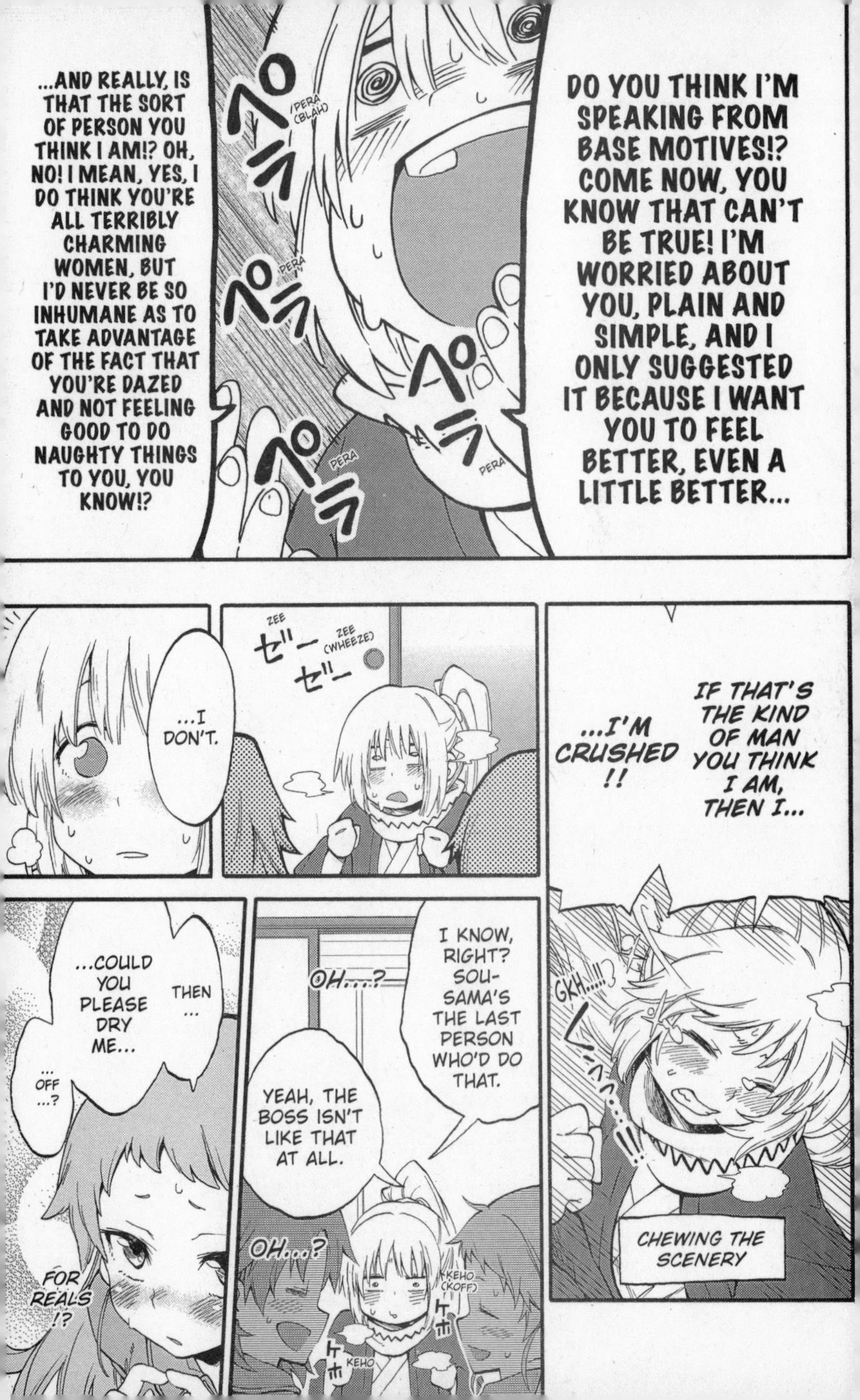
DO YOU THINK I'M SPEAKING FROM BASE MOTIVES!? COME NOW, YOU KNOW THAT CAN'T BE TRUE! I'M WORRIED ABOUT YOU, PLAIN AND SIMPLE, AND I ONLY SUGGESTED IT BECAUSE I WANT YOU TO FEEL BETTER, EVEN A LITTLE BETTER...
PERA (BLAH)
PERA
PERA
PERA
...AND REALLY, IS THAT THE SORT OF PERSON YOU THINK I AM!? OH, NO! I MEAN, YES, I DO THINK YOU'RE ALL TERRIBLY CHARMING WOMEN, BUT I'D NEVER BE SO INHUMANE AS TO TAKE ADVANTAGE OF THE FACT THAT YOU'RE DAZED AND NOT FEELING GOOD TO DO NAUGHTY THINGS TO YOU, YOU KNOW!?
IF THAT'S THE KIND OF MAN YOU THINK I AM, THEN I...
...I'M CRUSHED!!
ZEE
ZEE (WHEEZE)
...I DON'T.
GKH!!!!
CHEWING THE SCENERY
I KNOW, RIGHT? SOU-SAMA'S THE LAST PERSON WHO'D DO THAT.
OH...?
YEAH, THE BOSS ISN'T LIKE THAT AT ALL.
OH...?
KEHO (KOFF)
KEHO
THEN...
...COULD YOU PLEASE DRY ME...
...OFF...?
FOR REALS!?

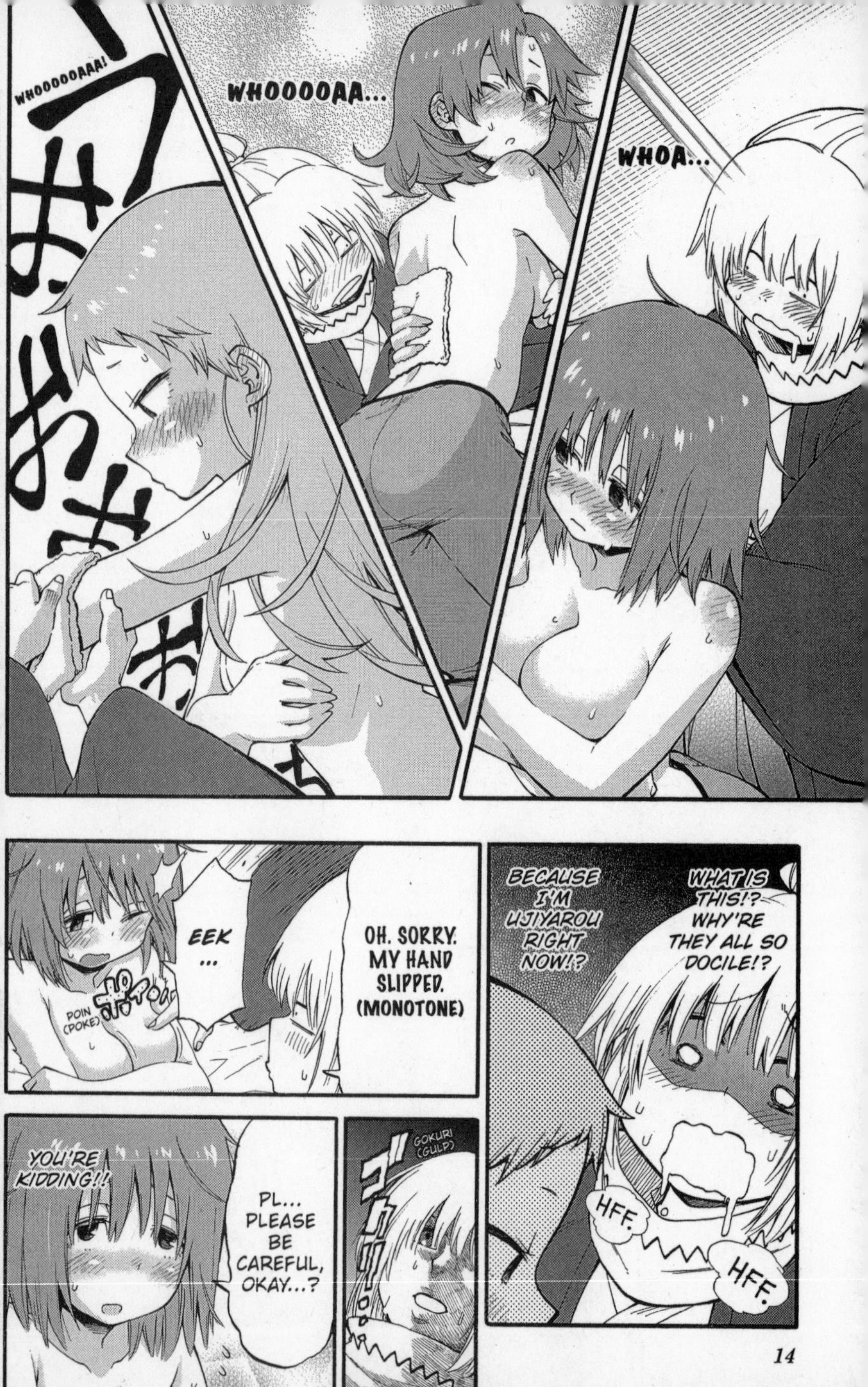
WHOA...
WHOOOOAA...
WHOOOOOAAA!
WHAT IS THIS!? WHY'RE THEY ALL SO DOCILE!?
BECAUSE I'M UJIYAROU RIGHT NOW!?
HFF.
HFF.
OH. SORRY. MY HAND SLIPPED. (MONOTONE)
EEK ...
POIN (POKE)
GOKURI (GULP)
PL... PLEASE BE CAREFUL, OKAY...?
YOU'RE KIDDING!!

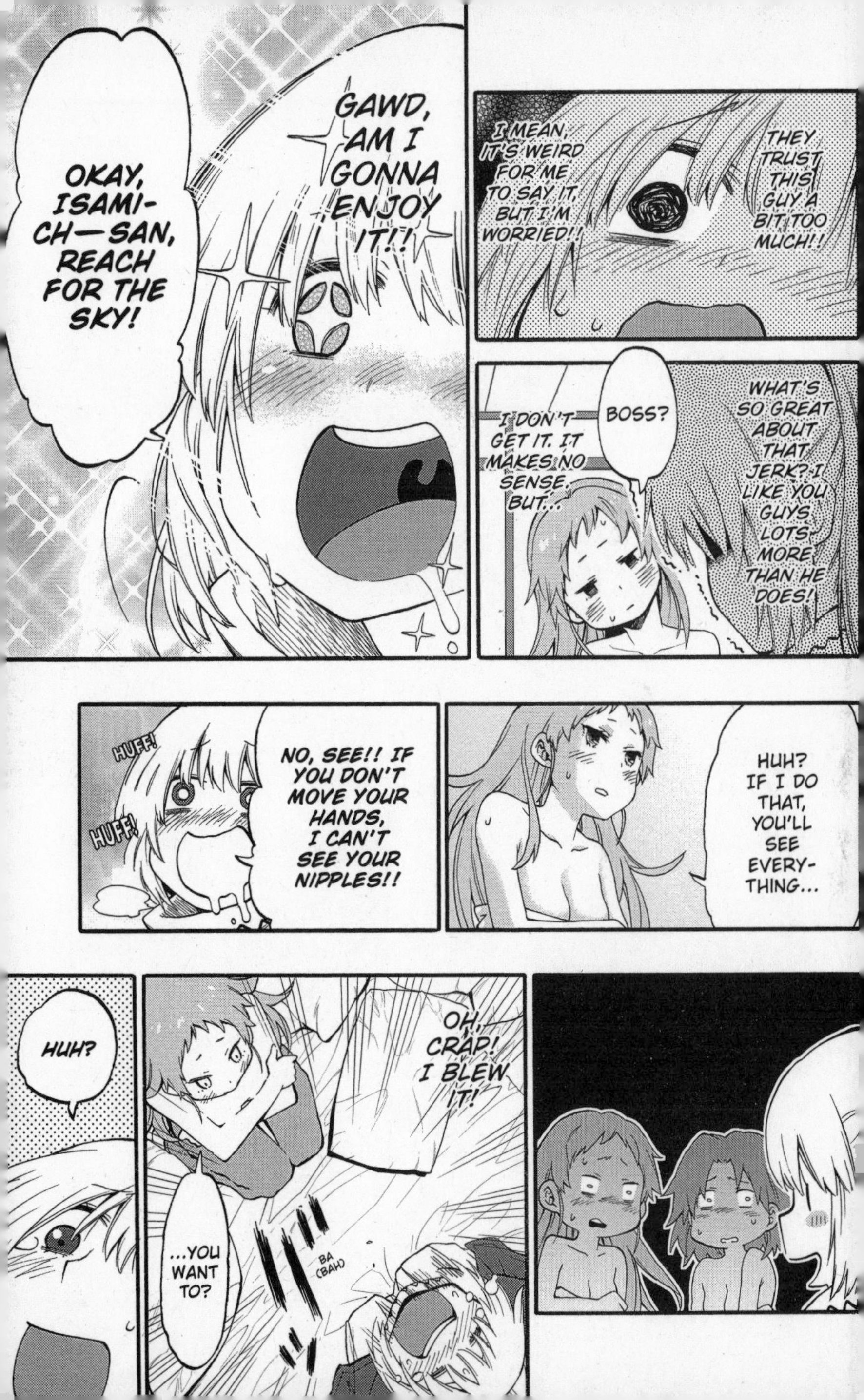
THEY TRUST THIS GUY A BIT TOO MUCH!!
I MEAN, IT'S WEIRD FOR ME TO SAY IT, BUT I'M WORRIED!!
WHAT'S SO GREAT ABOUT THAT JERK? I LIKE YOU GUYS LOTS MORE THAN HE DOES!
BOSS?
I DON'T GET IT. IT MAKES NO SENSE. BUT...
GAWD, AM I GONNA ENJOY IT!!
OKAY, ISAMI-CH—SAN, REACH FOR THE SKY!
HUH? IF I DO THAT, YOU'LL SEE EVERY-THING...
NO, SEE!! IF YOU DON'T MOVE YOUR HANDS, I CAN'T SEE YOUR NIPPLES!!
HUFF!
HUFF!
OH, CRAP! I BLEW IT!
...YOU WANT TO?
BA (BAH)
HUH?

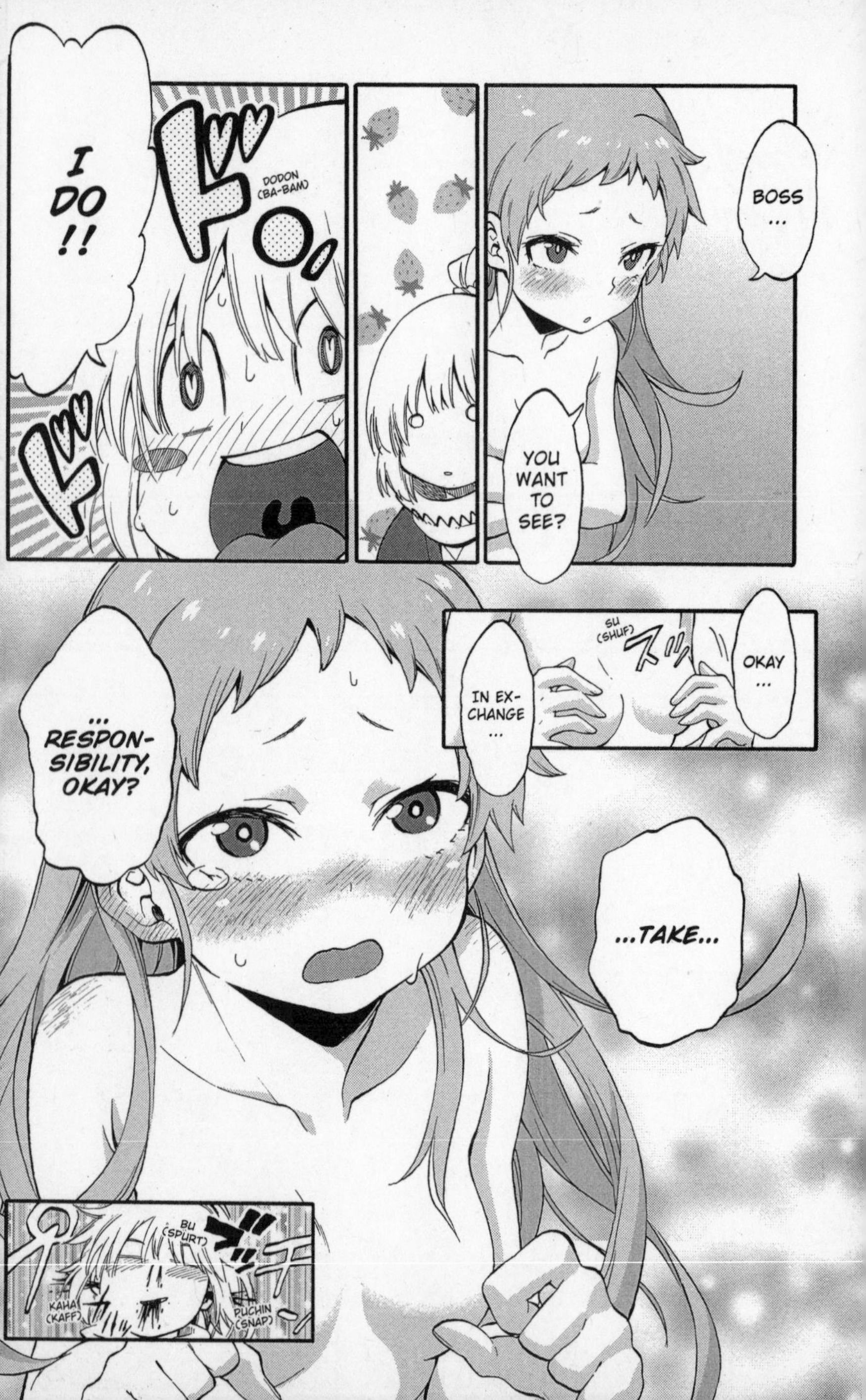
BOSS ...
YOU WANT TO SEE?
DODON (BA-BAM)
I DO !!
OKAY ...
SU (SHUF)
IN EX-CHANGE ...
...TAKE...
... RESPON-SIBILITY, OKAY?
BU (SPURT)
PUCHIN (SNAP)
KAHA (KAFF)

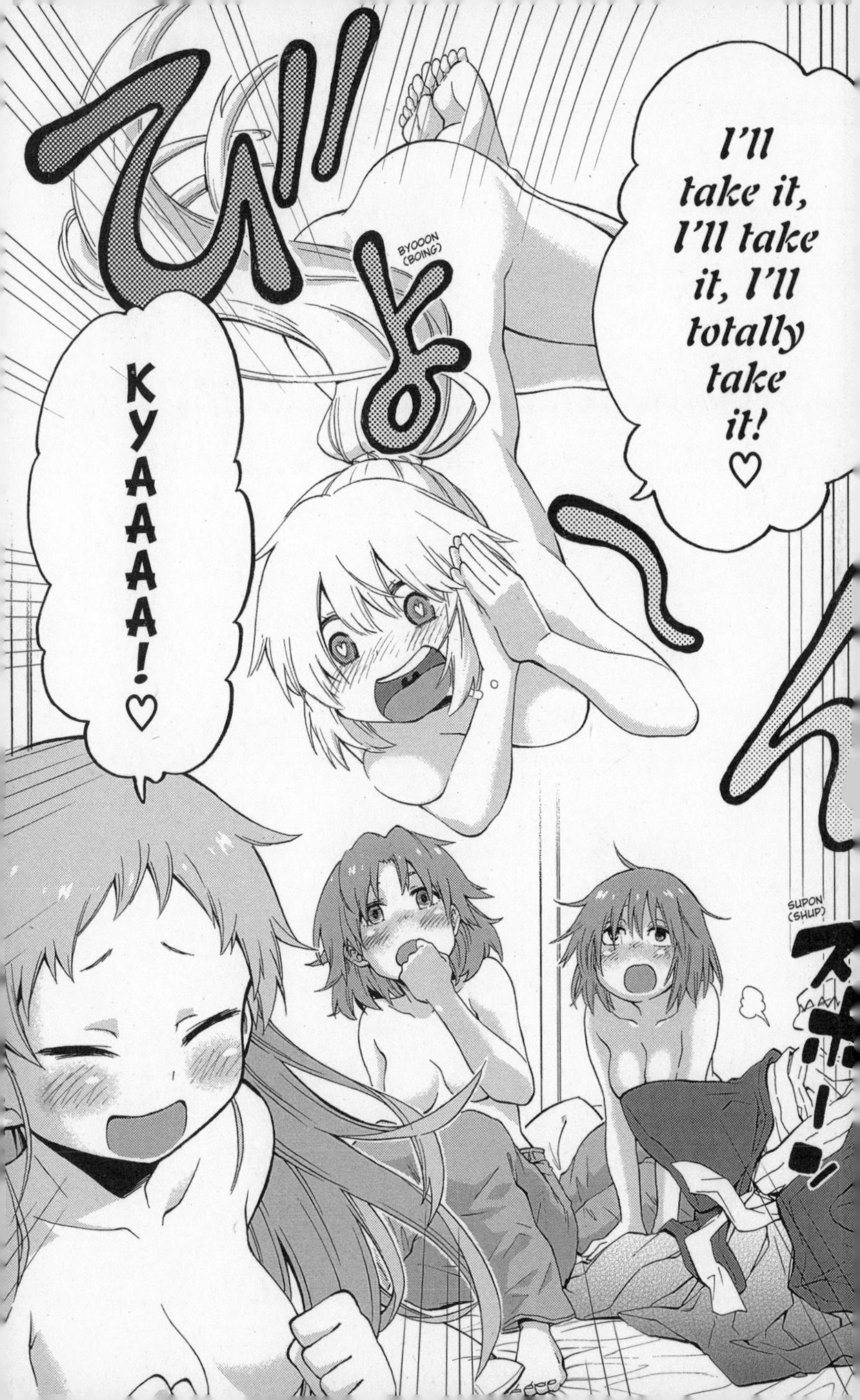
I'll take it, I'll take it, I'll take it, I'll totally take it! ♡
BYOOON (BOING)
KYAAAAA! ♡
SUPON (SHUP)

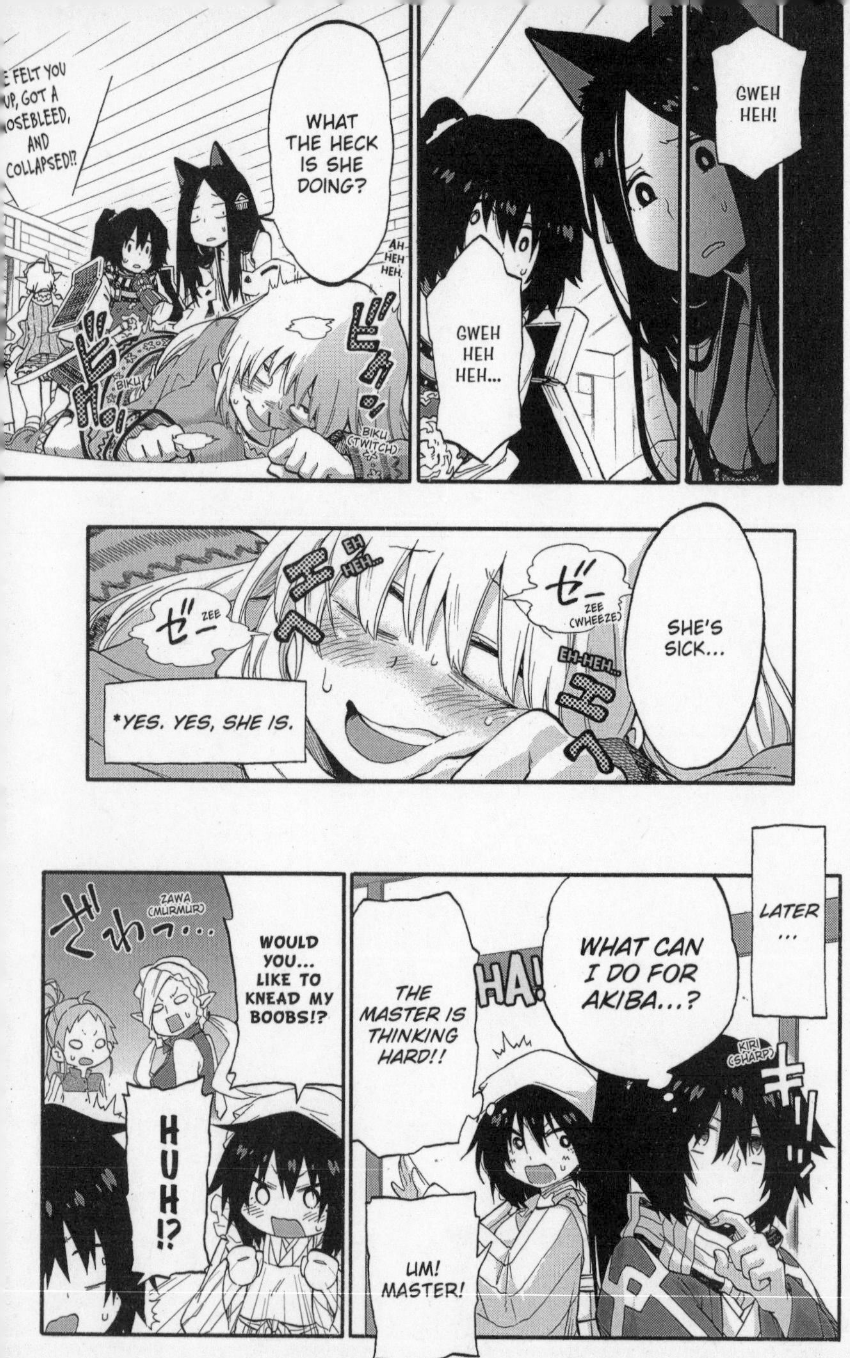
GWEH HEH!
GWEH HEH HEH...
WHAT THE HECK IS SHE DOING?
AH HEH HEH.
BIKU (TWITCH)
BIKU
E FELT YOU UP, GOT A OSEBLEED, AND COLLAPSED!?
SHE'S SICK...
ZEE (WHEEZE)
EH-HEH...
EH HEH...
ZEE
*YES. YES, SHE IS.
LATER...
WHAT CAN I DO FOR AKIBA...?
KIRI (SHARP)
HA!
THE MASTER IS THINKING HARD!!
UM! MASTER!
WOULD YOU... LIKE TO KNEAD MY BOOBS!?
ZAWA (MURMUR)
HUH!?

LOG HORIZON
THE WEST WIND BRIGADE

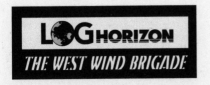

LOG HORIZON

THE WEST WIND BRIGADE

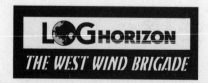

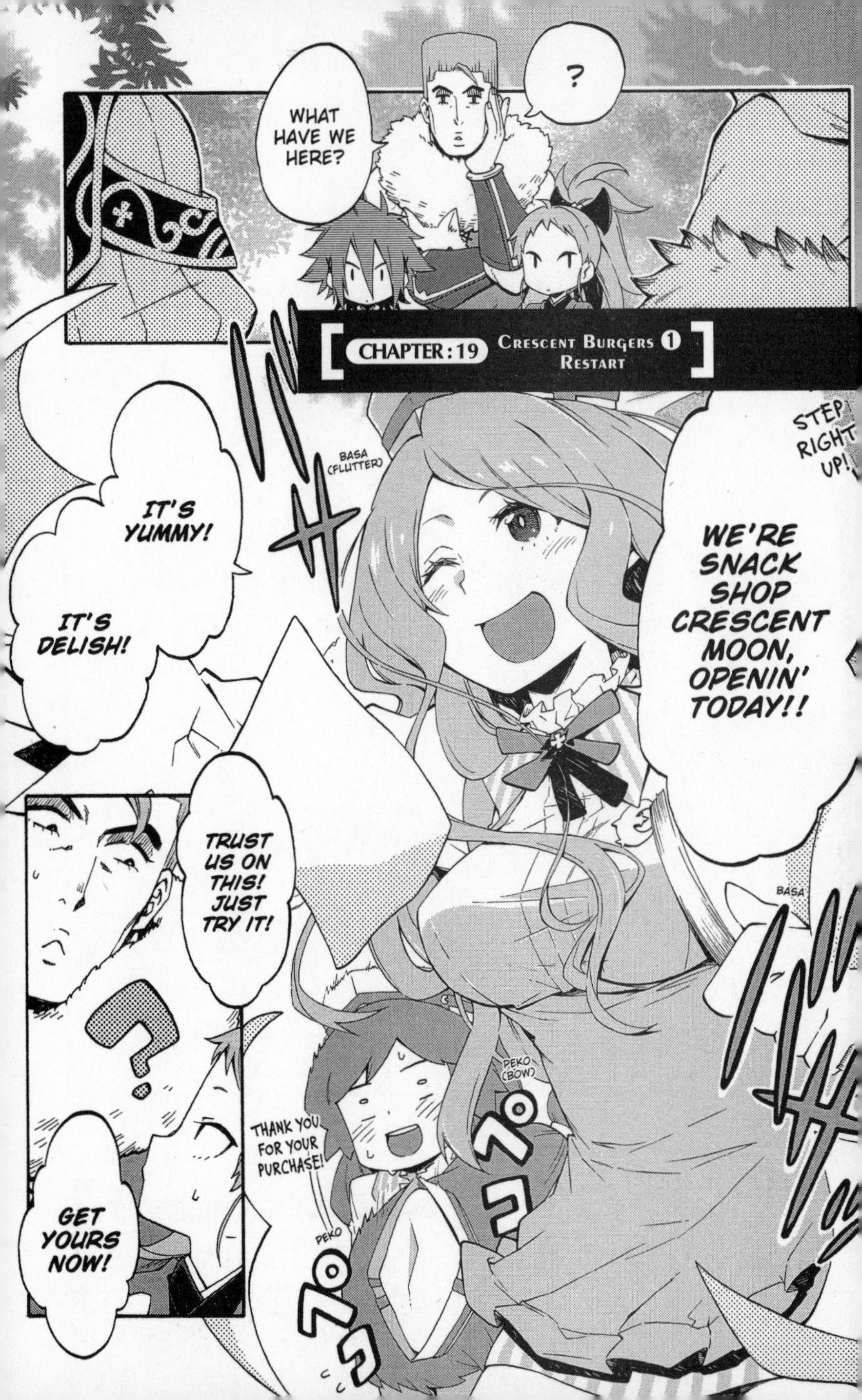
?
WHAT HAVE WE HERE?
CHAPTER : 19 Crescent Burgers 1 Restart
STEP RIGHT UP!
WE'RE SNACK SHOP CRESCENT MOON, OPENIN' TODAY!!
BASA
BASA (FLUTTER)
IT'S YUMMY!
IT'S DELISH!
PEKO (BOW)
THANK YOU FOR YOUR PURCHASE!
PEKO
TRUST US ON THIS! JUST TRY IT!
GET YOURS NOW!

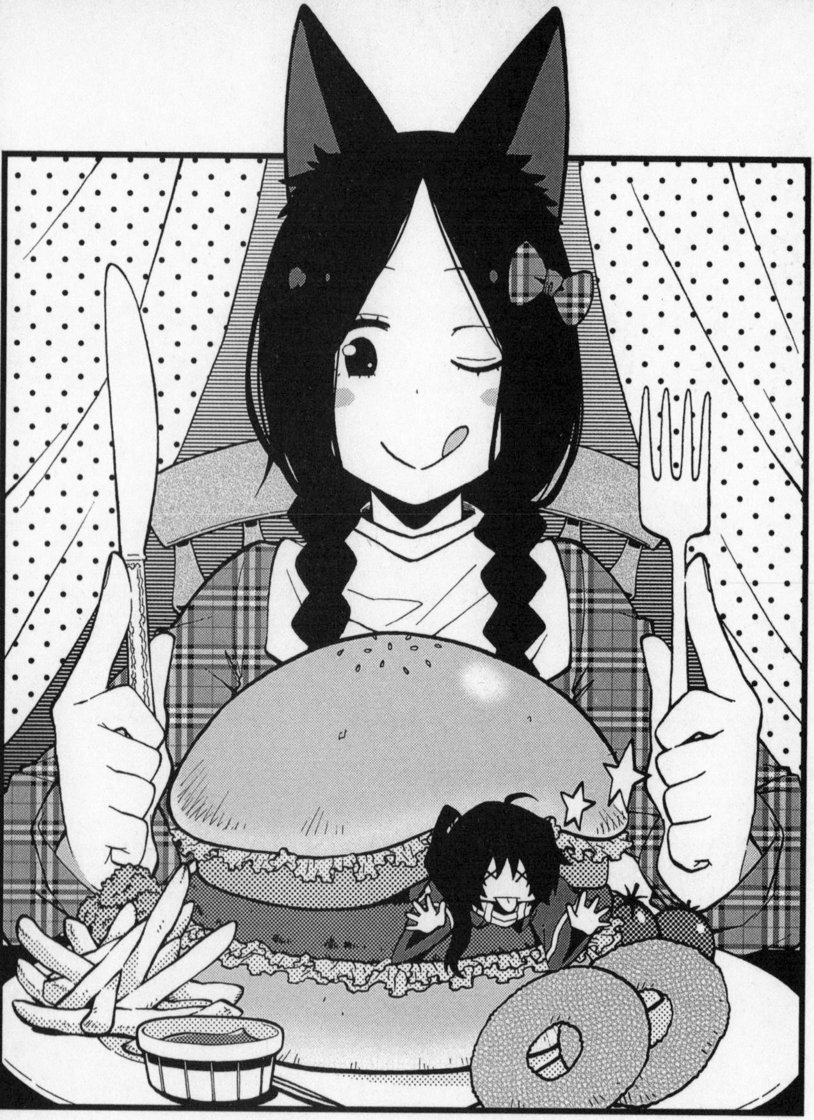

CHAPTER : 19 Crescent Burgers 1 Restart

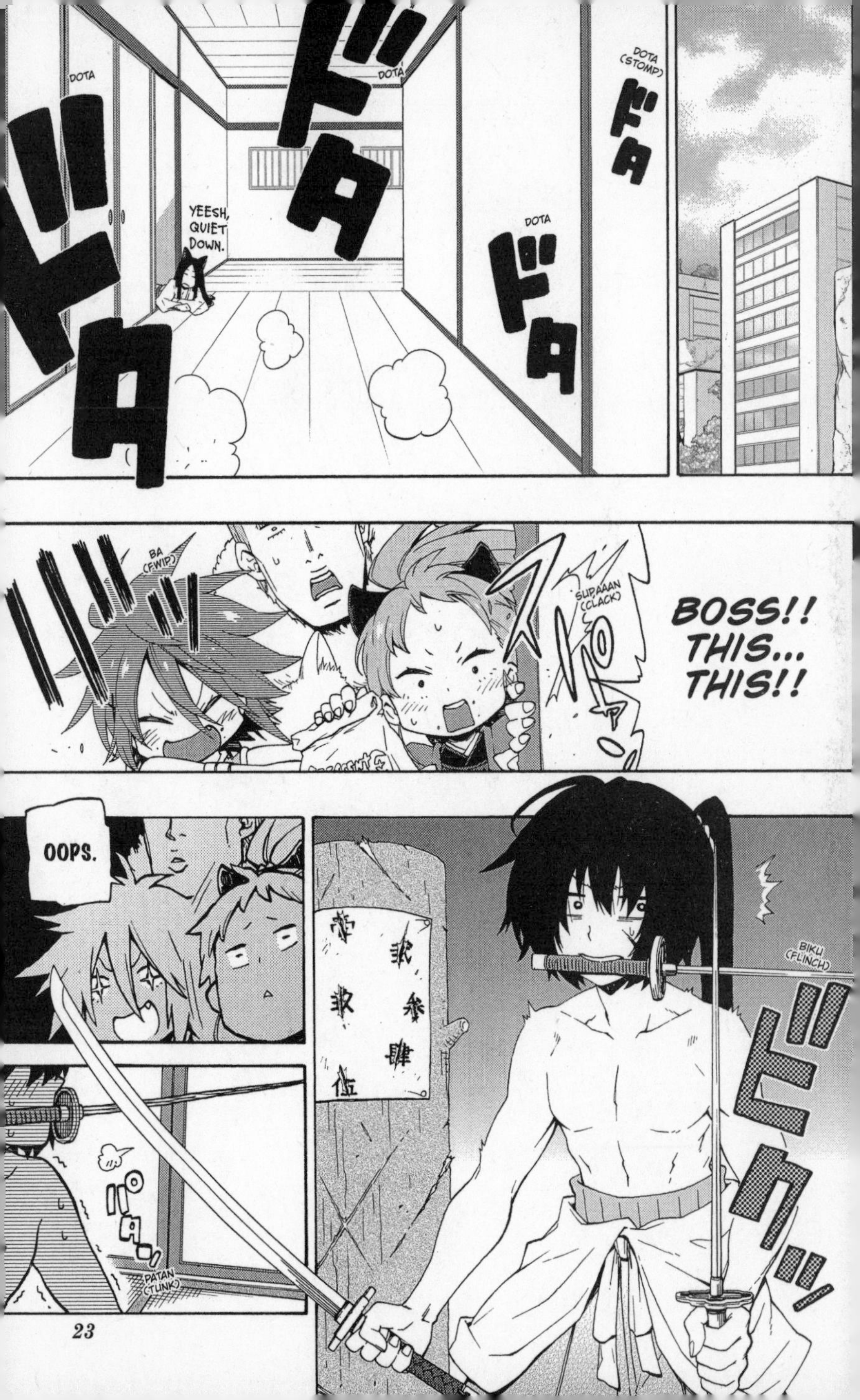

DOTA (STOMP)
DOTA
DOTA
YEESH, QUIET DOWN.
DOTA
BOSS!! THIS... THIS!!
SUPAAAN (CLACK)
BA (FWIP)
BIKU (FLINCH)
OOPS.
PATAN (TUNK)

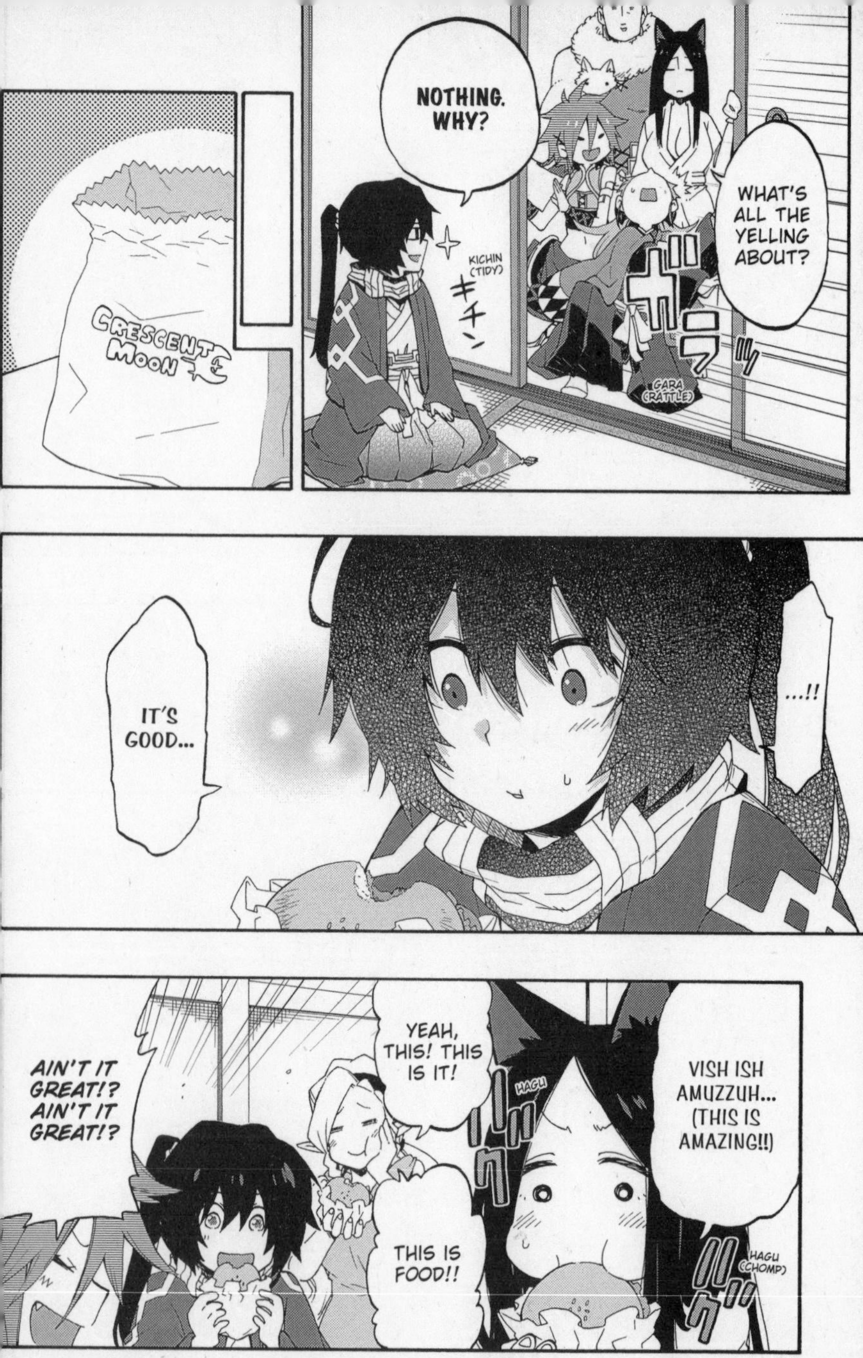
WHAT'S ALL THE YELLING ABOUT?
GARA (RATTLE)
NOTHING. WHY?
KICHIN (TIDY)
CRESCENT MOON
...!!
IT'S GOOD...
VISH ISH AMUZZUH... (THIS IS AMAZING!!)
HAGU (CHOMP)
HAGU
YEAH, THIS! THIS IS IT!
THIS IS FOOD!!
AIN'T IT GREAT!? AIN'T IT GREAT!?

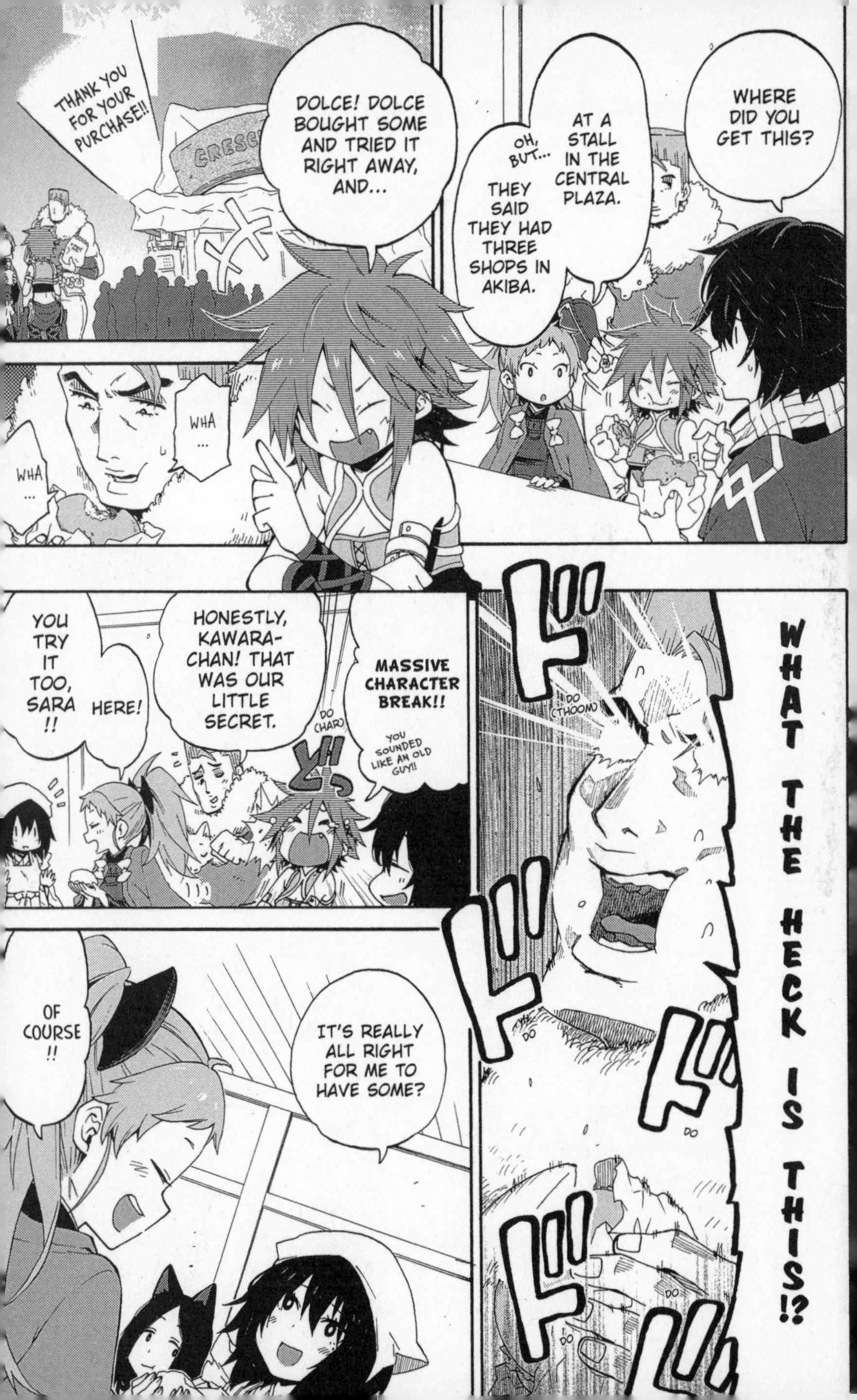

WHERE DID YOU GET THIS?
AT A STALL IN THE CENTRAL PLAZA.
OH, BUT...
THEY SAID THEY HAD THREE SHOPS IN AKIBA.
DOLCE! DOLCE BOUGHT SOME AND TRIED IT RIGHT AWAY, AND...
THANK YOU FOR YOUR PURCHASE!!
WHA ...
WHA ...
WHAT THE HECK IS THIS!?
DO (THOOM)
DO
DO
DO
DO
MASSIVE CHARACTER BREAK!!
YOU SOUNDED LIKE AN OLD GUY!!
DO (CHAR)
HONESTLY, KAWARA-CHAN! THAT WAS OUR LITTLE SECRET.
HERE!
YOU TRY IT TOO, SARA !!
IT'S REALLY ALL RIGHT FOR ME TO HAVE SOME?
OF COURSE !!

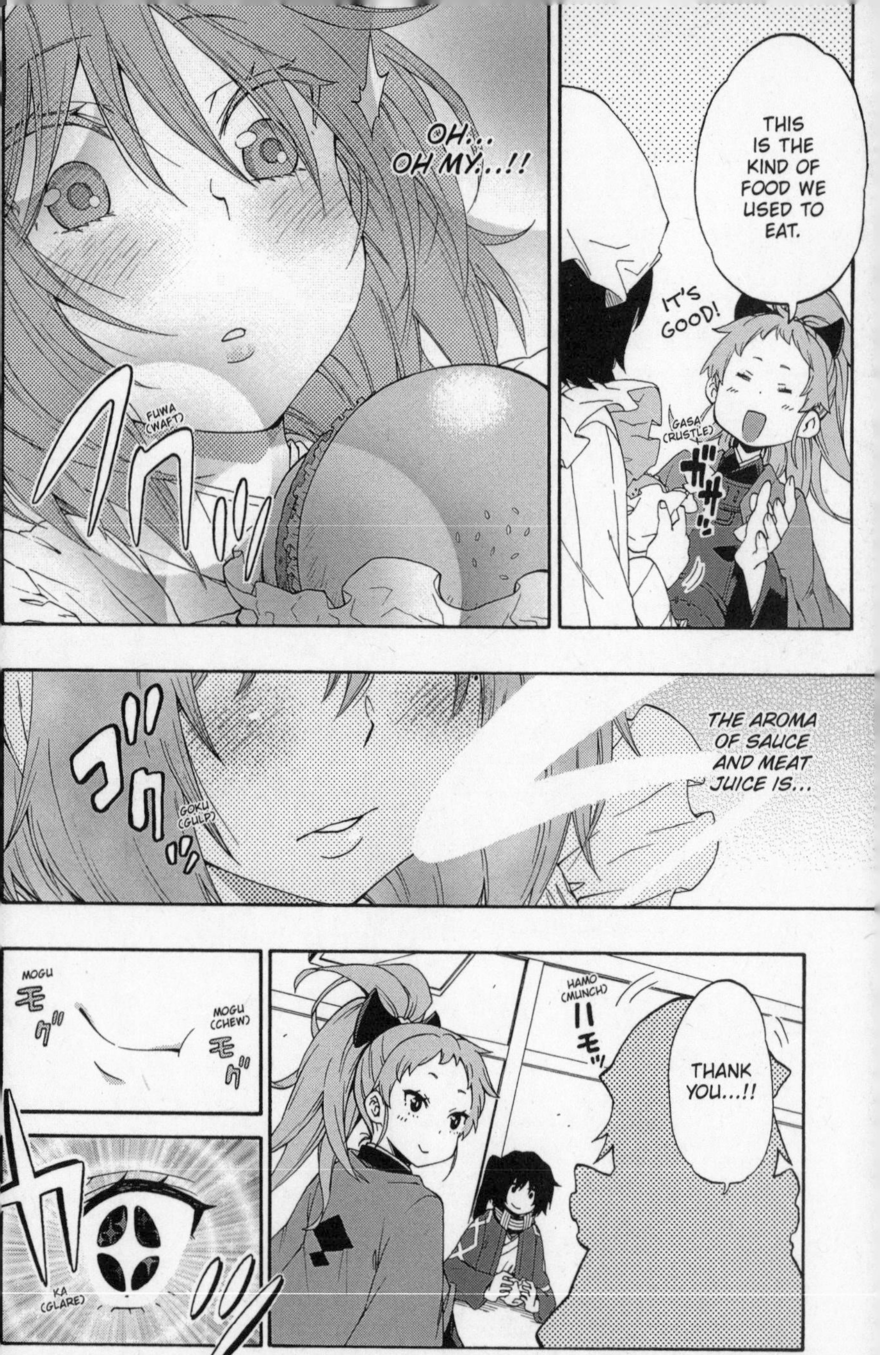
THIS IS THE KIND OF FOOD WE USED TO EAT.
IT'S GOOD!
GASA (RUSTLE)
OH... OH MY...!!
FUWA (WAFT)
THE AROMA OF SAUCE AND MEAT JUICE IS...
GOKU (GULP)
THANK YOU...!!
HAMO (MUNCH)
MOGU (CHEW)
MOGU
KA (GLARE)

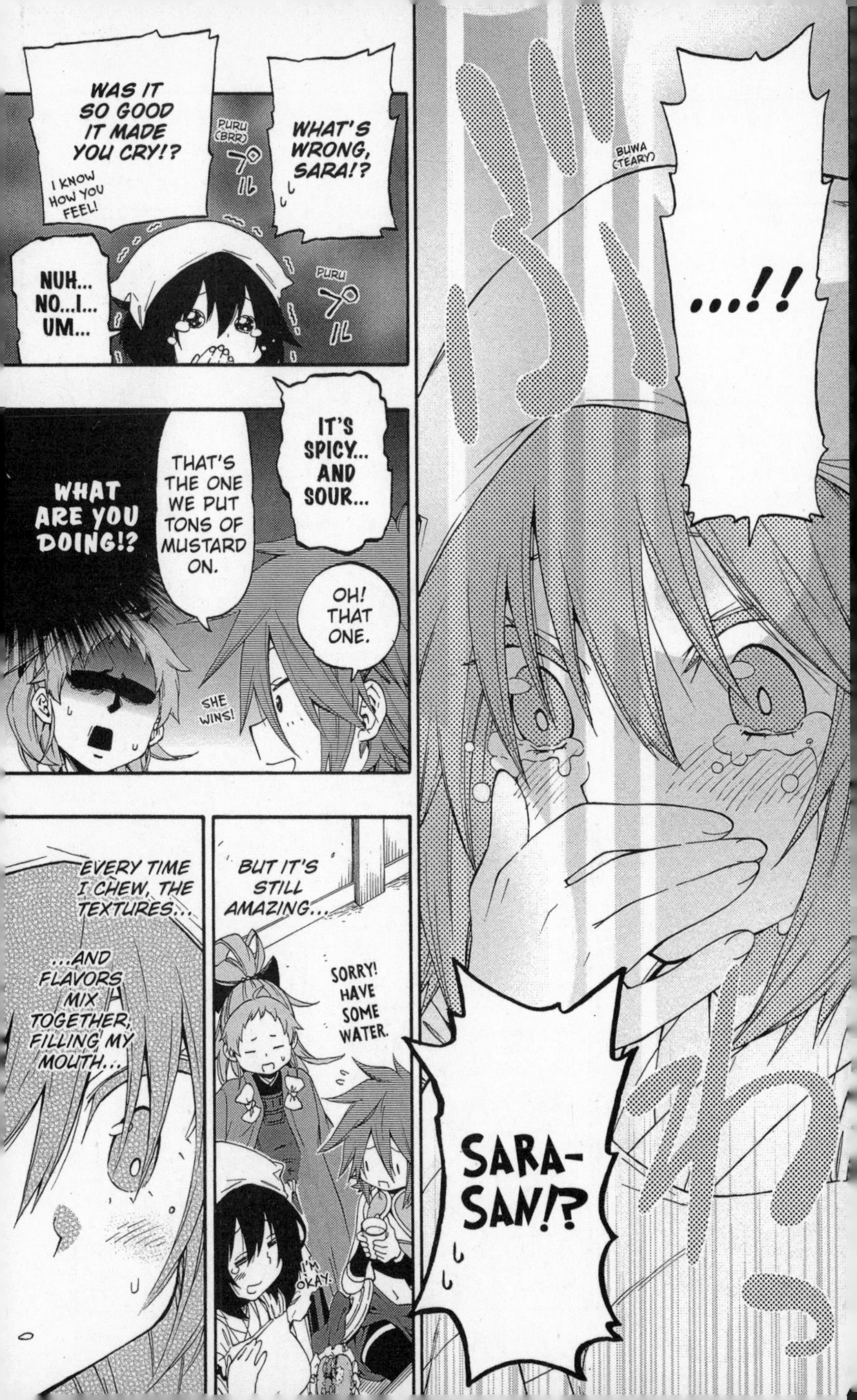

...!!
BUWA (TEARY)
SARA-SAN!?
WHAT'S WRONG, SARA!?
PURU (BRR)
WAS IT SO GOOD IT MADE YOU CRY!?
I KNOW HOW YOU FEEL!
PURU
NUH... NO...I... UM...
IT'S SPICY... AND SOUR...
THAT'S THE ONE WE PUT TONS OF MUSTARD ON.
OH! THAT ONE.
WHAT ARE YOU DOING!?
SHE WINS!
BUT IT'S STILL AMAZING...
SORRY! HAVE SOME WATER.
I'M OKAY.
EVERY TIME I CHEW, THE TEXTURES...
...AND FLAVORS MIX TOGETHER, FILLING MY MOUTH...

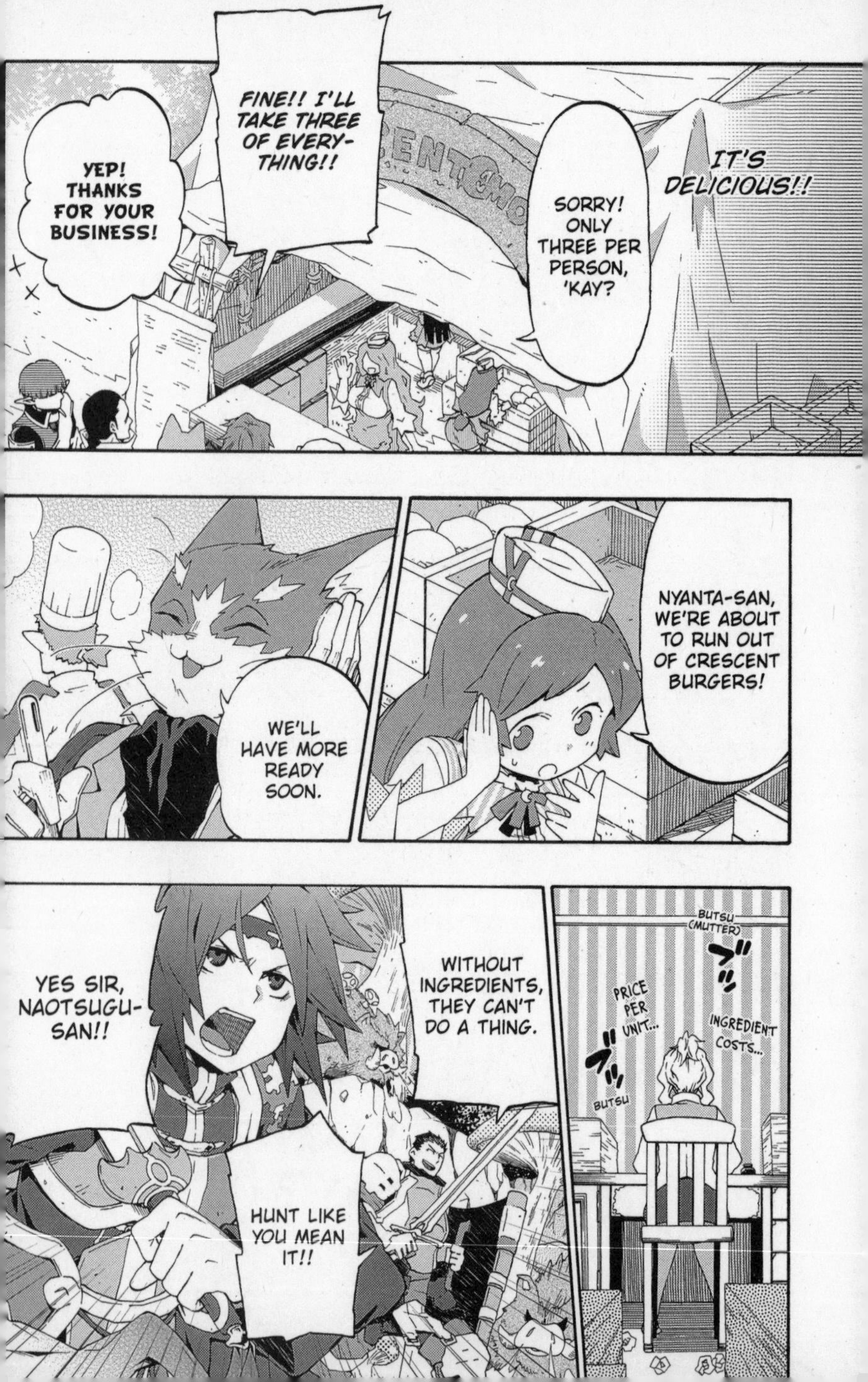
IT'S DELICIOUS!!
SORRY! ONLY THREE PER PERSON, 'KAY?
FINE!! I'LL TAKE THREE OF EVERY-THING!!
YEP! THANKS FOR YOUR BUSINESS!
NYANTA-SAN, WE'RE ABOUT TO RUN OUT OF CRESCENT BURGERS!
WE'LL HAVE MORE READY SOON.
BUTSU (MUTTER)
INGREDIENT COSTS...
PRICE PER UNIT...
BUTSU
WITHOUT INGREDIENTS, THEY CAN'T DO A THING.
YES SIR, NAOTSUGU-SAN!!
HUNT LIKE YOU MEAN IT!!

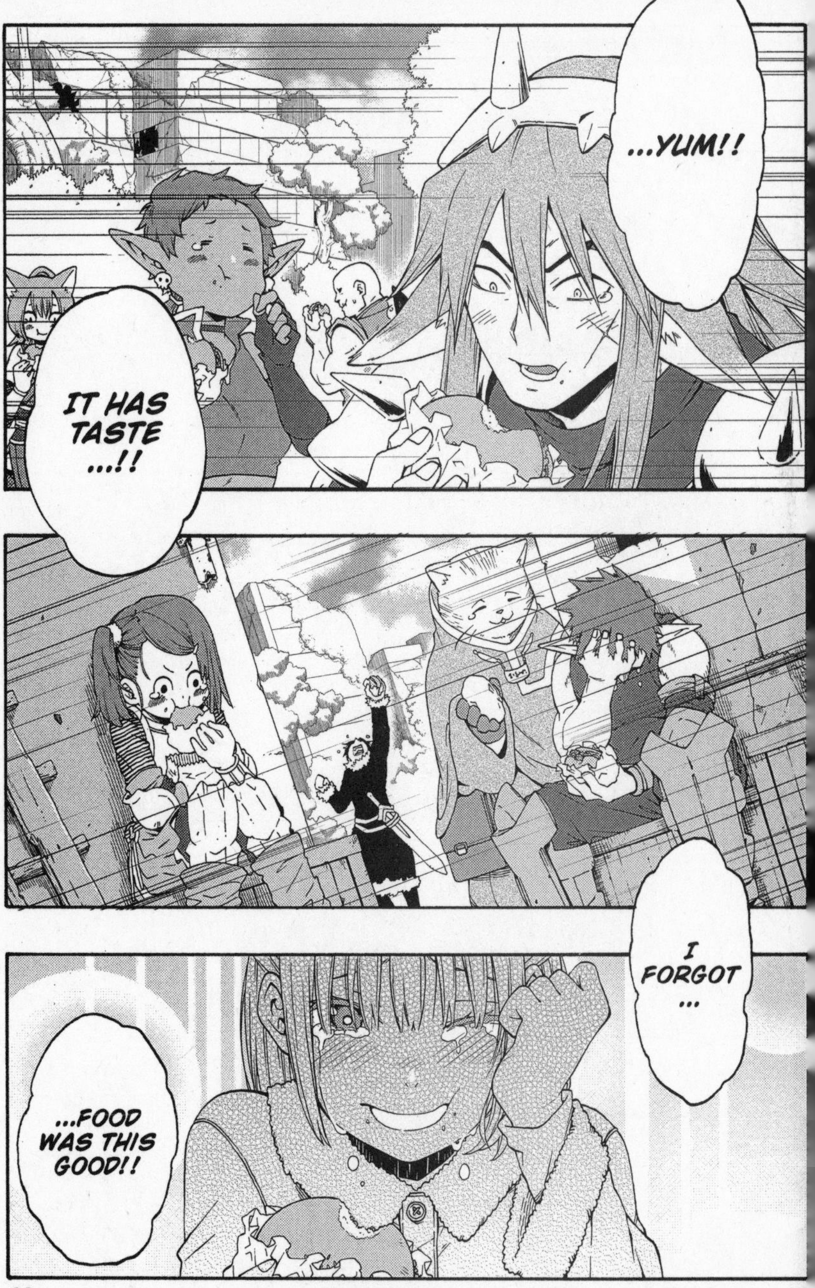
...YUM!!
IT HAS TASTE ...!!
I FORGOT ...
...FOOD WAS THIS GOOD!!

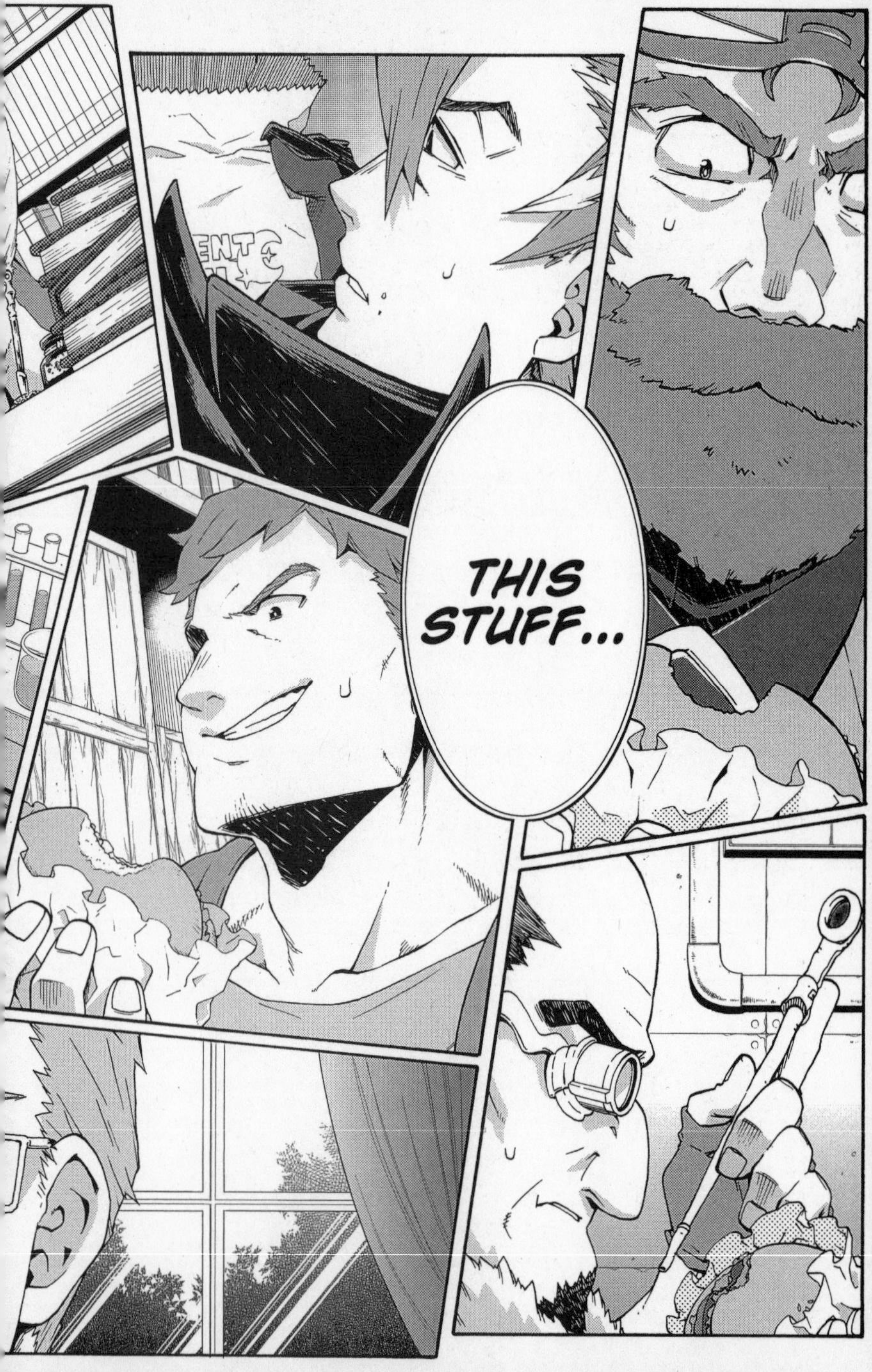
THIS STUFF...

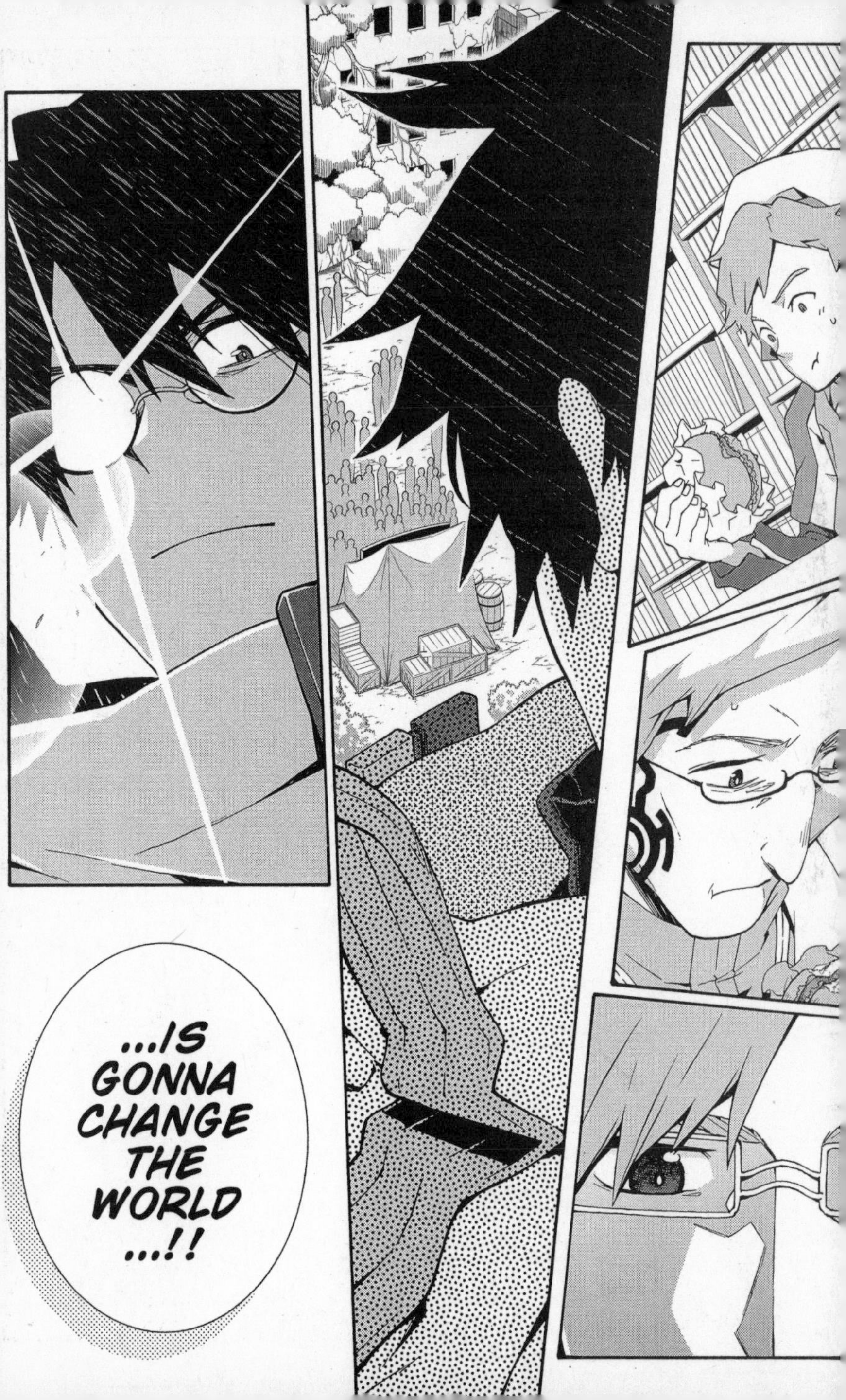
...IS GONNA CHANGE THE WORLD ...!!

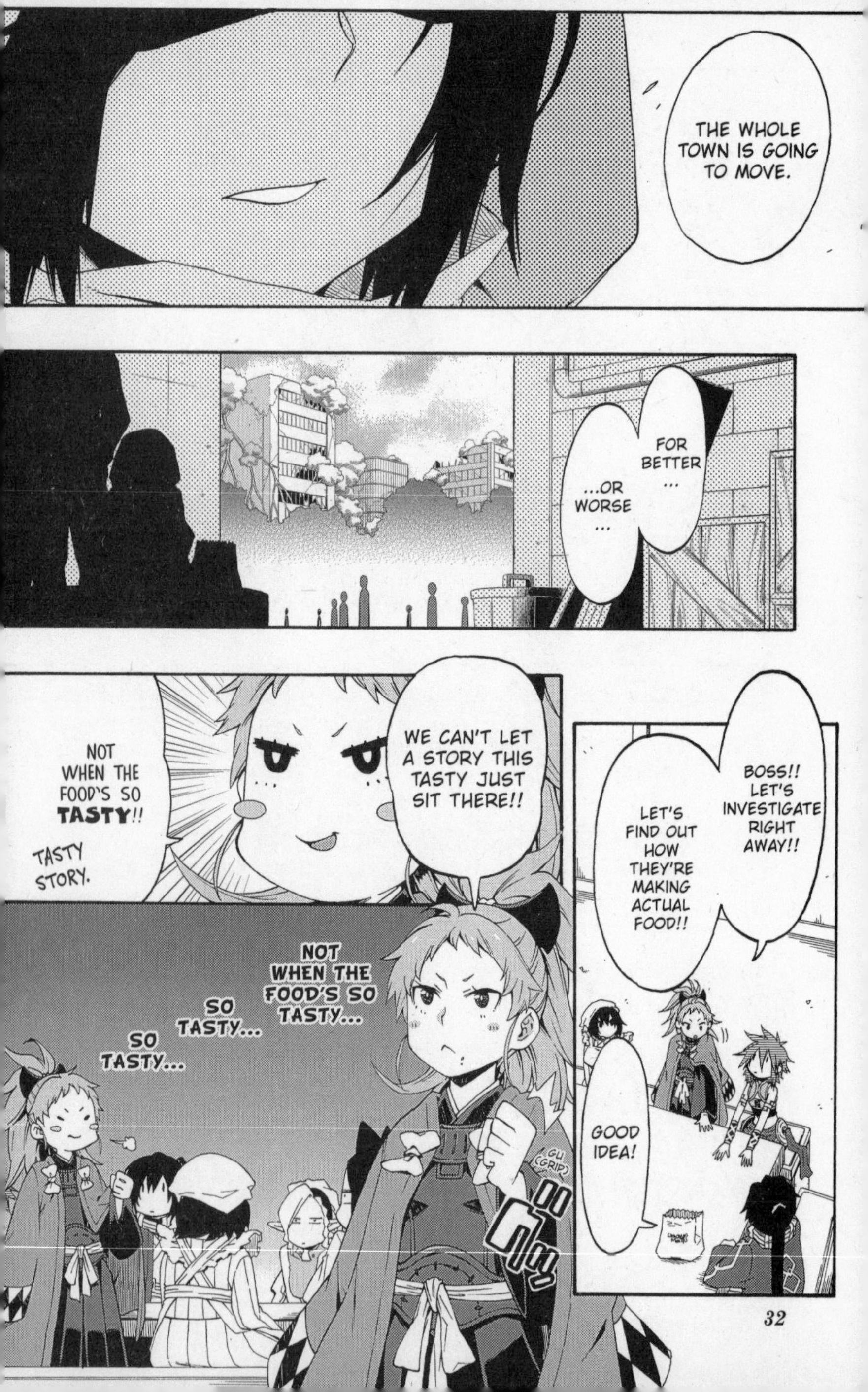
THE WHOLE TOWN IS GOING TO MOVE.
FOR BETTER ...
...OR WORSE ...
BOSS!! LET'S INVESTIGATE RIGHT AWAY!!
LET'S FIND OUT HOW THEY'RE MAKING ACTUAL FOOD!!
GOOD IDEA!
WE CAN'T LET A STORY THIS TASTY JUST SIT THERE!!
NOT WHEN THE FOOD'S SO **TASTY**!!
TASTY STORY.
GU (GRIP)
NOT WHEN THE FOOD'S SO TASTY...
SO TASTY...
SO TASTY...

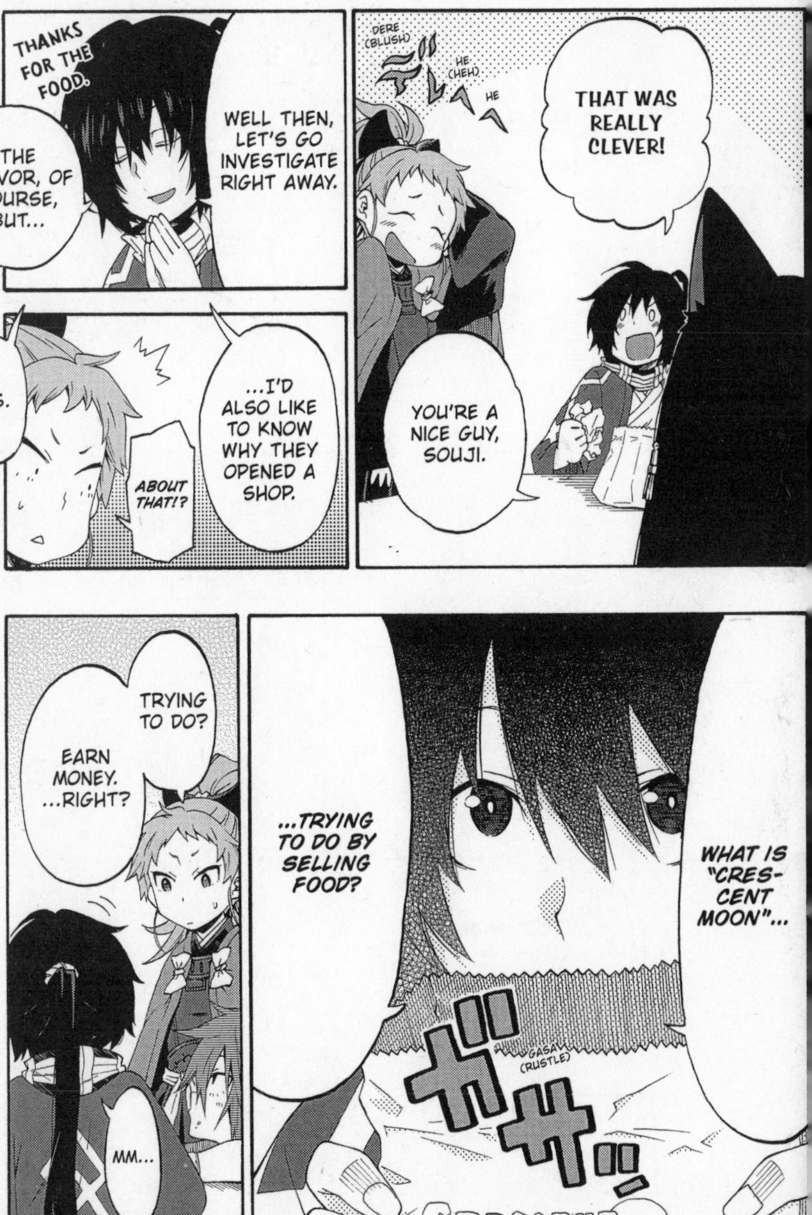
THAT WAS REALLY CLEVER!
HE (HEH)
HE
DERE (BLUSH)
YOU'RE A NICE GUY, SOUJI.
WELL THEN, LET'S GO INVESTIGATE RIGHT AWAY.
THANKS FOR THE FOOD.
THE FLAVOR, OF COURSE, BUT...
...I'D ALSO LIKE TO KNOW WHY THEY OPENED A SHOP.
ABOUT THAT!?
YES.
WHAT IS "CRES-CENT MOON"...
...TRYING TO DO BY SELLING FOOD?
GASA (RUSTLE)
CRESCENT
TRYING TO DO?
EARN MONEY. ...RIGHT?
MM...

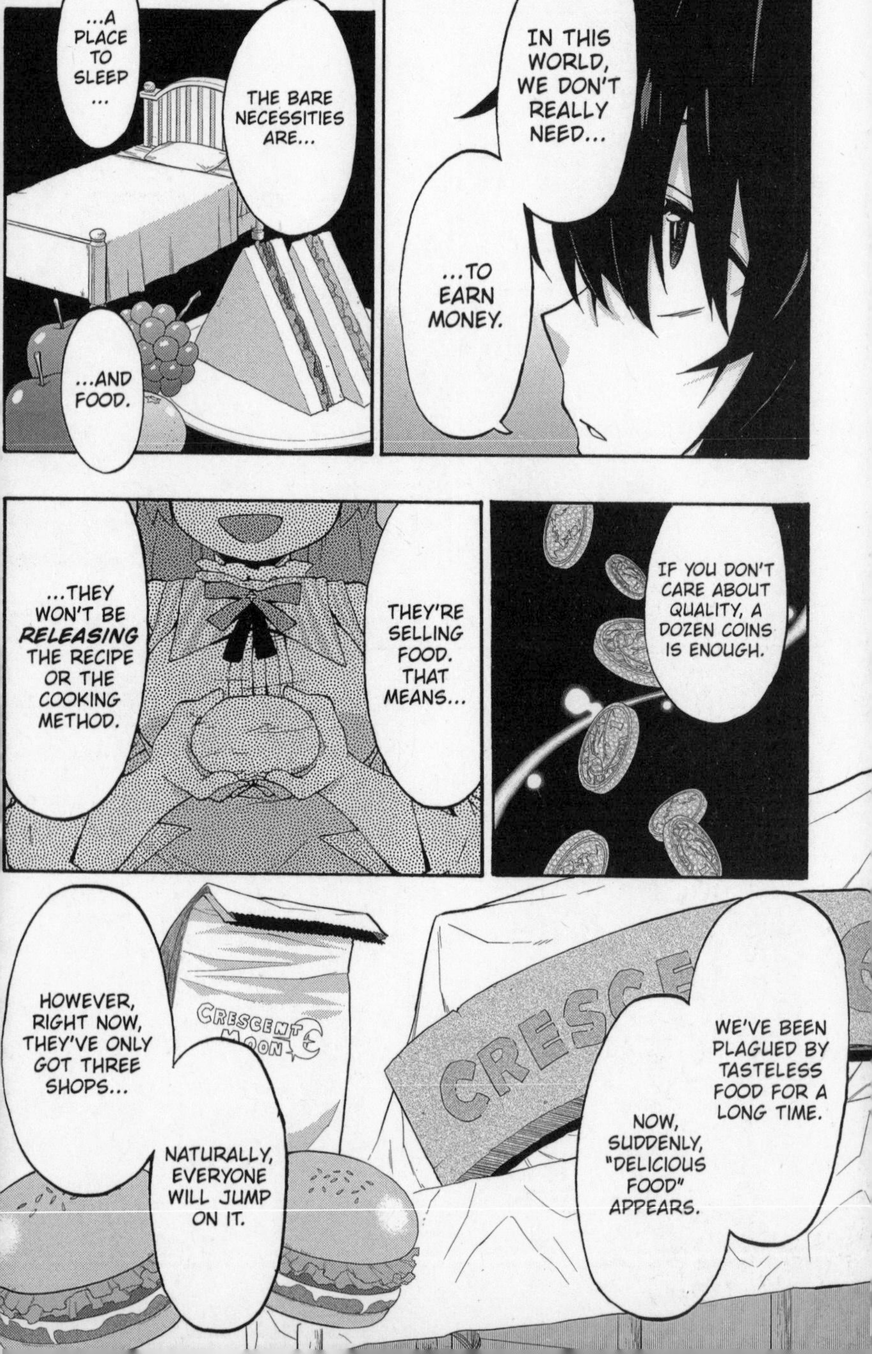
IN THIS WORLD, WE DON'T REALLY NEED...
...TO EARN MONEY.
THE BARE NECESSITIES ARE...
...A PLACE TO SLEEP...
...AND FOOD.
IF YOU DON'T CARE ABOUT QUALITY, A DOZEN COINS IS ENOUGH.
THEY'RE SELLING FOOD. THAT MEANS...
...THEY WON'T BE *RELEASING* THE RECIPE OR THE COOKING METHOD.
WE'VE BEEN PLAGUED BY TASTELESS FOOD FOR A LONG TIME.
NOW, SUDDENLY, "DELICIOUS FOOD" APPEARS.
HOWEVER, RIGHT NOW, THEY'VE ONLY GOT THREE SHOPS...
CRESCENT MOON
NATURALLY, EVERYONE WILL JUMP ON IT.

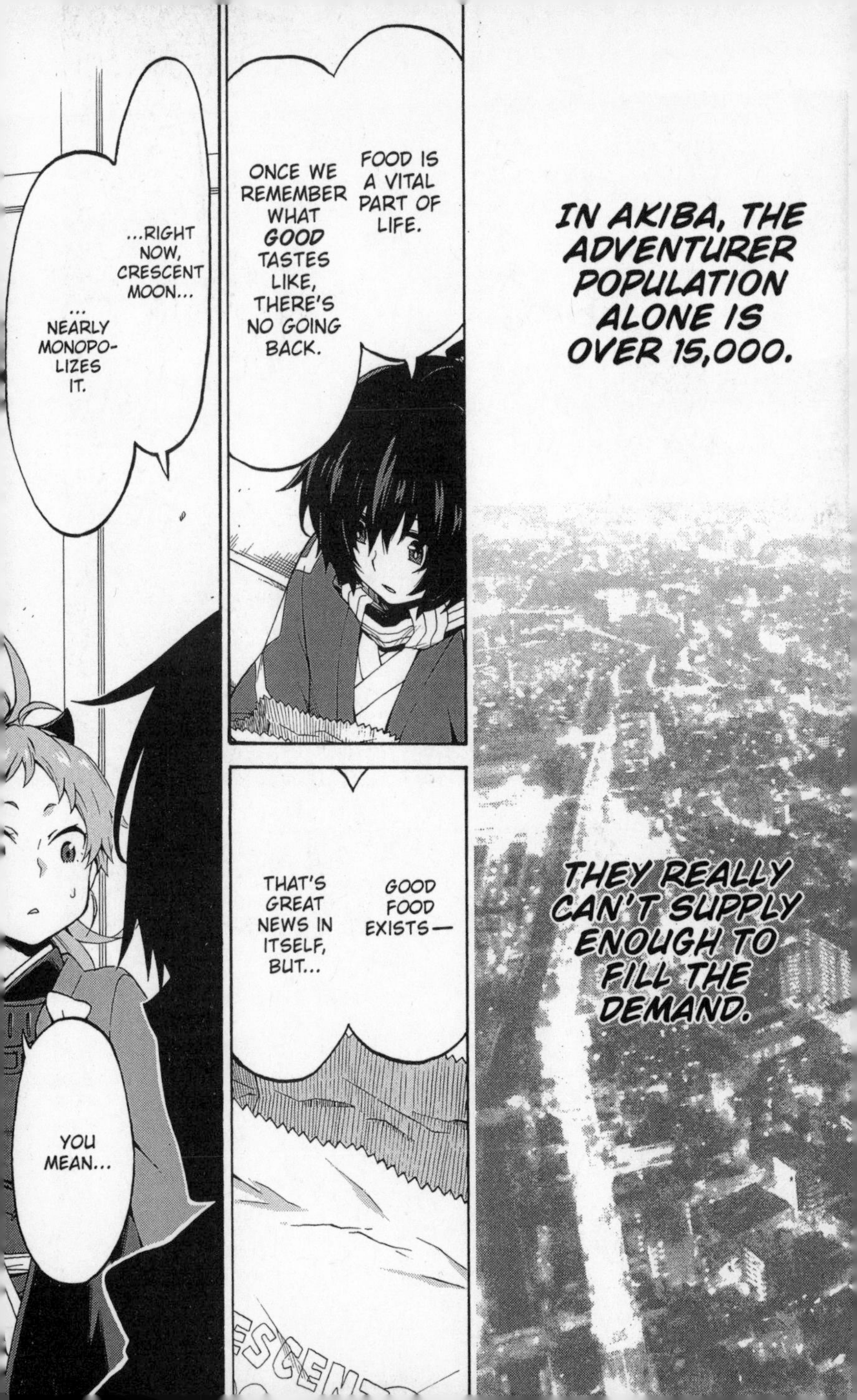
IN AKIBA, THE ADVENTURER POPULATION ALONE IS OVER 15,000.
THEY REALLY CAN'T SUPPLY ENOUGH TO FILL THE DEMAND.
FOOD IS A VITAL PART OF LIFE.
ONCE WE REMEMBER WHAT GOOD TASTES LIKE, THERE'S NO GOING BACK.
GOOD FOOD EXISTS—
THAT'S GREAT NEWS IN ITSELF, BUT...
...RIGHT NOW, CRESCENT MOON...
...NEARLY MONOPOLIZES IT.
YOU MEAN...

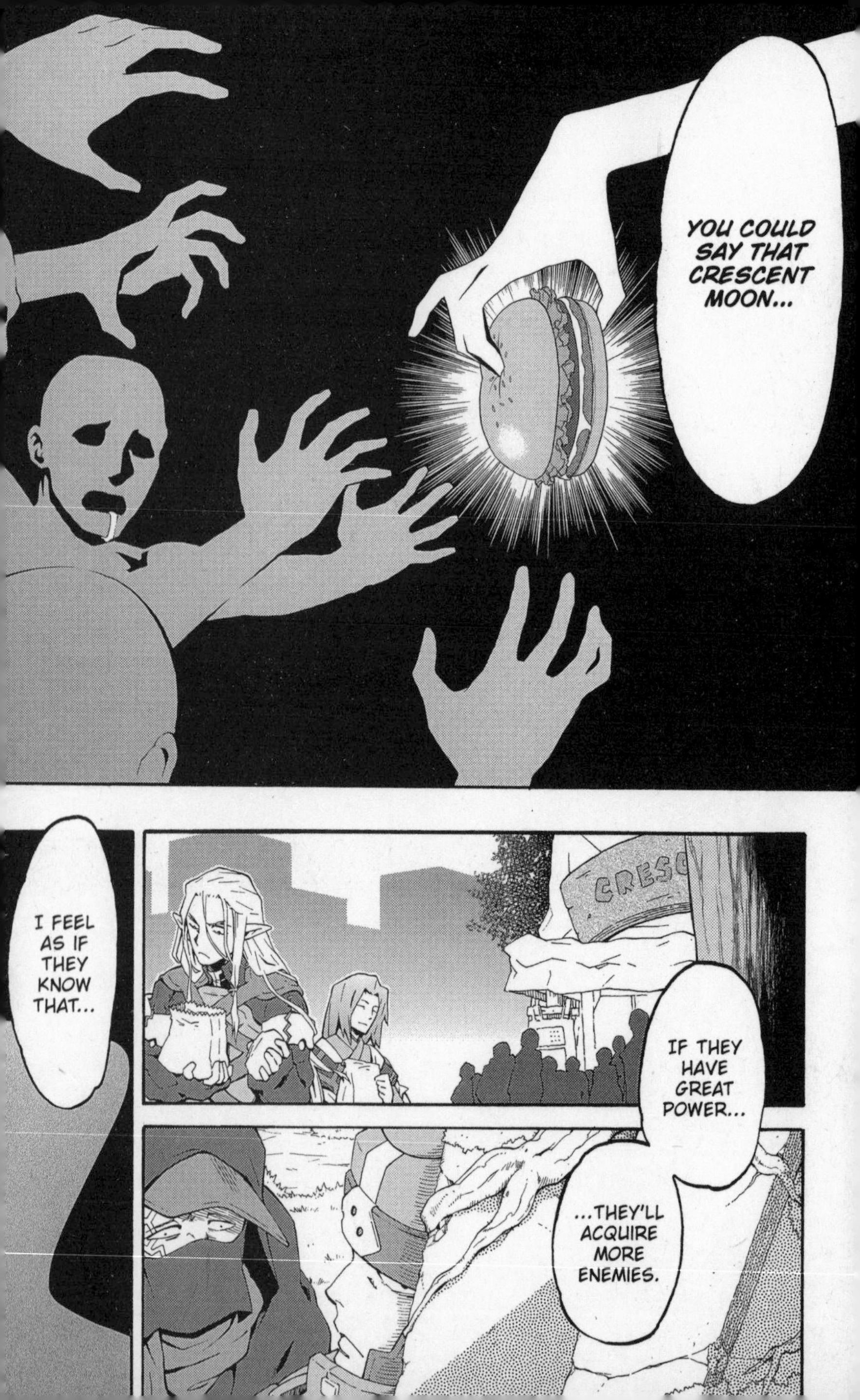
YOU COULD SAY THAT CRESCENT MOON...
CRESC
IF THEY HAVE GREAT POWER...
...THEY'LL ACQUIRE MORE ENEMIES.
I FEEL AS IF THEY KNOW THAT...

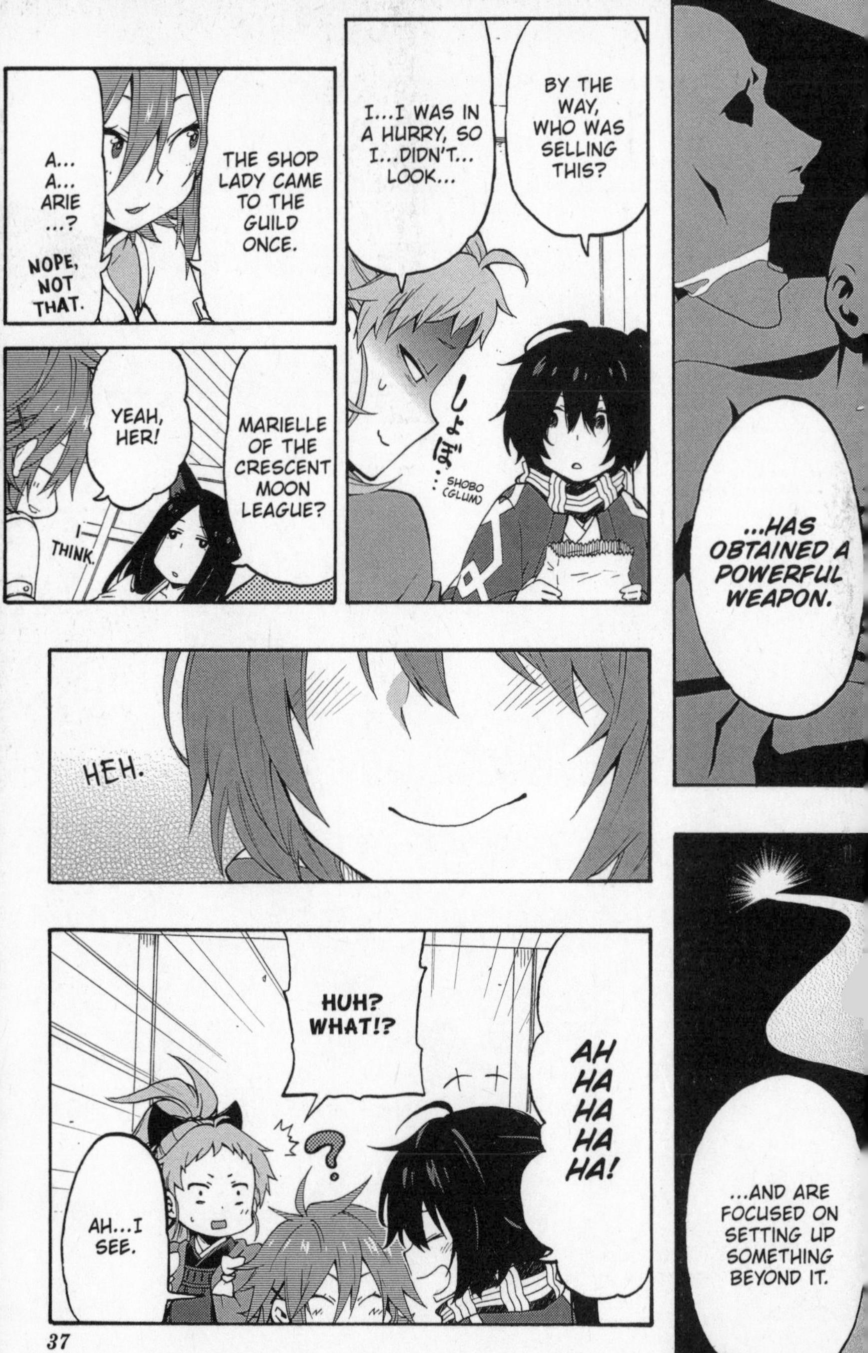
...HAS OBTAINED A POWERFUL WEAPON.
...AND ARE FOCUSED ON SETTING UP SOMETHING BEYOND IT.
BY THE WAY, WHO WAS SELLING THIS?
I...I WAS IN A HURRY, SO I...DIDN'T... LOOK...
しょぼ…
SHOBO (GLUM)
THE SHOP LADY CAME TO THE GUILD ONCE.
A... A... ARIE ...?
NOPE, NOT THAT.
MARIELLE OF THE CRESCENT MOON LEAGUE?
YEAH, HER!
I— THINK.
HEH.
AH HA HA HA HA!
HUH? WHAT!?
AH...I SEE.

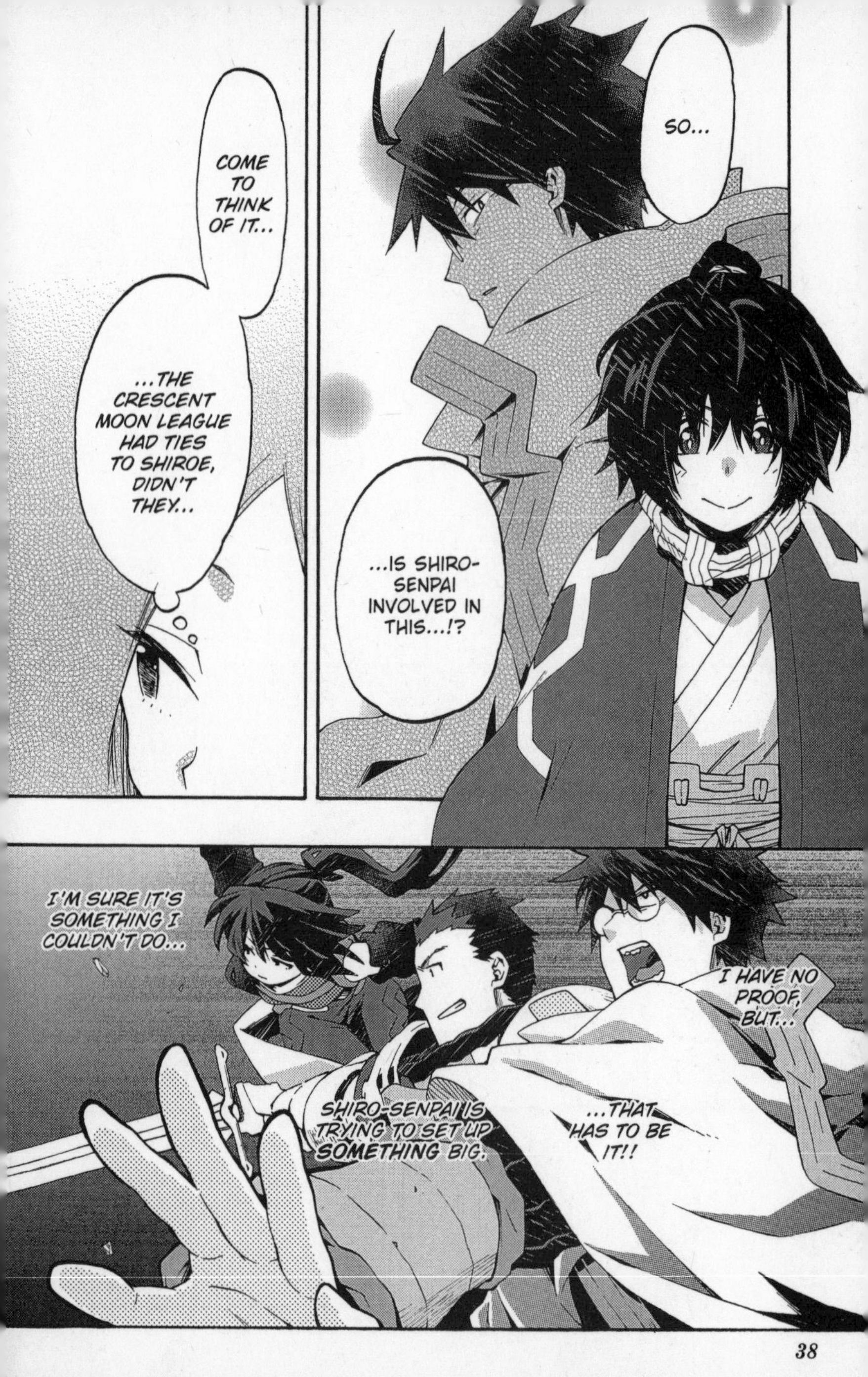
SO...
...IS SHIRO-SENPAI INVOLVED IN THIS...!?
COME TO THINK OF IT...
...THE CRESCENT MOON LEAGUE HAD TIES TO SHIROE, DIDN'T THEY...
I HAVE NO PROOF, BUT...
SHIRO-SENPAI IS TRYING TO SET UP SOMETHING BIG.
...THAT HAS TO BE IT!!
I'M SURE IT'S SOMETHING I COULDN'T DO...

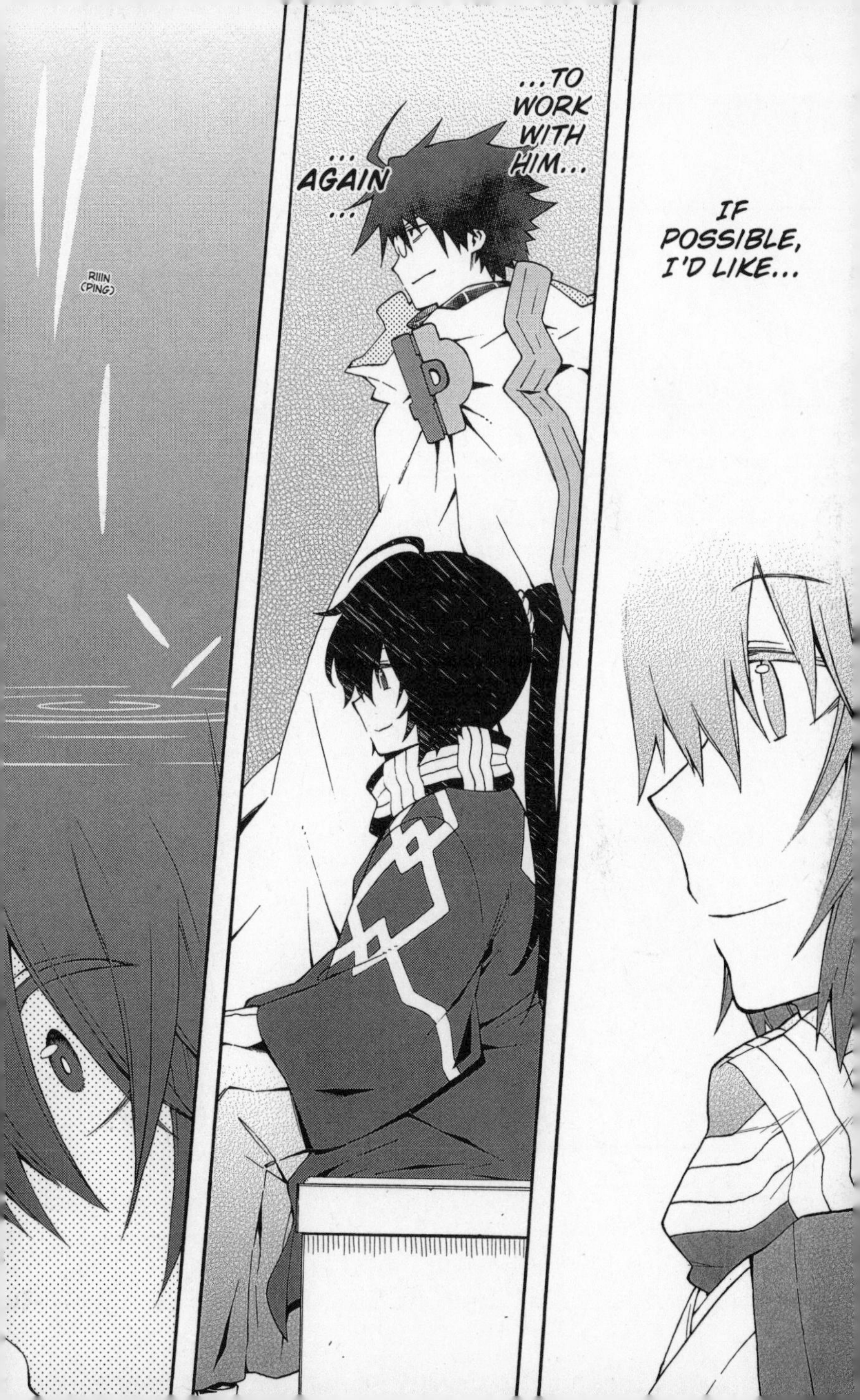
IF POSSIBLE, I'D LIKE...
...TO WORK WITH HIM...
...AGAIN...
RIIIN (PING)

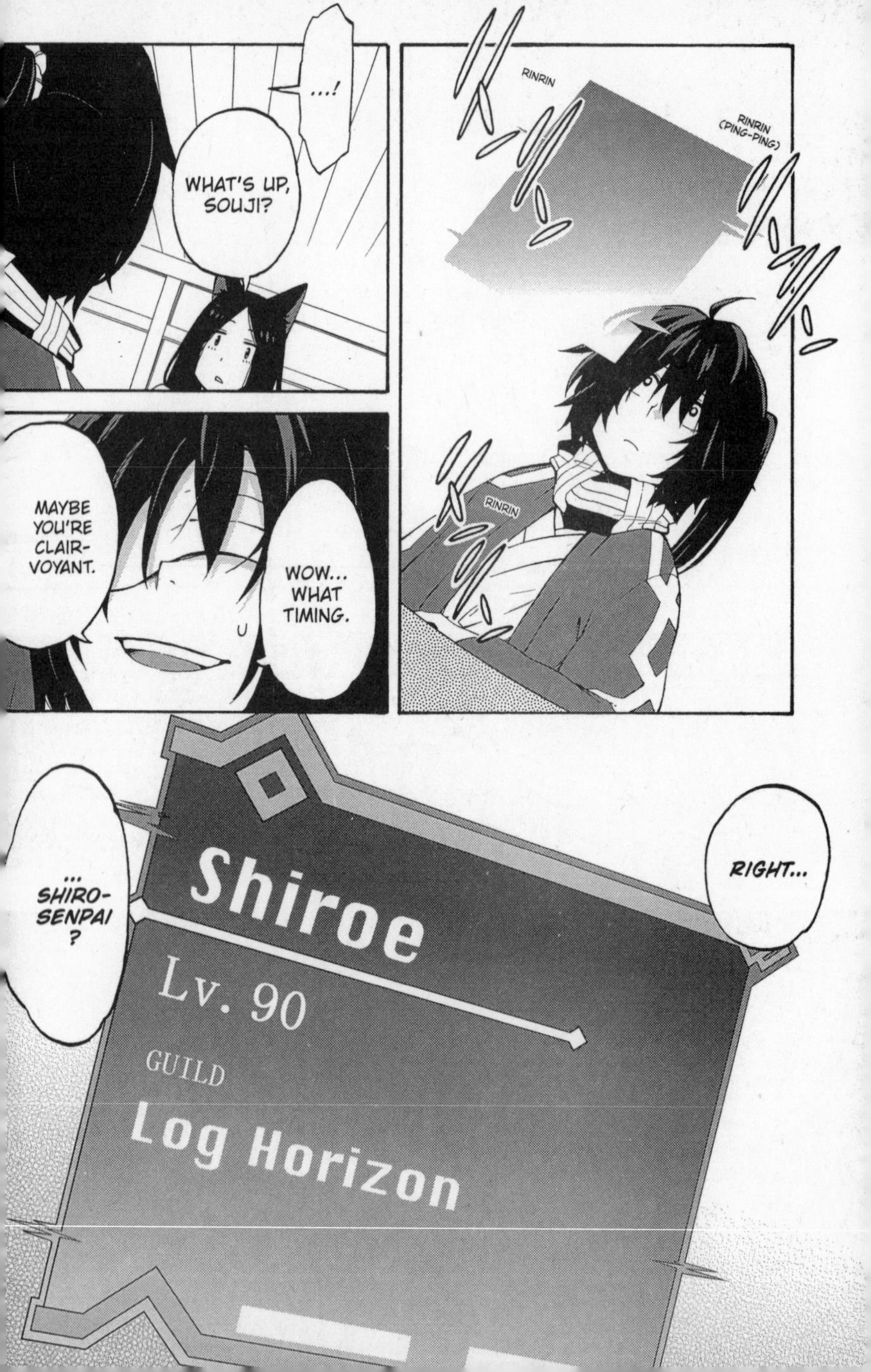
RINRIN
RINRIN (PING-PING)
RINRIN
...!
WHAT'S UP, SOUJI?
WOW... WHAT TIMING.
MAYBE YOU'RE CLAIR-VOYANT.
RIGHT...
... SHIRO-SENPAI?
Shiroe
Lv. 90
GUILD
Log Horizon

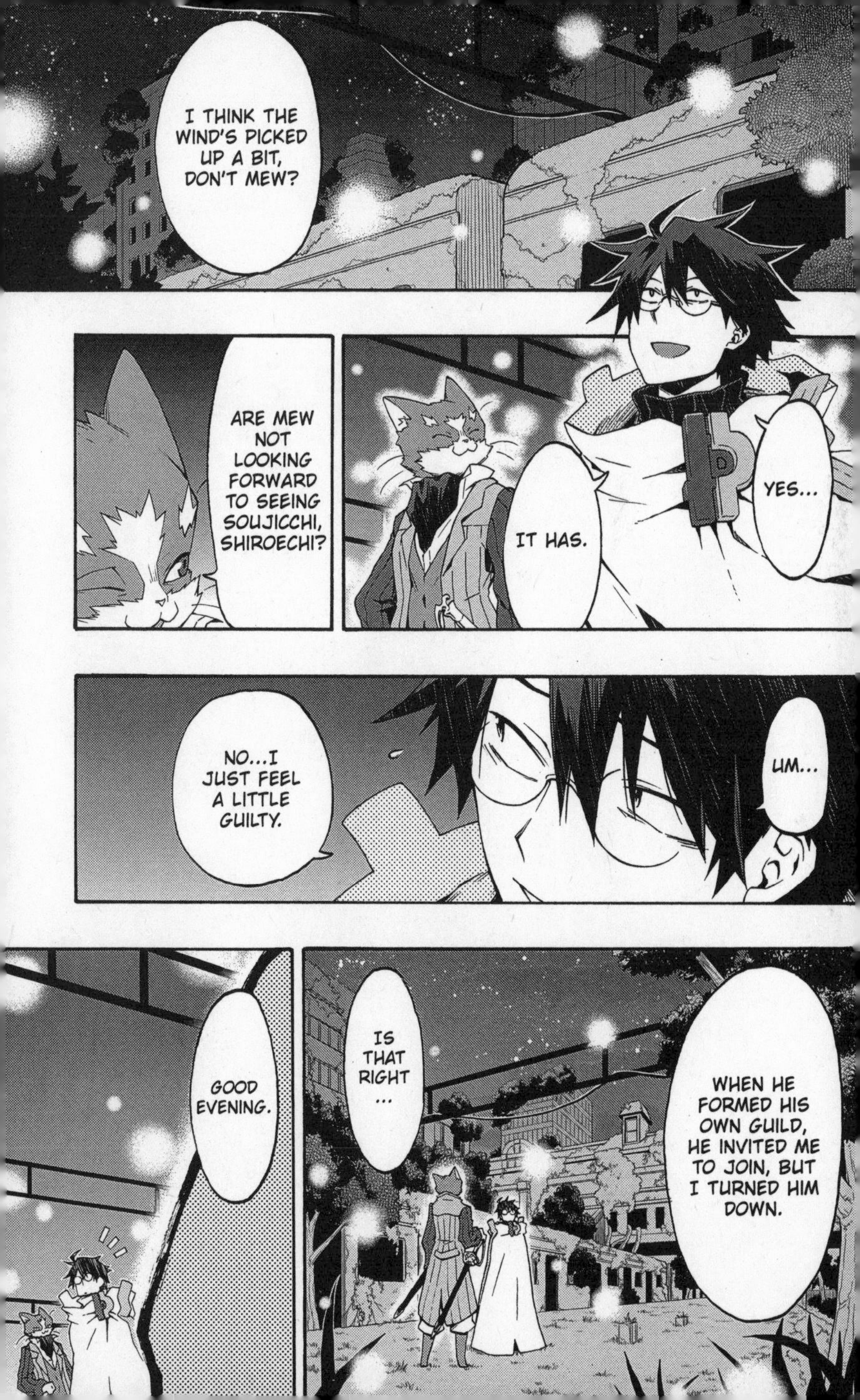
I THINK THE WIND'S PICKED UP A BIT, DON'T MEW?
YES...
IT HAS.
ARE MEW NOT LOOKING FORWARD TO SEEING SOUJICCHI, SHIROECHI?
UM...
NO...I JUST FEEL A LITTLE GUILTY.
WHEN HE FORMED HIS OWN GUILD, HE INVITED ME TO JOIN, BUT I TURNED HIM DOWN.
IS THAT RIGHT...
GOOD EVENING.

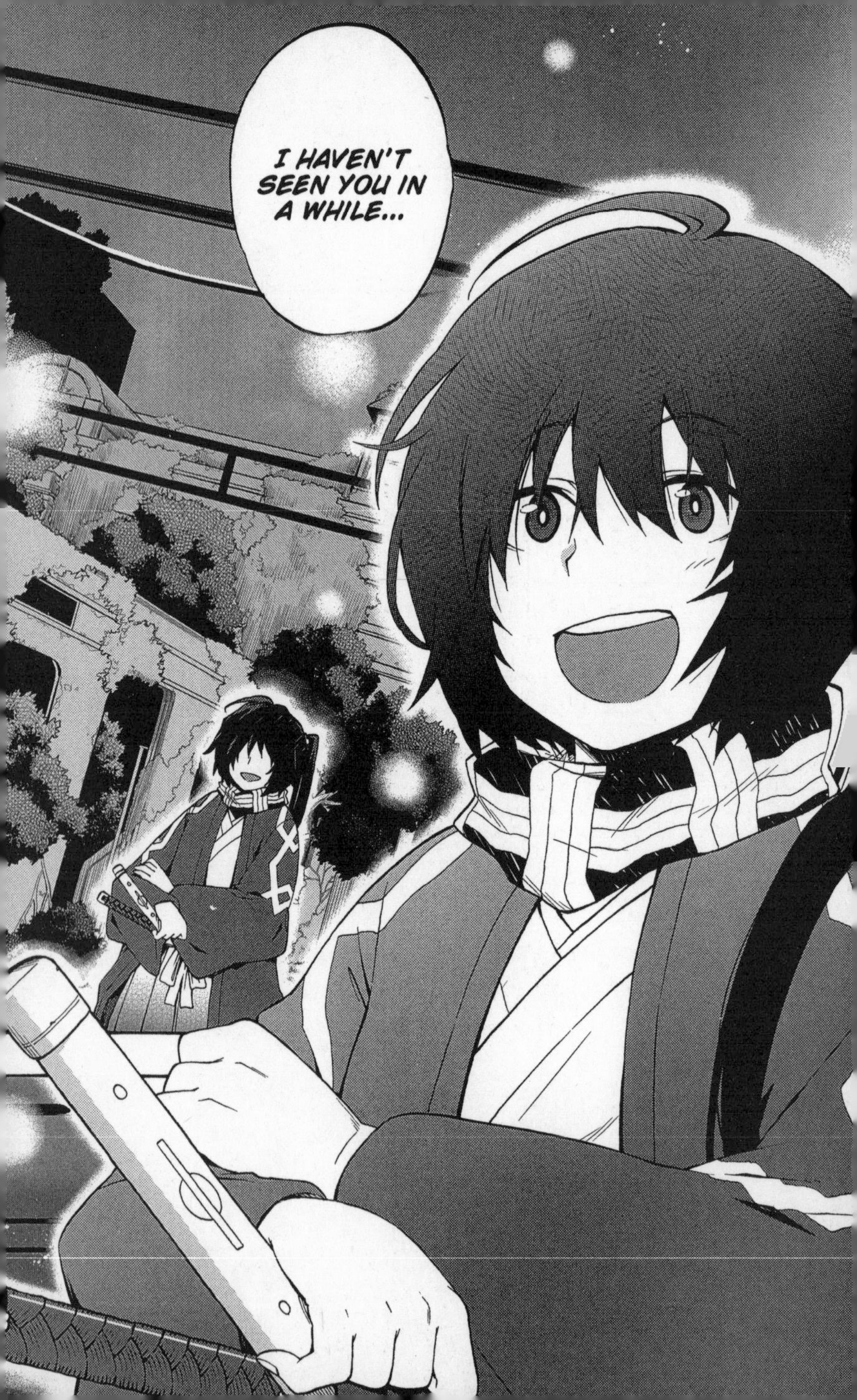
I HAVEN'T SEEN YOU IN A WHILE...

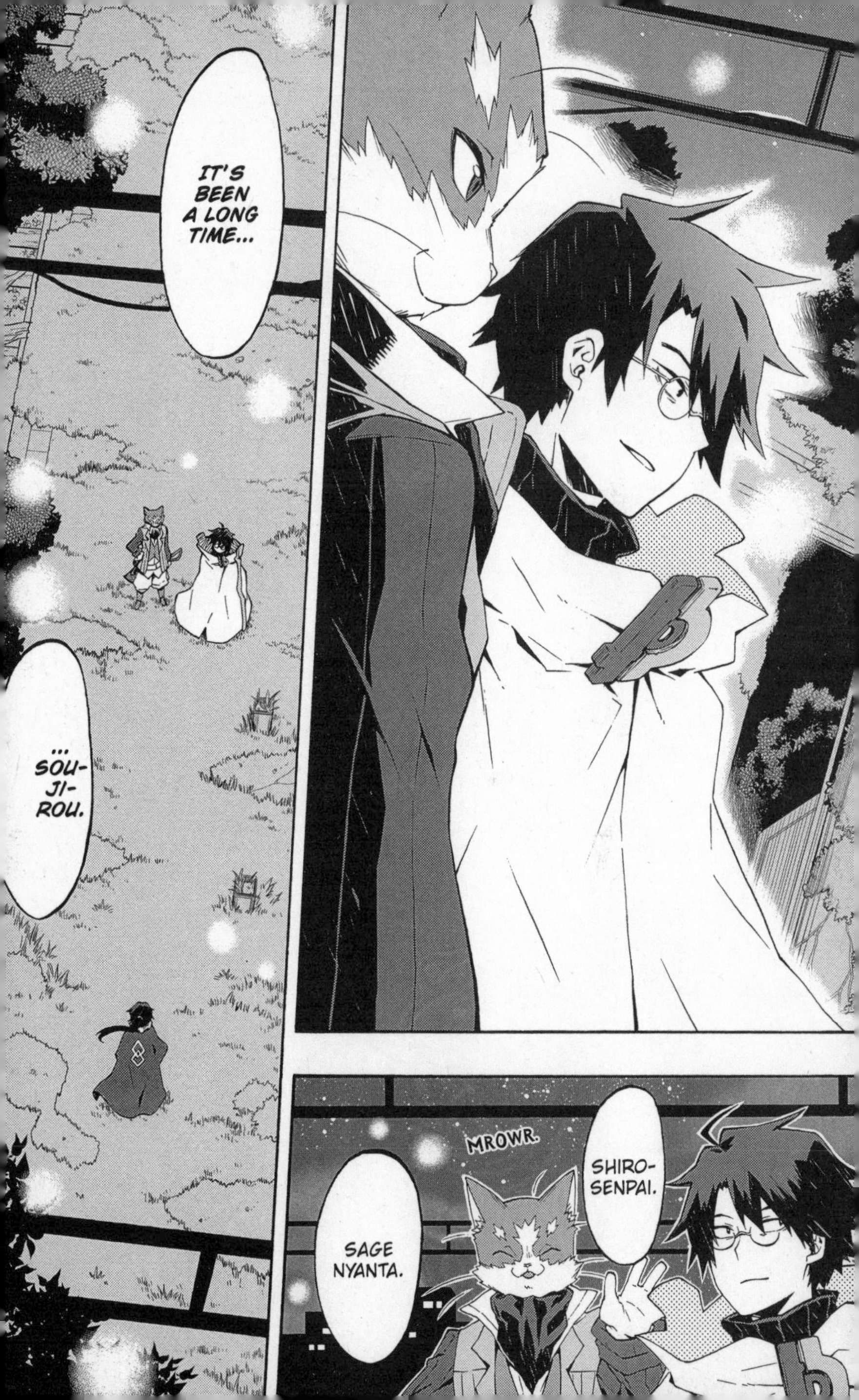
SHIRO-SENPAI.
MROWR.
SAGE NYANTA.
IT'S BEEN A LONG TIME...
... SOU-JI-ROU.

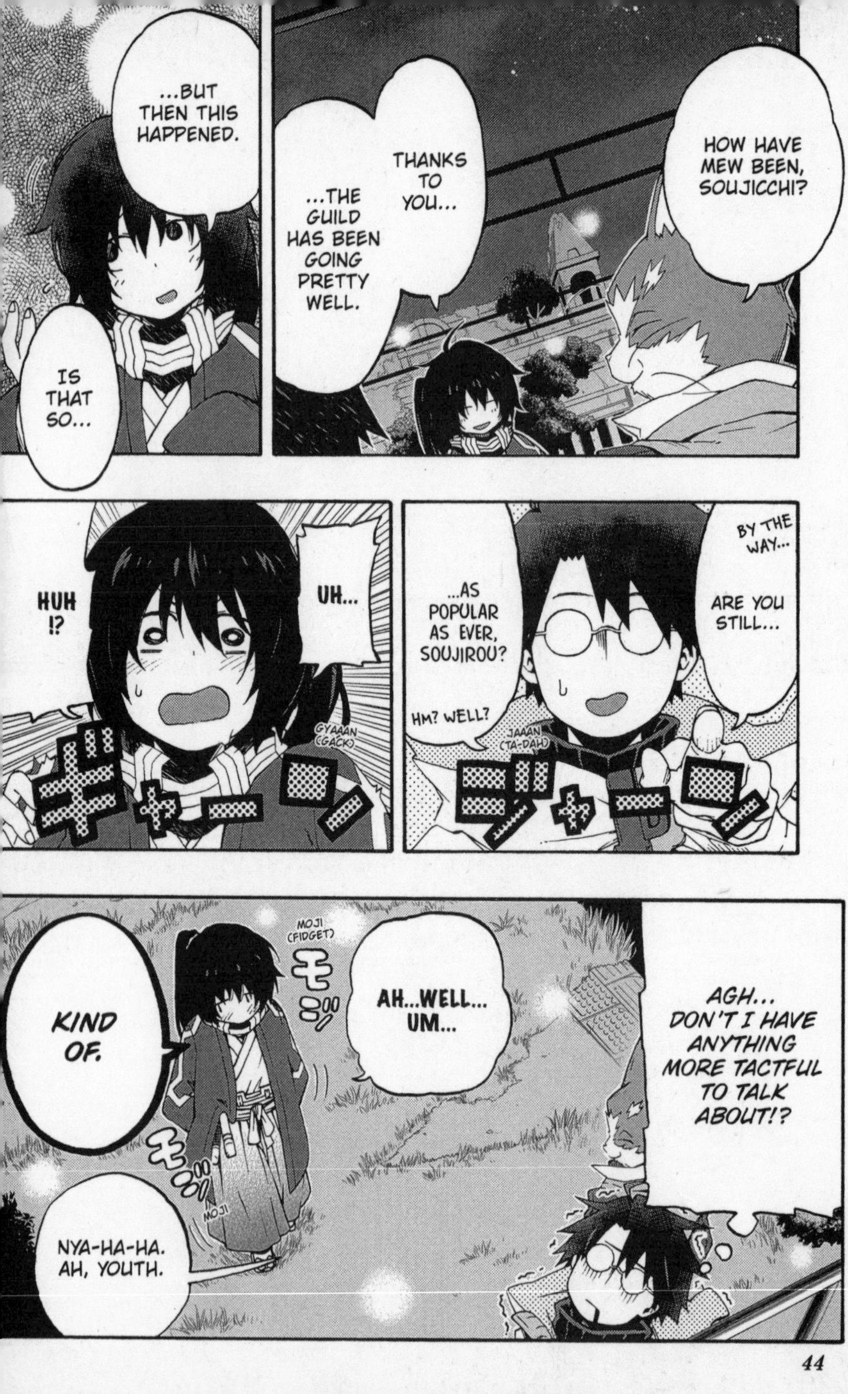
HOW HAVE MEW BEEN, SOUJICCHI?
THANKS TO YOU...
...THE GUILD HAS BEEN GOING PRETTY WELL.
...BUT THEN THIS HAPPENED.
IS THAT SO...
BY THE WAY...
ARE YOU STILL...
...AS POPULAR AS EVER, SOUJIROU?
HM? WELL?
JAAAN (TA-DAH)
UH...
HUH !?
GYAAAN (GACK)
AGH... DON'T I HAVE ANYTHING MORE TACTFUL TO TALK ABOUT!?
AH...WELL... UM...
MOJI (FIDGET)
KIND OF.
MOJI
NYA-HA-HA. AH, YOUTH.

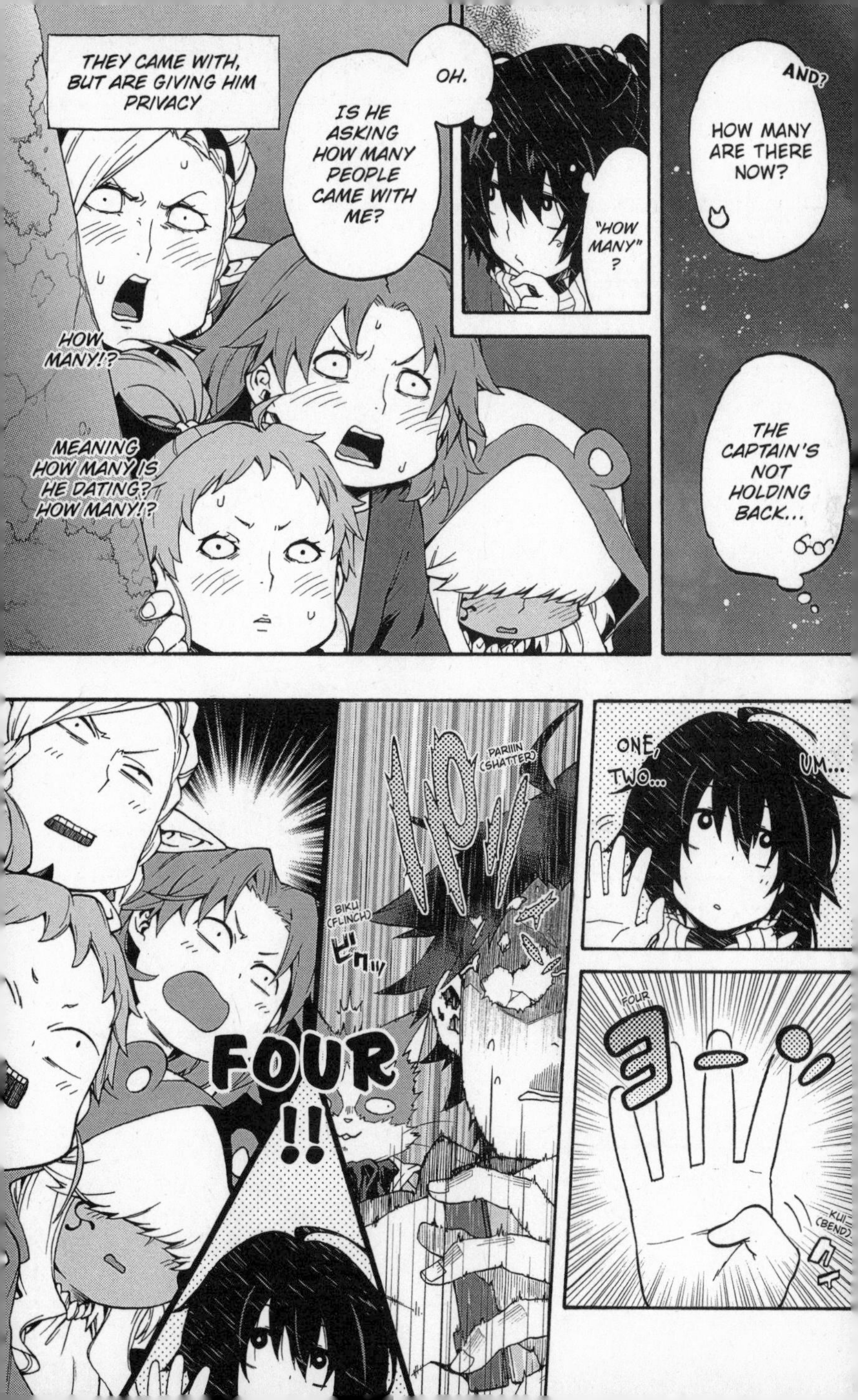
AND?
HOW MANY ARE THERE NOW?
THE CAPTAIN'S NOT HOLDING BACK...
"HOW MANY" ?
OH.
IS HE ASKING HOW MANY PEOPLE CAME WITH ME?
THEY CAME WITH, BUT ARE GIVING HIM PRIVACY
HOW MANY!?
MEANING HOW MANY IS HE DATING? HOW MANY!?
UM...
ONE, TWO...
FOUR
KUI (BEND)
PARIIIN (SHATTER)
BIKU (FLINCH)
FOUR !!

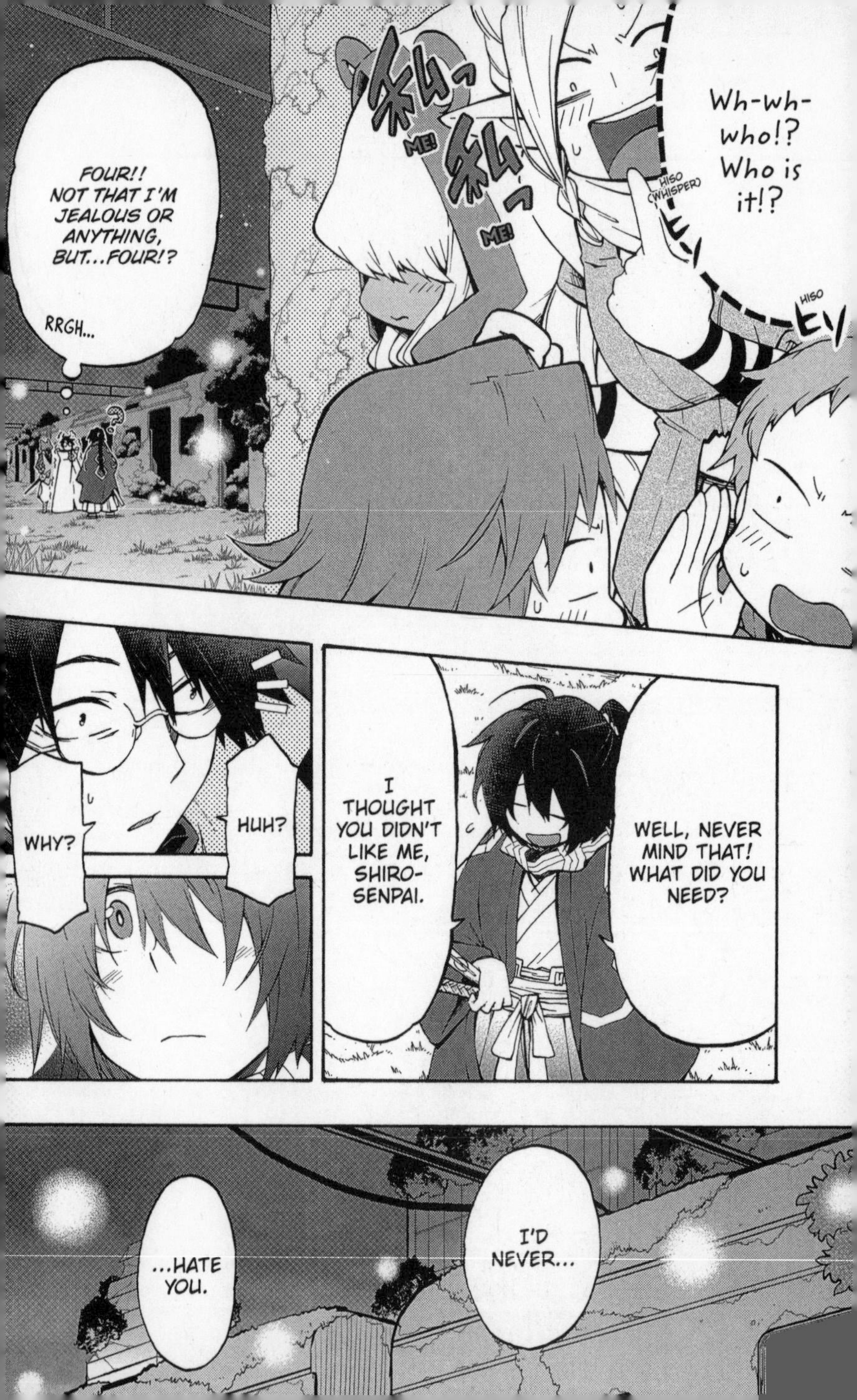
Wh-wh-who!? Who is it!?
私っ
ME!
私っ
ME!
HISO (WHISPER)
HISO
FOUR!! NOT THAT I'M JEALOUS OR ANYTHING, BUT...FOUR!?
RRGH...
WELL, NEVER MIND THAT! WHAT DID YOU NEED?
I THOUGHT YOU DIDN'T LIKE ME, SHIRO-SENPAI.
HUH?
WHY?
I'D NEVER...
...HATE YOU.

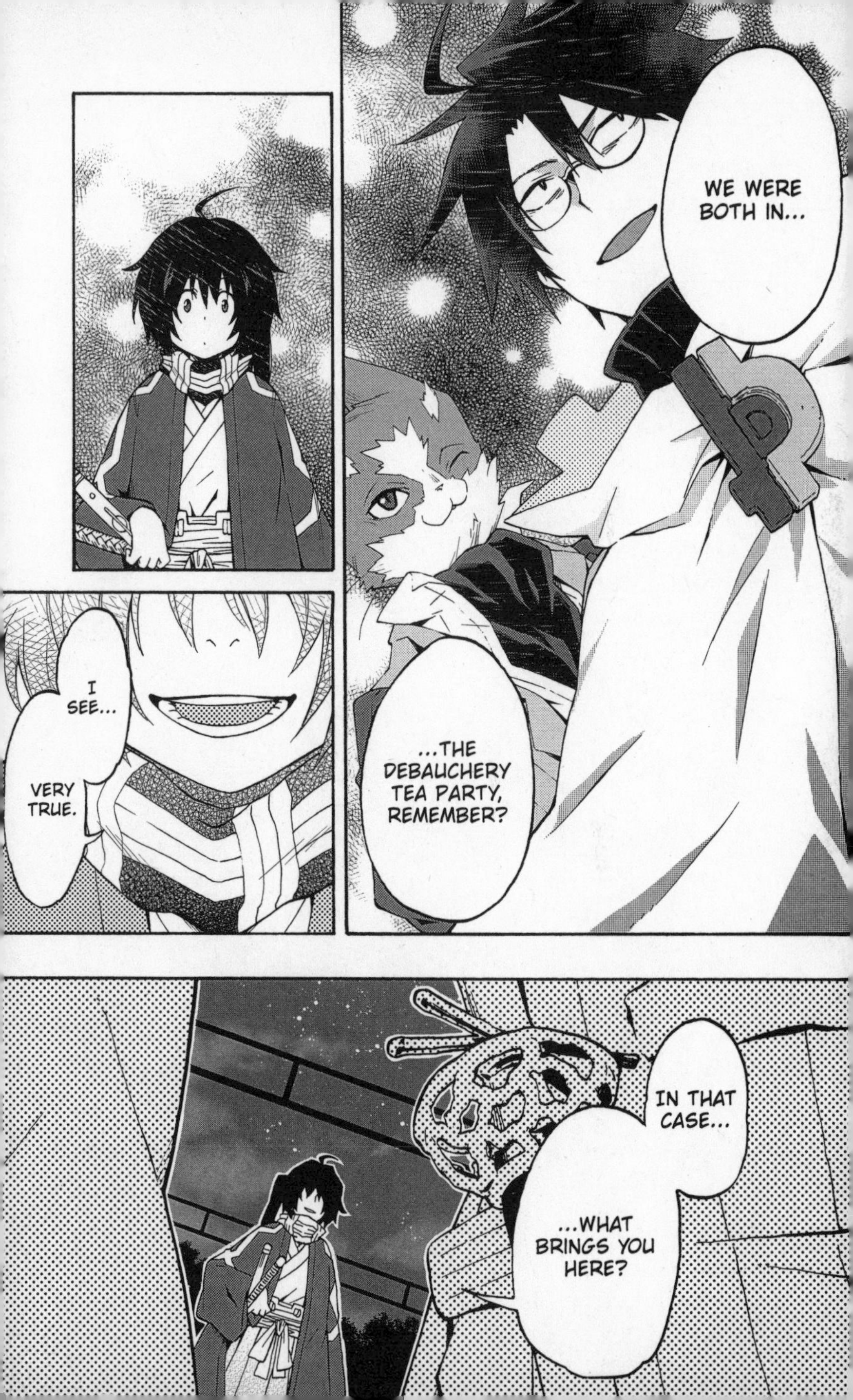
WE WERE BOTH IN...
...THE DEBAUCHERY TEA PARTY, REMEMBER?
I SEE...
VERY TRUE.
IN THAT CASE...
...WHAT BRINGS YOU HERE?

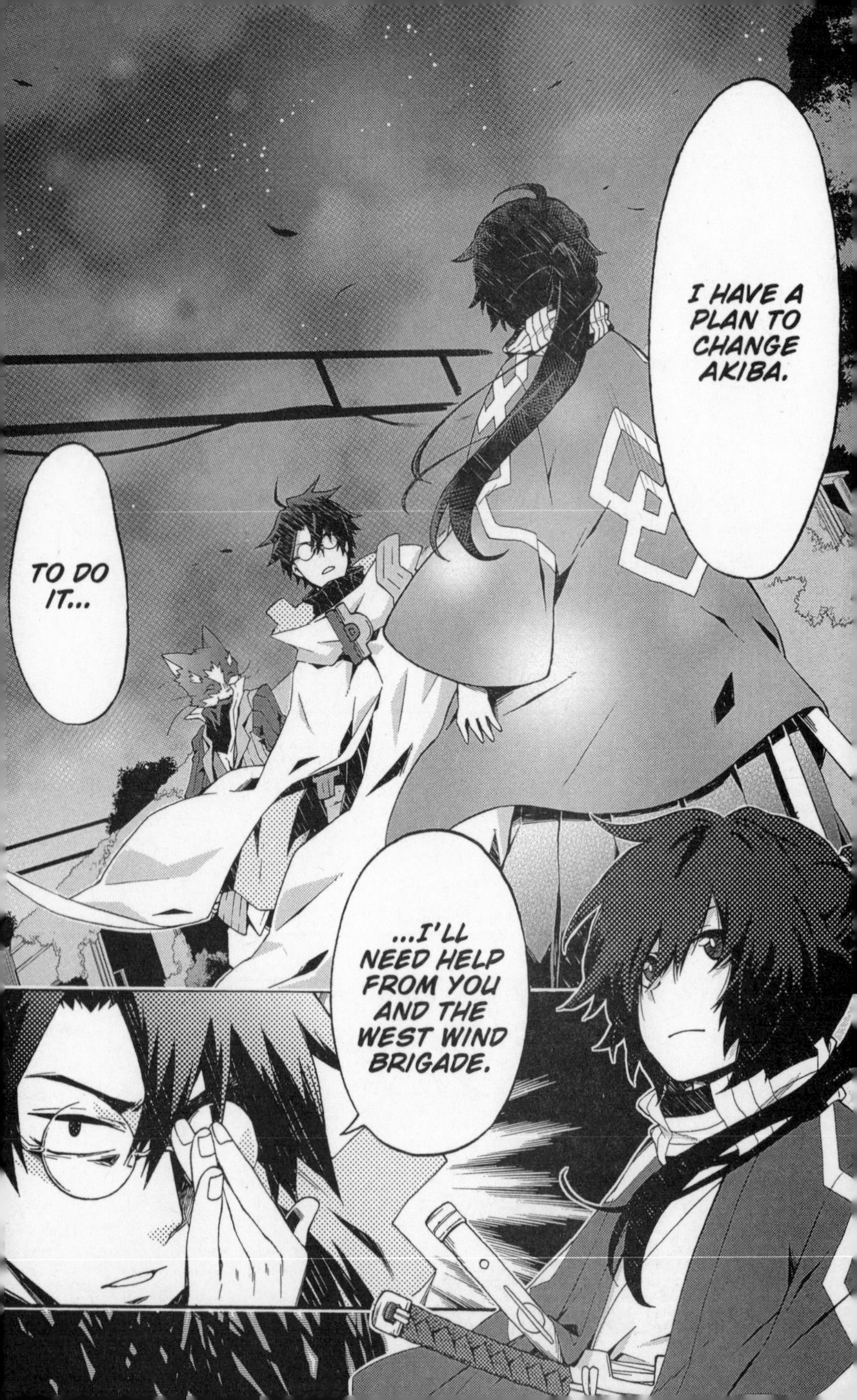
I HAVE A PLAN TO CHANGE AKIBA.
TO DO IT...
...I'LL NEED HELP FROM YOU AND THE WEST WIND BRIGADE.

LOG HORIZON
THE WEST WIND BRIGADE

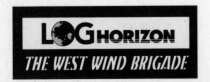

LOG HORIZON

THE WEST WIND BRIGADE

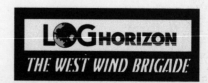

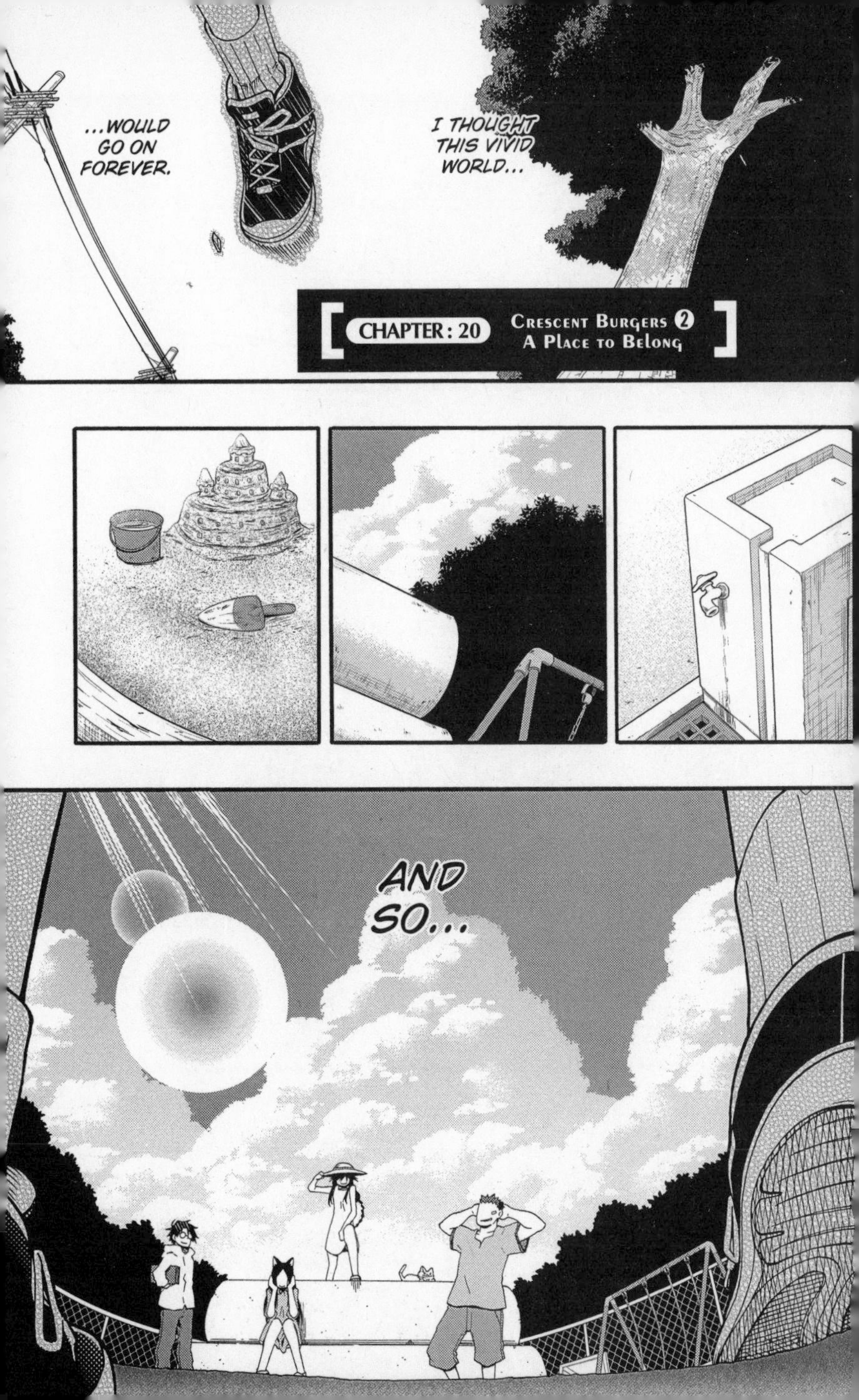
I THOUGHT THIS VIVID WORLD...
...WOULD GO ON FOREVER.
CHAPTER: 20
CRESCENT BURGERS 2
A PLACE TO BELONG
AND SO...

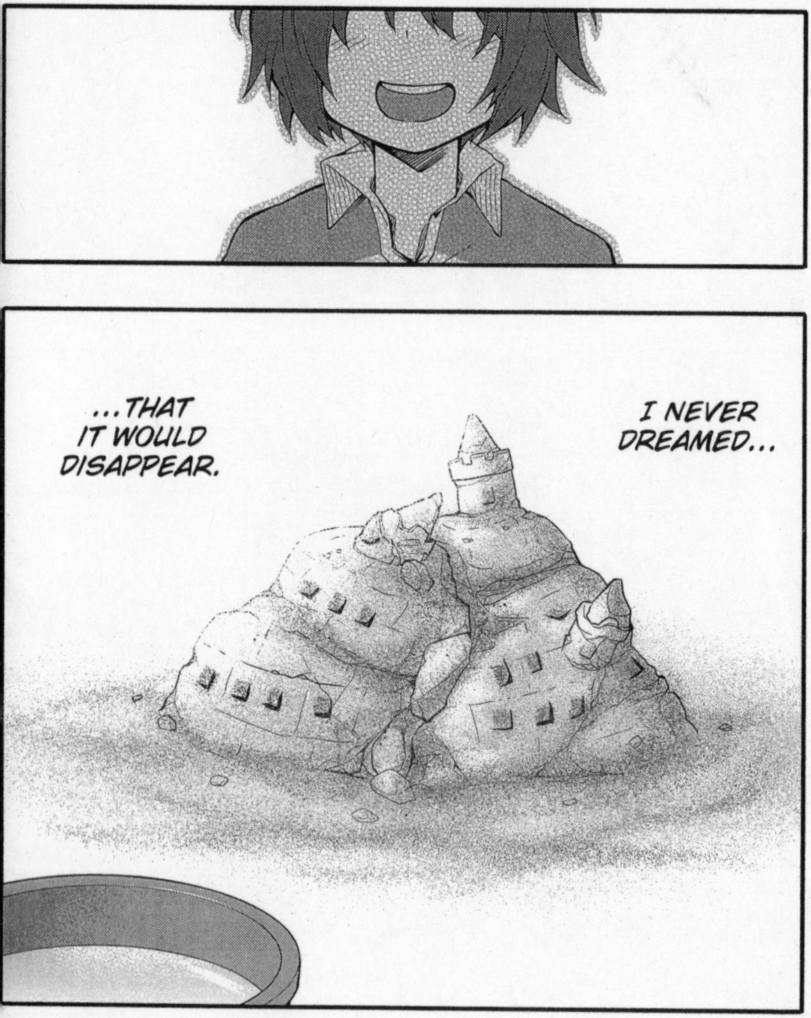
I NEVER DREAMED...
...THAT IT WOULD DISAPPEAR.

CHAPTER: 20 Crescent Burgers 2 A Place to Belong

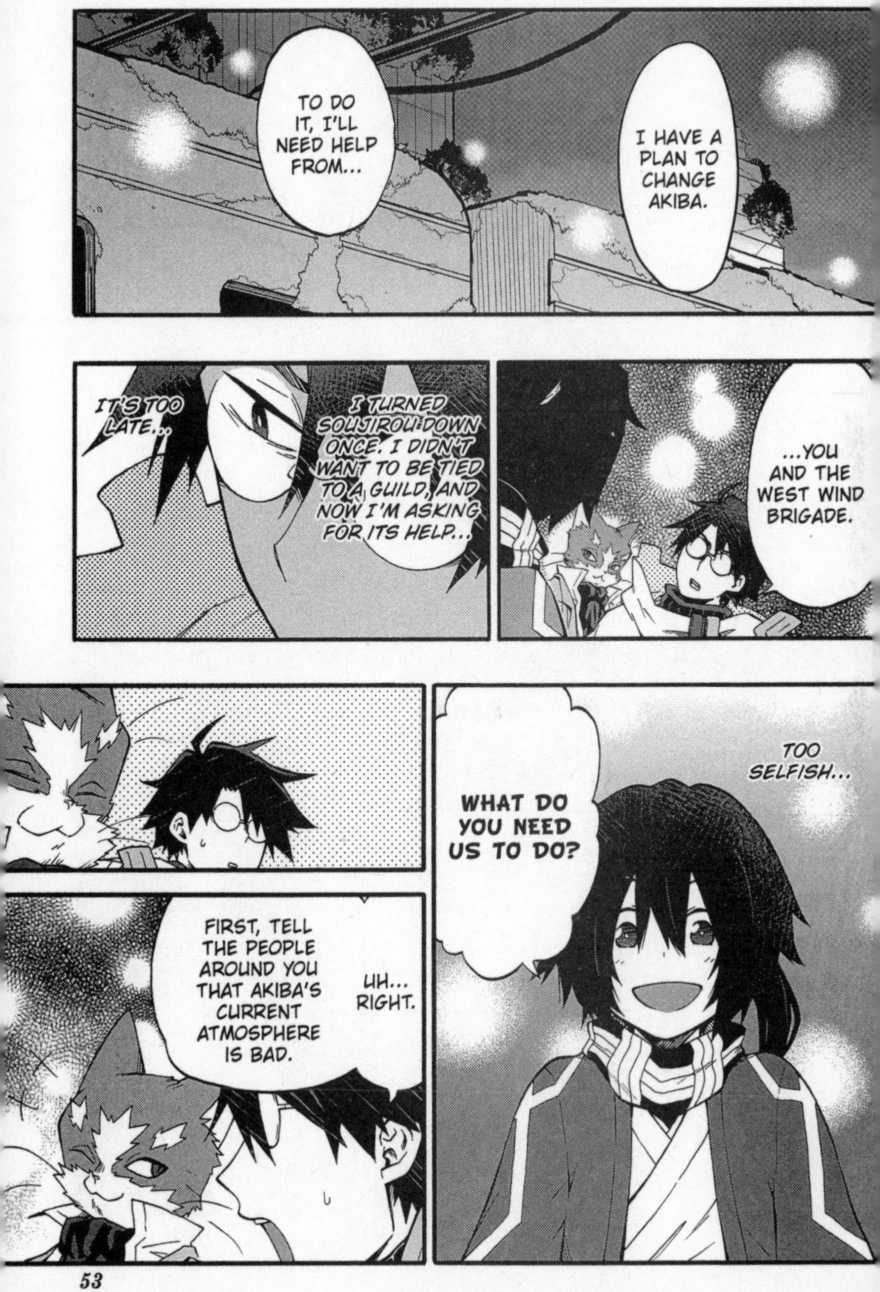
I HAVE A PLAN TO CHANGE AKIBA.
TO DO IT, I'LL NEED HELP FROM...
...YOU AND THE WEST WIND BRIGADE.
I TURNED SOUJIROU DOWN ONCE. I DIDN'T WANT TO BE TIED TO A GUILD, AND NOW I'M ASKING FOR ITS HELP...
IT'S TOO LATE...
TOO SELFISH...
WHAT DO YOU NEED US TO DO?
FIRST, TELL THE PEOPLE AROUND YOU THAT AKIBA'S CURRENT ATMOSPHERE IS BAD.
UH... RIGHT.

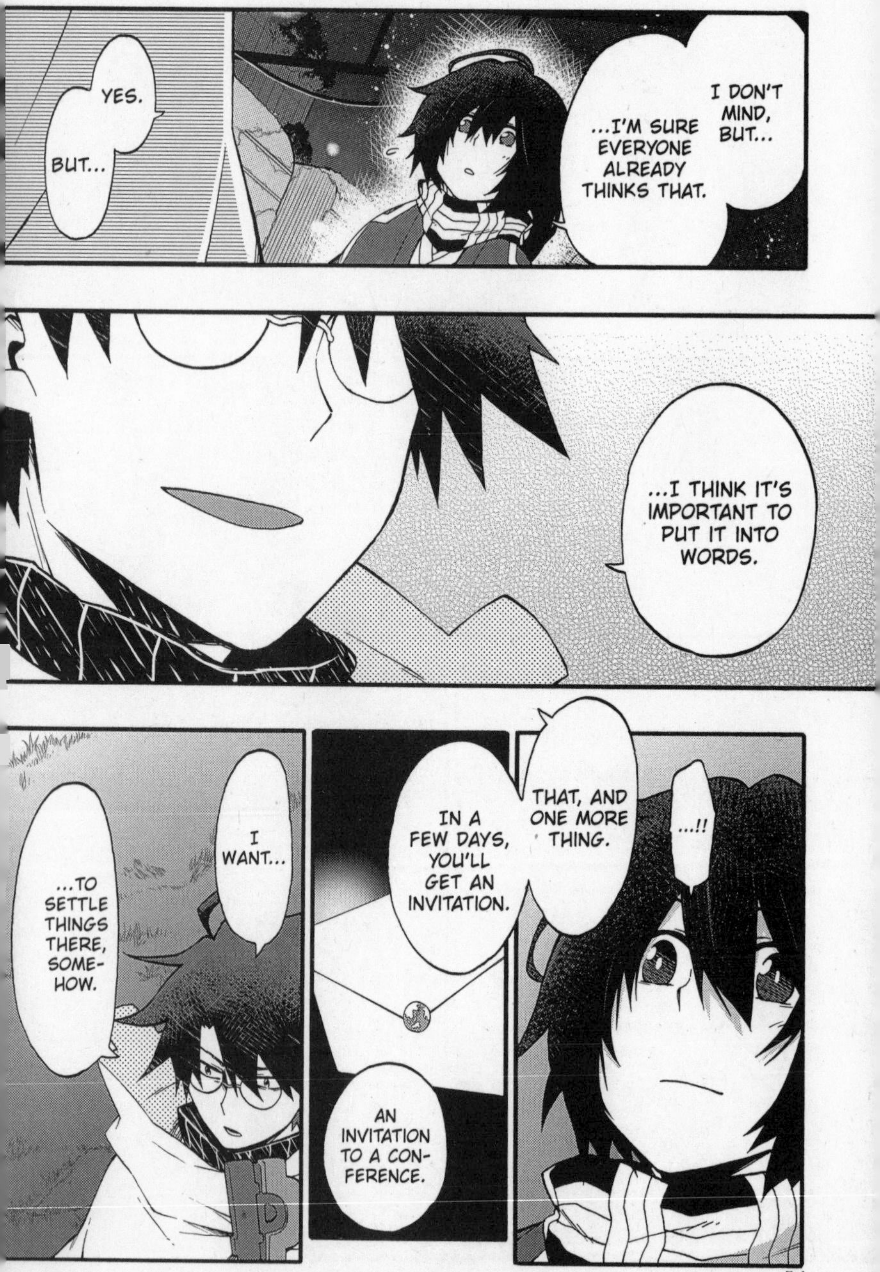
I DON'T MIND, BUT...
...I'M SURE EVERYONE ALREADY THINKS THAT.
YES.
BUT...
...I THINK IT'S IMPORTANT TO PUT IT INTO WORDS.
...!!
THAT, AND ONE MORE THING.
IN A FEW DAYS, YOU'LL GET AN INVITATION.
AN INVITATION TO A CONFERENCE.
I WANT...
...TO SETTLE THINGS THERE, SOMEHOW.

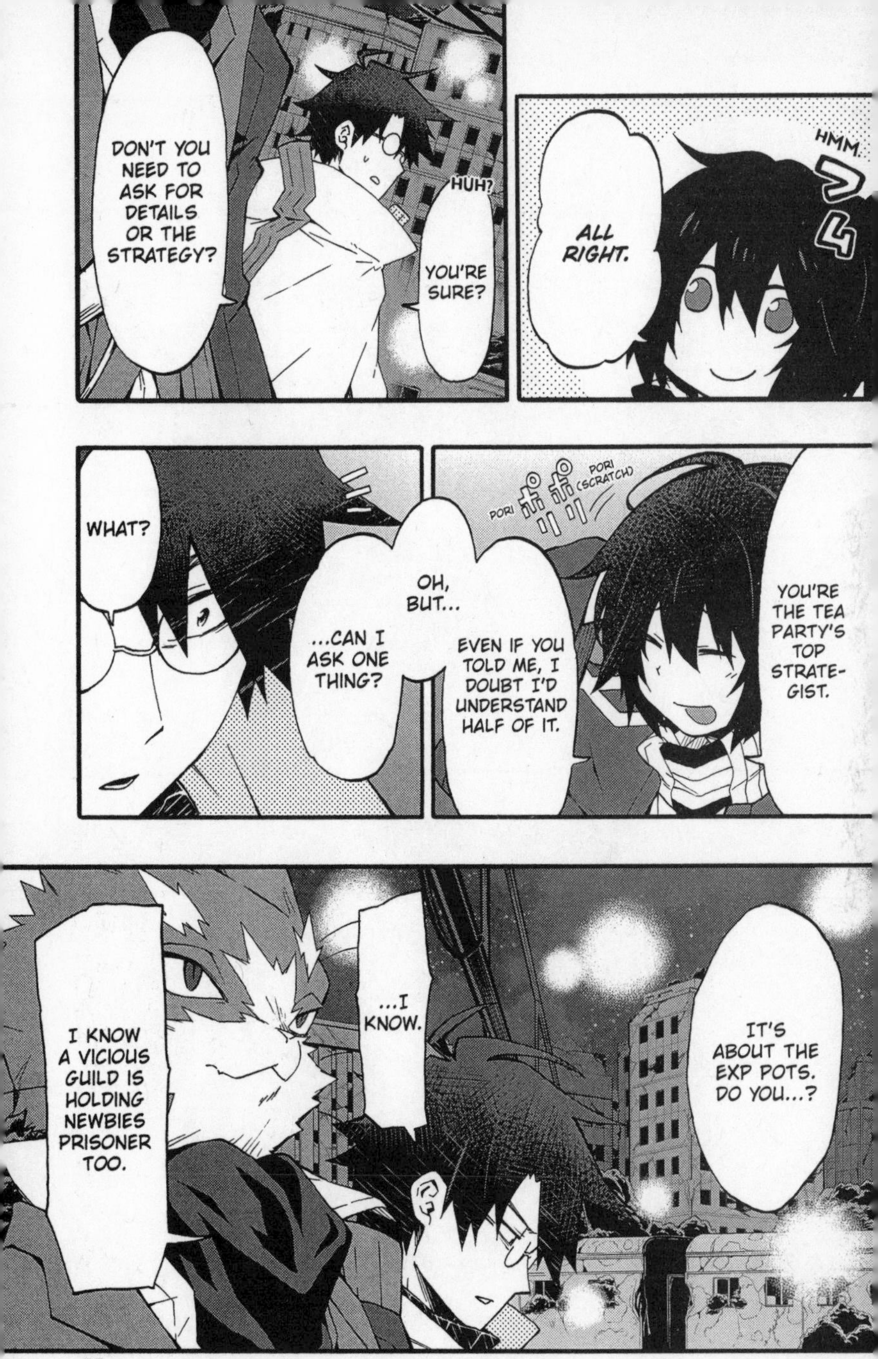
HMM.
ALL RIGHT.
HUH?
YOU'RE SURE?
DON'T YOU NEED TO ASK FOR DETAILS OR THE STRATEGY?
YOU'RE THE TEA PARTY'S TOP STRATEGIST.
PORI PORI (SCRATCH)
EVEN IF YOU TOLD ME, I DOUBT I'D UNDERSTAND HALF OF IT.
OH, BUT...
...CAN I ASK ONE THING?
WHAT?
IT'S ABOUT THE EXP POTS. DO YOU...?
...I KNOW.
I KNOW A VICIOUS GUILD IS HOLDING NEWBIES PRISONER TOO.

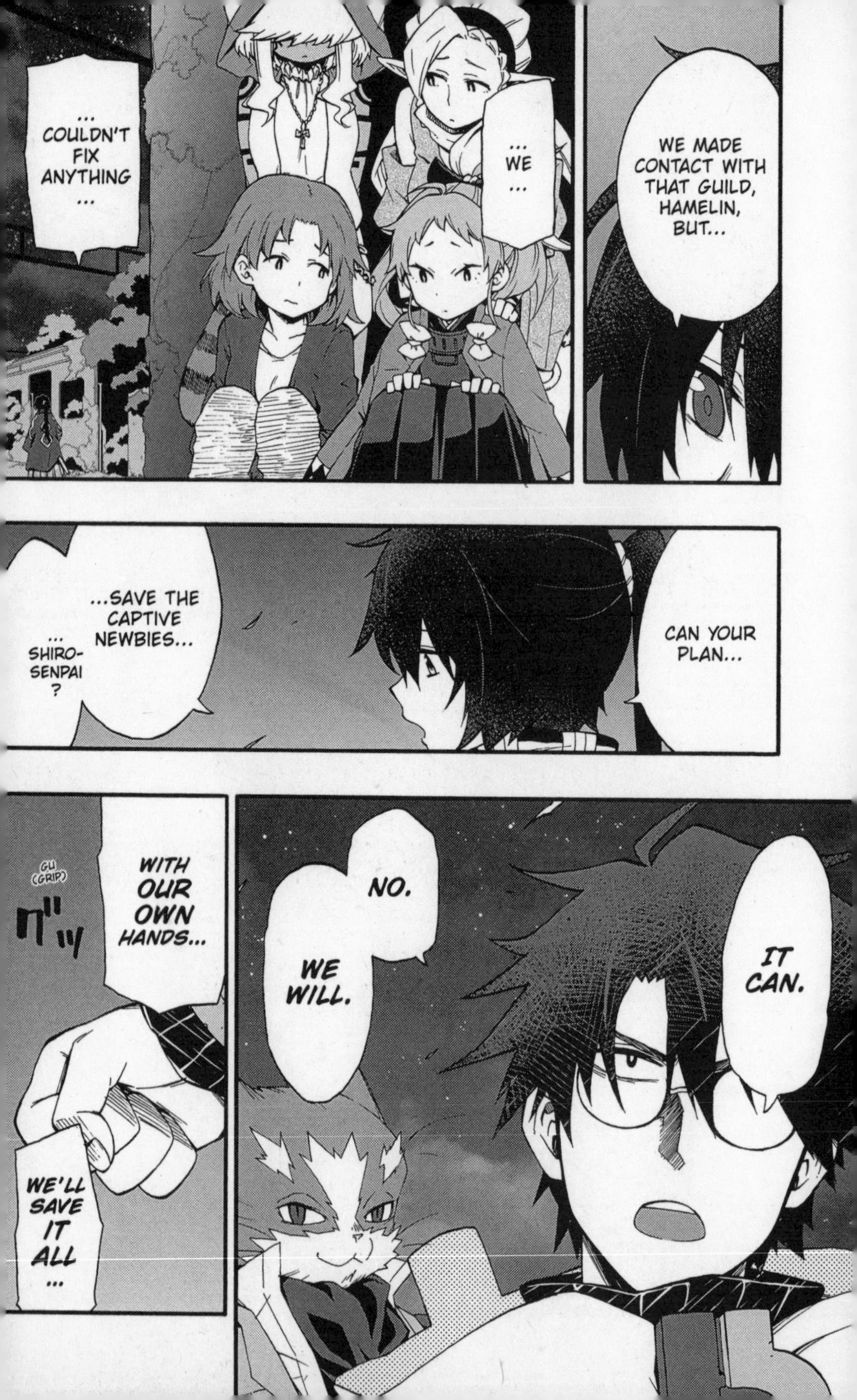
WE MADE CONTACT WITH THAT GUILD, HAMELIN, BUT...
... WE ...
... COULDN'T FIX ANYTHING ...
CAN YOUR PLAN...
...SAVE THE CAPTIVE NEWBIES...
... SHIRO-SENPAI ?
IT CAN.
NO.
WE WILL.
WITH OUR OWN HANDS...
GU (GRIP)
WE'LL SAVE IT ALL ...

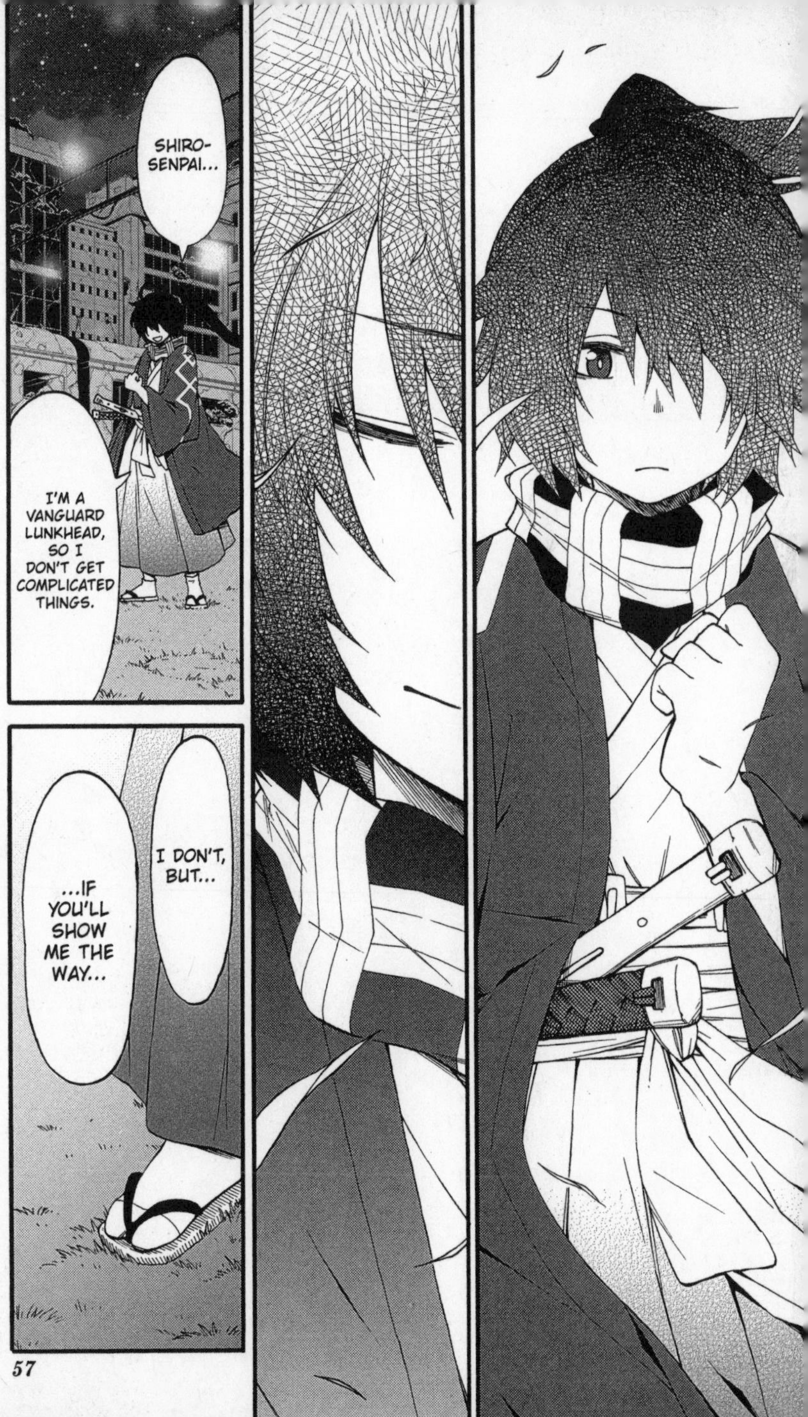
SHIRO-SENPAI…
I'M A VANGUARD LUNKHEAD, SO I DON'T GET COMPLICATED THINGS.
I DON'T, BUT…
…IF YOU'LL SHOW ME THE WAY…

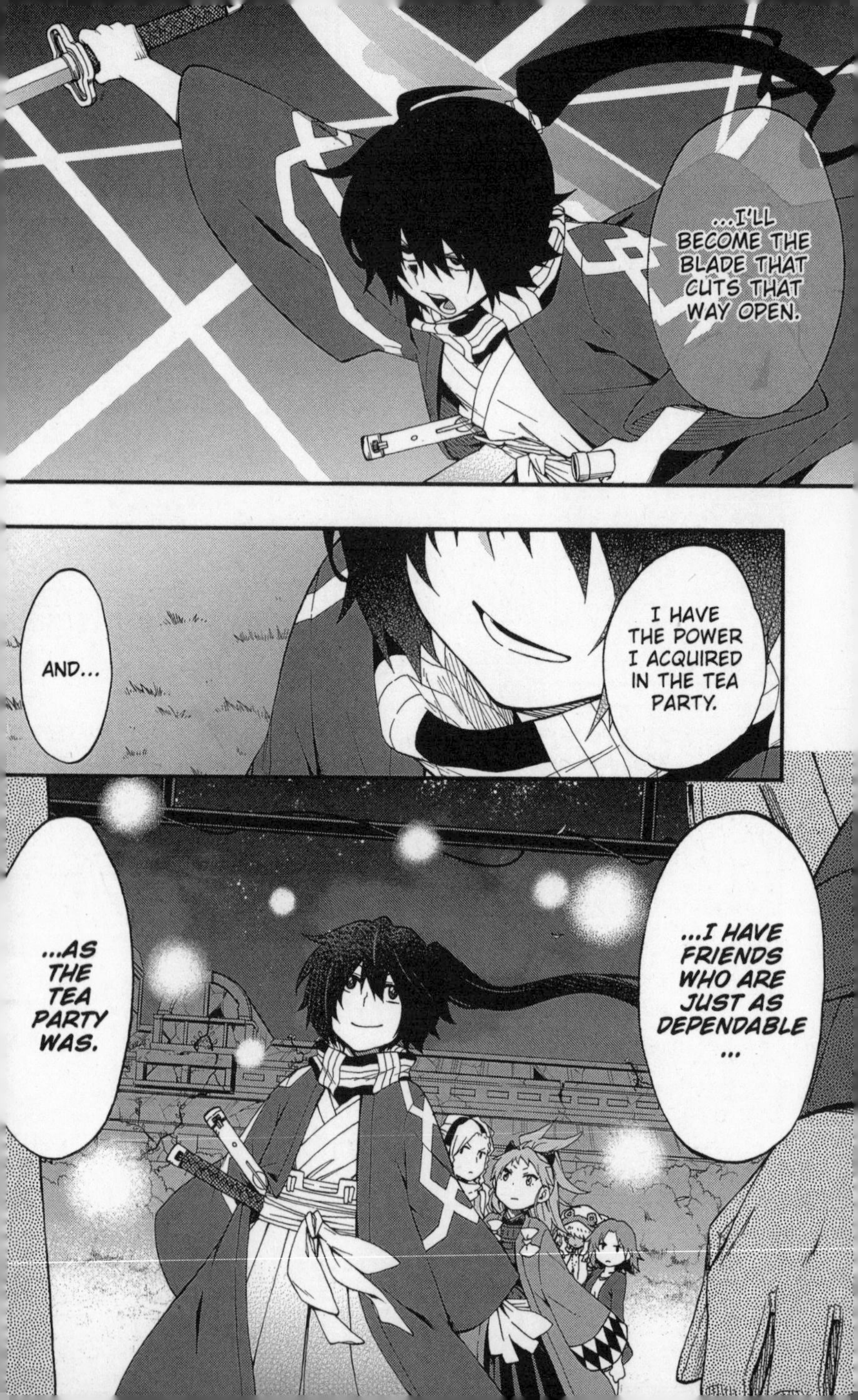
...I'LL BECOME THE BLADE THAT CUTS THAT WAY OPEN.
I HAVE THE POWER I ACQUIRED IN THE TEA PARTY.
AND...
...I HAVE FRIENDS WHO ARE JUST AS DEPENDABLE ...
...AS THE TEA PARTY WAS.

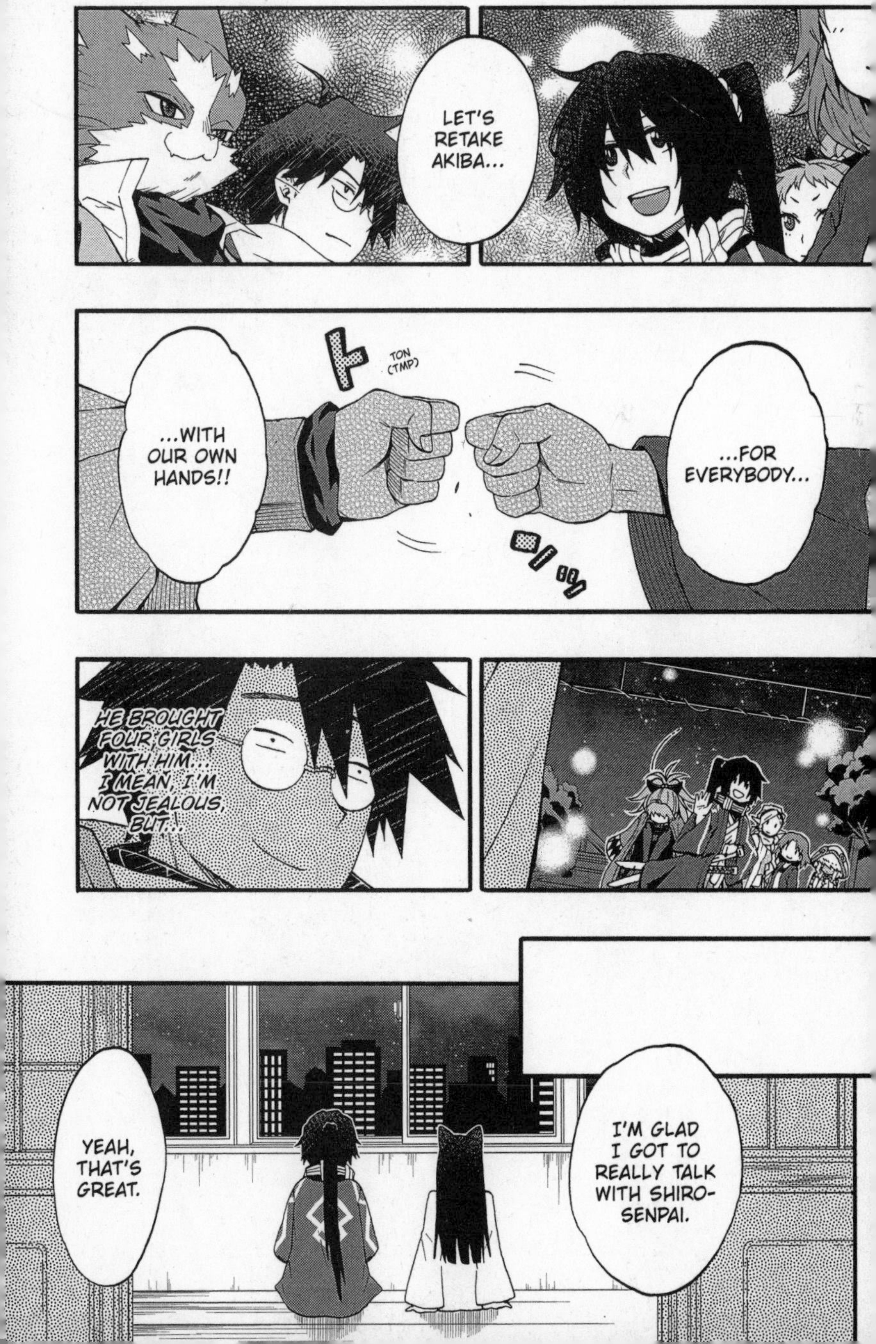
LET'S RETAKE AKIBA...
...FOR EVERYBODY...
TON (TMP)
...WITH OUR OWN HANDS!!
HE BROUGHT FOUR GIRLS WITH HIM... I MEAN, I'M NOT JEALOUS, BUT...
I'M GLAD I GOT TO REALLY TALK WITH SHIRO-SENPAI.
YEAH, THAT'S GREAT.

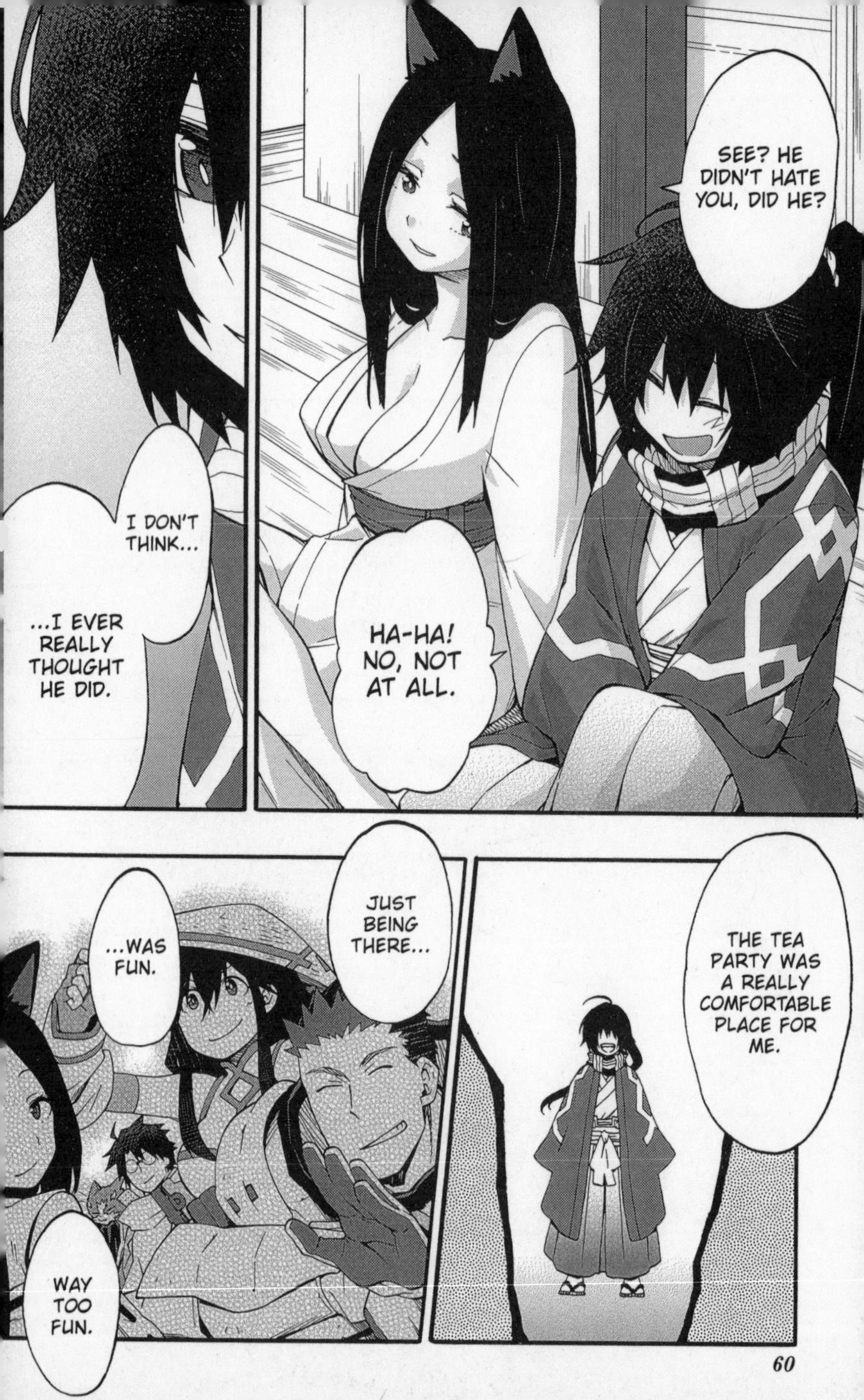
SEE? HE DIDN'T HATE YOU, DID HE?
HA-HA! NO, NOT AT ALL.
I DON'T THINK...
...I EVER REALLY THOUGHT HE DID.
THE TEA PARTY WAS A REALLY COMFORTABLE PLACE FOR ME.
JUST BEING THERE...
...WAS FUN.
WAY TOO FUN.

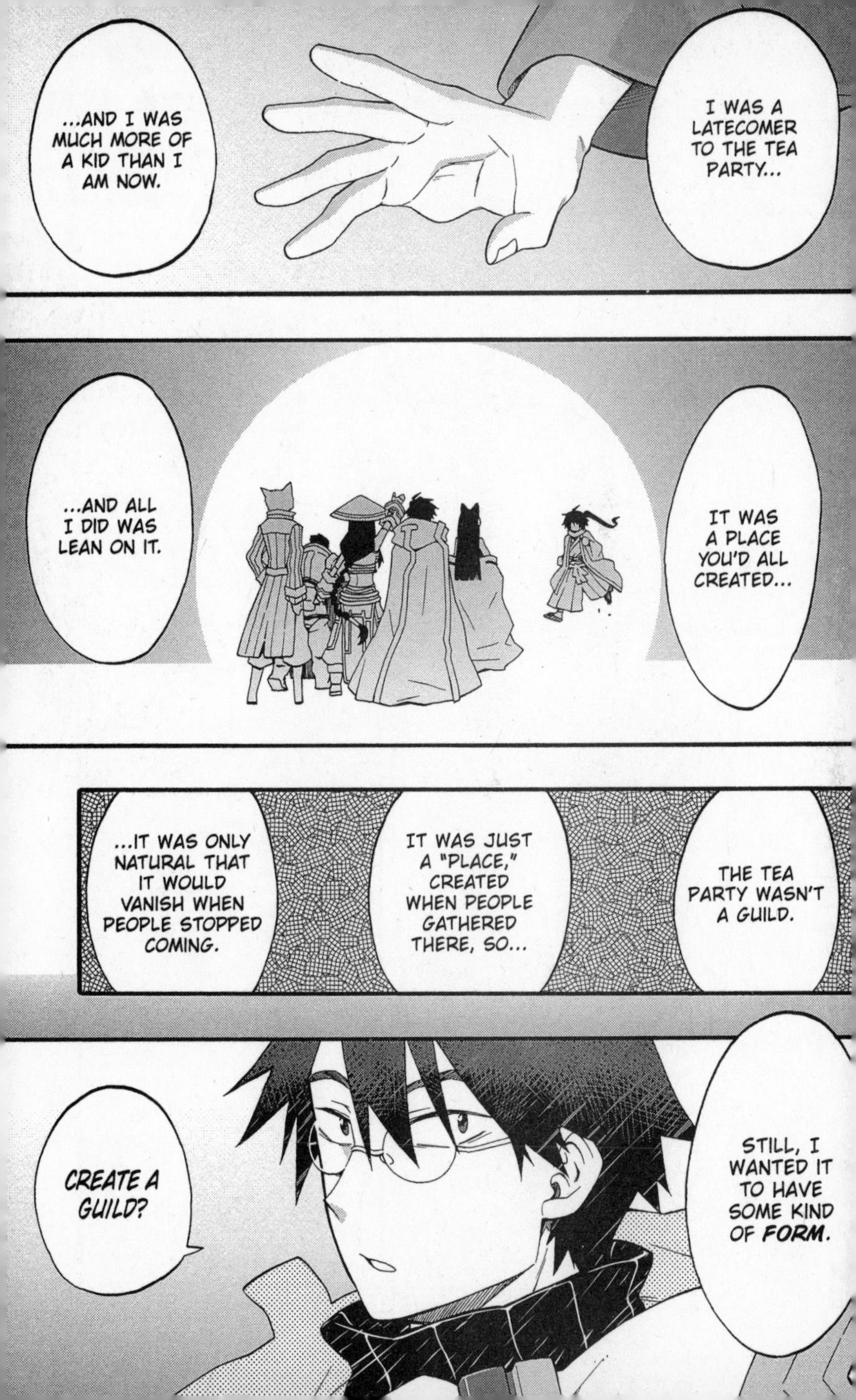
I WAS A LATECOMER TO THE TEA PARTY...
...AND I WAS MUCH MORE OF A KID THAN I AM NOW.
IT WAS A PLACE YOU'D ALL CREATED...
...AND ALL I DID WAS LEAN ON IT.
THE TEA PARTY WASN'T A GUILD.
IT WAS JUST A "PLACE," CREATED WHEN PEOPLE GATHERED THERE, SO...
...IT WAS ONLY NATURAL THAT IT WOULD VANISH WHEN PEOPLE STOPPED COMING.
STILL, I WANTED IT TO HAVE SOME KIND OF *FORM*.
CREATE A GUILD?

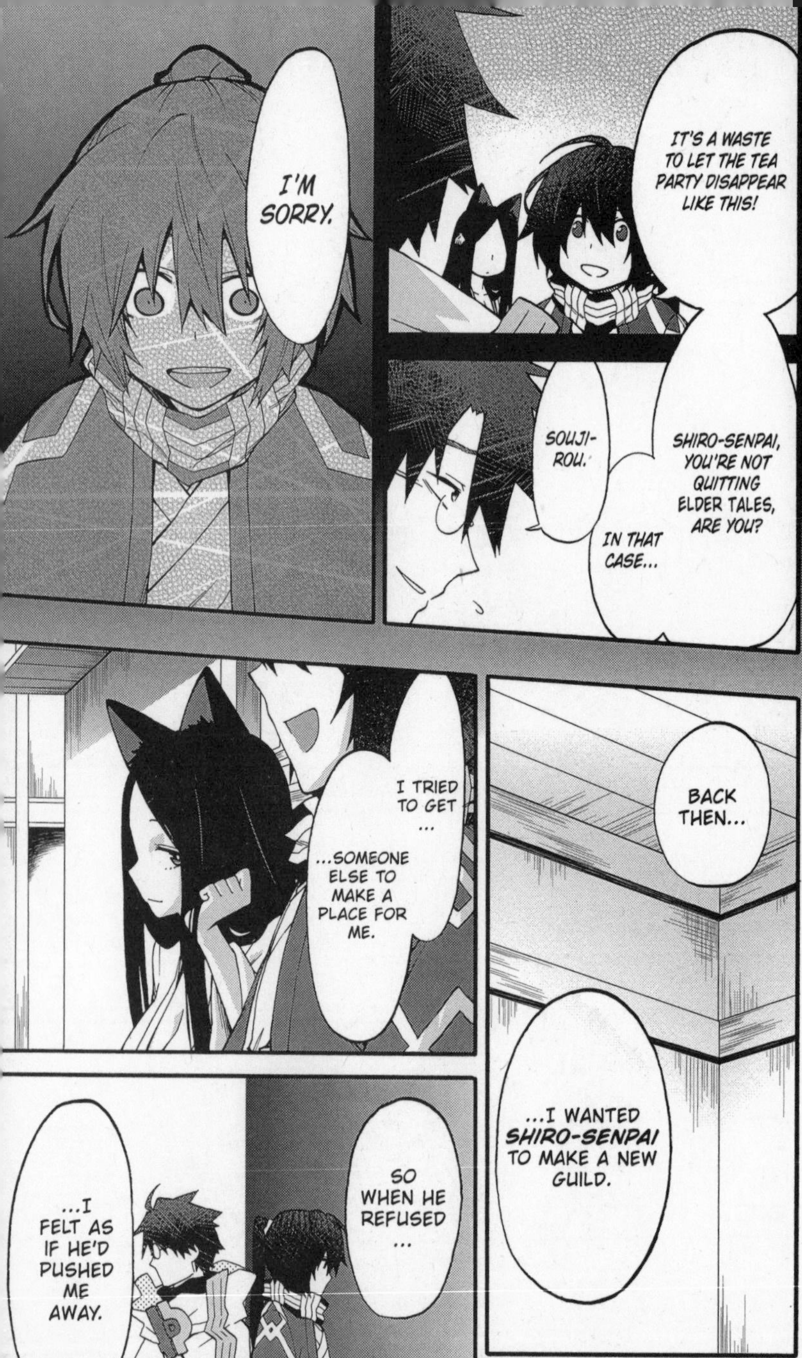
IT'S A WASTE TO LET THE TEA PARTY DISAPPEAR LIKE THIS!
SHIRO-SENPAI, YOU'RE NOT QUITTING ELDER TALES, ARE YOU?
IN THAT CASE...
SOUJI-ROU.
I'M SORRY.
BACK THEN...
...I WANTED *SHIRO-SENPAI* TO MAKE A NEW GUILD.
I TRIED TO GET ...
...SOMEONE ELSE TO MAKE A PLACE FOR ME.
SO WHEN HE REFUSED ...
...I FELT AS IF HE'D PUSHED ME AWAY.

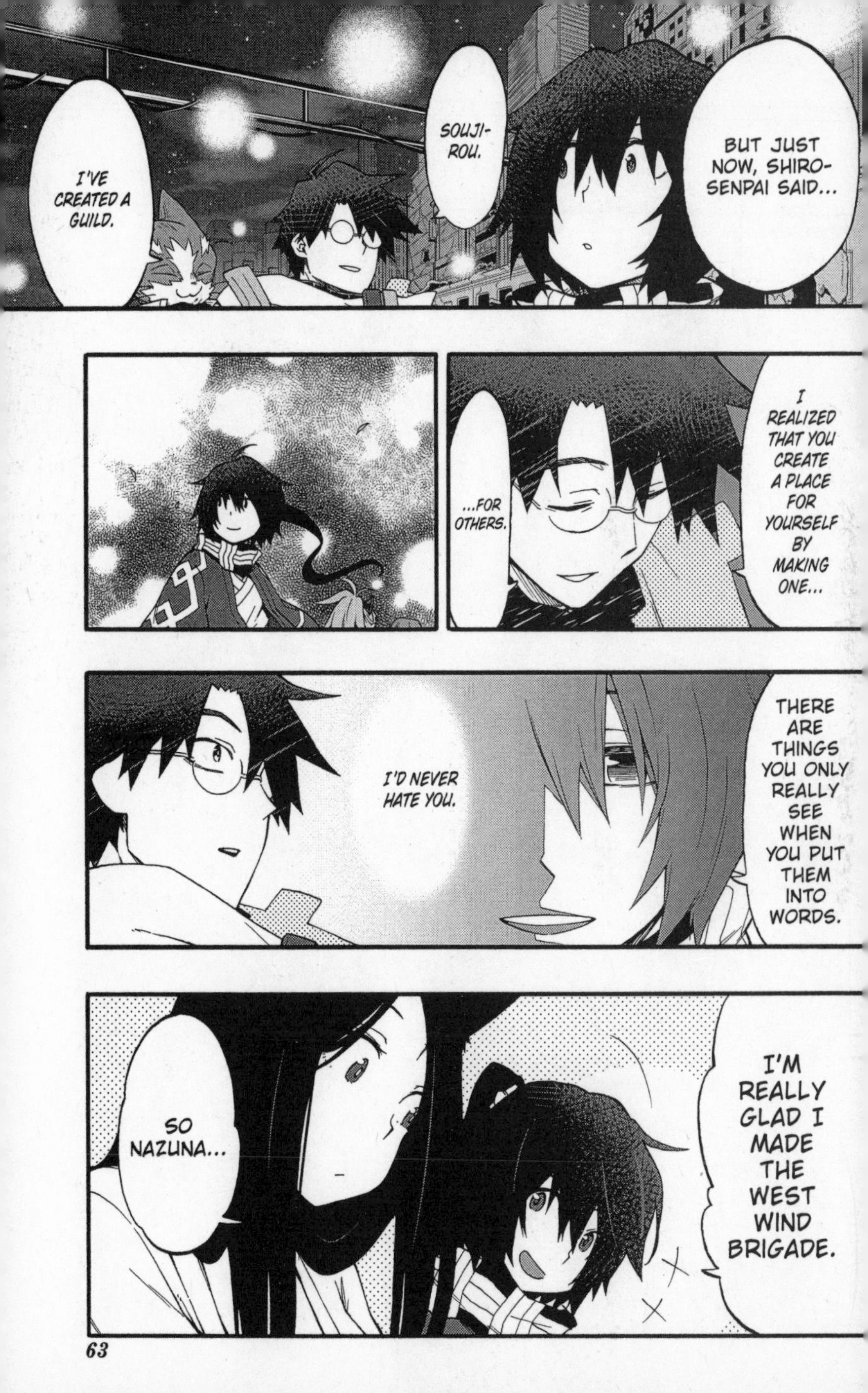
BUT JUST NOW, SHIRO-SENPAI SAID...
SOUJI-ROU.
I'VE CREATED A GUILD.
I REALIZED THAT YOU CREATE A PLACE FOR YOURSELF BY MAKING ONE...
...FOR OTHERS.
THERE ARE THINGS YOU ONLY REALLY SEE WHEN YOU PUT THEM INTO WORDS.
I'D NEVER HATE YOU.
I'M REALLY GLAD I MADE THE WEST WIND BRIGADE.
SO NAZUNA...

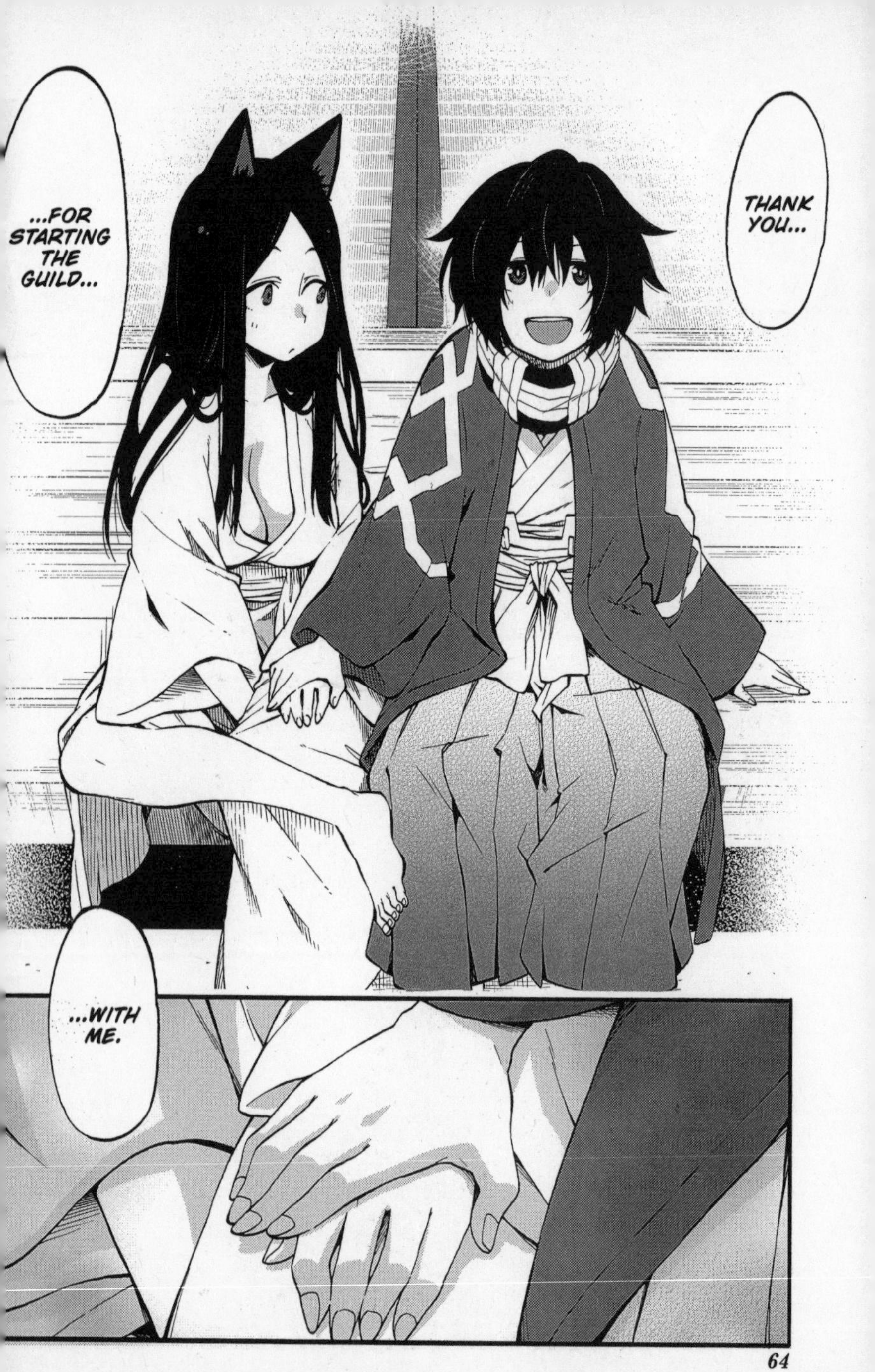
THANK YOU...
...FOR STARTING THE GUILD...
...WITH ME.

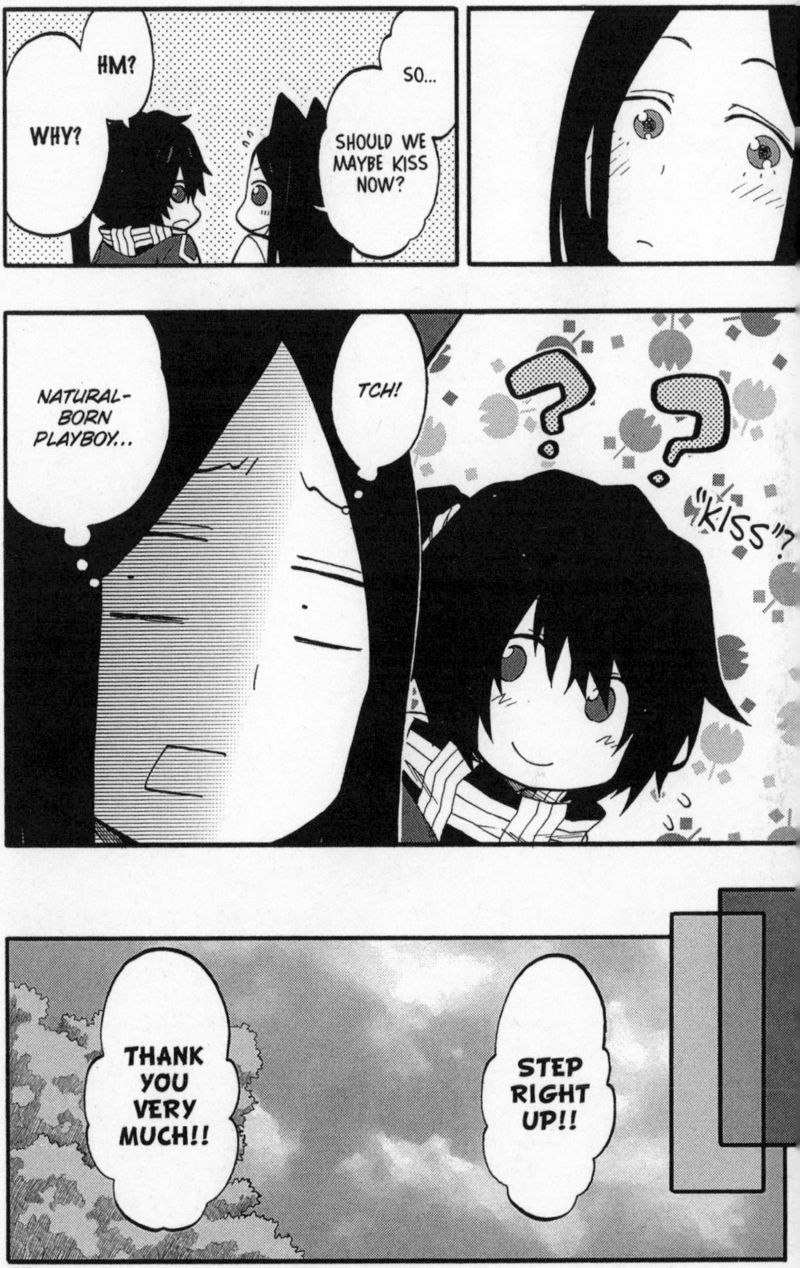
SO...
SHOULD WE MAYBE KISS NOW?
HM?
WHY?
"KISS"?
TCH!
NATURAL-BORN PLAYBOY...
STEP RIGHT UP!!
THANK YOU VERY MUCH!!

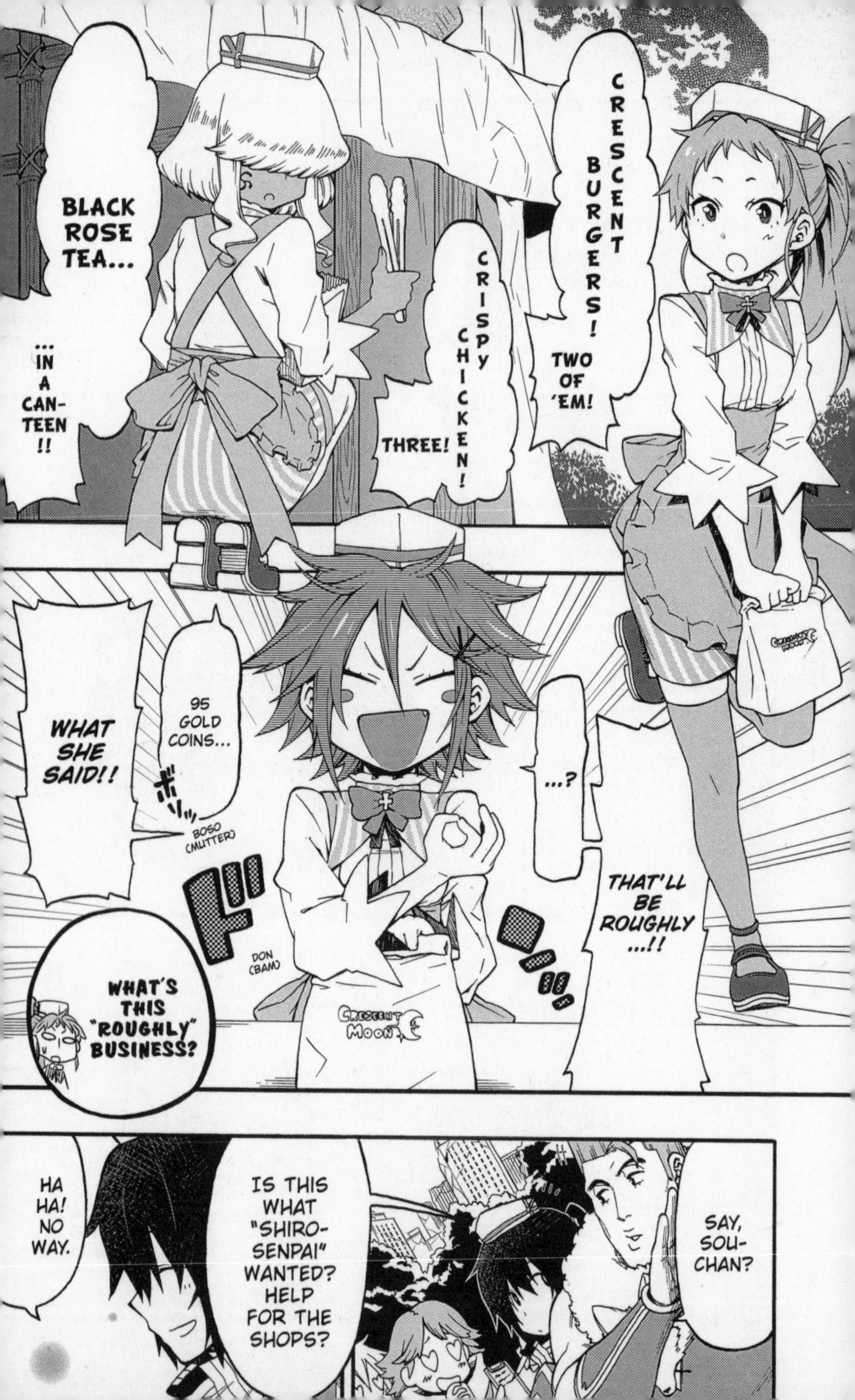
CRESCENT BURGERS!
TWO OF 'EM!
CRISPY CHICKEN!
THREE!
BLACK ROSE TEA...
...IN A CAN-TEEN!!
THAT'LL BE ROUGHLY ...!!
...?
DON (BAM)
CRESENT MOON
95 GOLD COINS...
BOSO (MUTTER)
WHAT SHE SAID!!
WHAT'S THIS "ROUGHLY" BUSINESS?
SAY, SOU-CHAN?
IS THIS WHAT "SHIRO-SENPAI" WANTED? HELP FOR THE SHOPS?
HA HA! NO WAY.

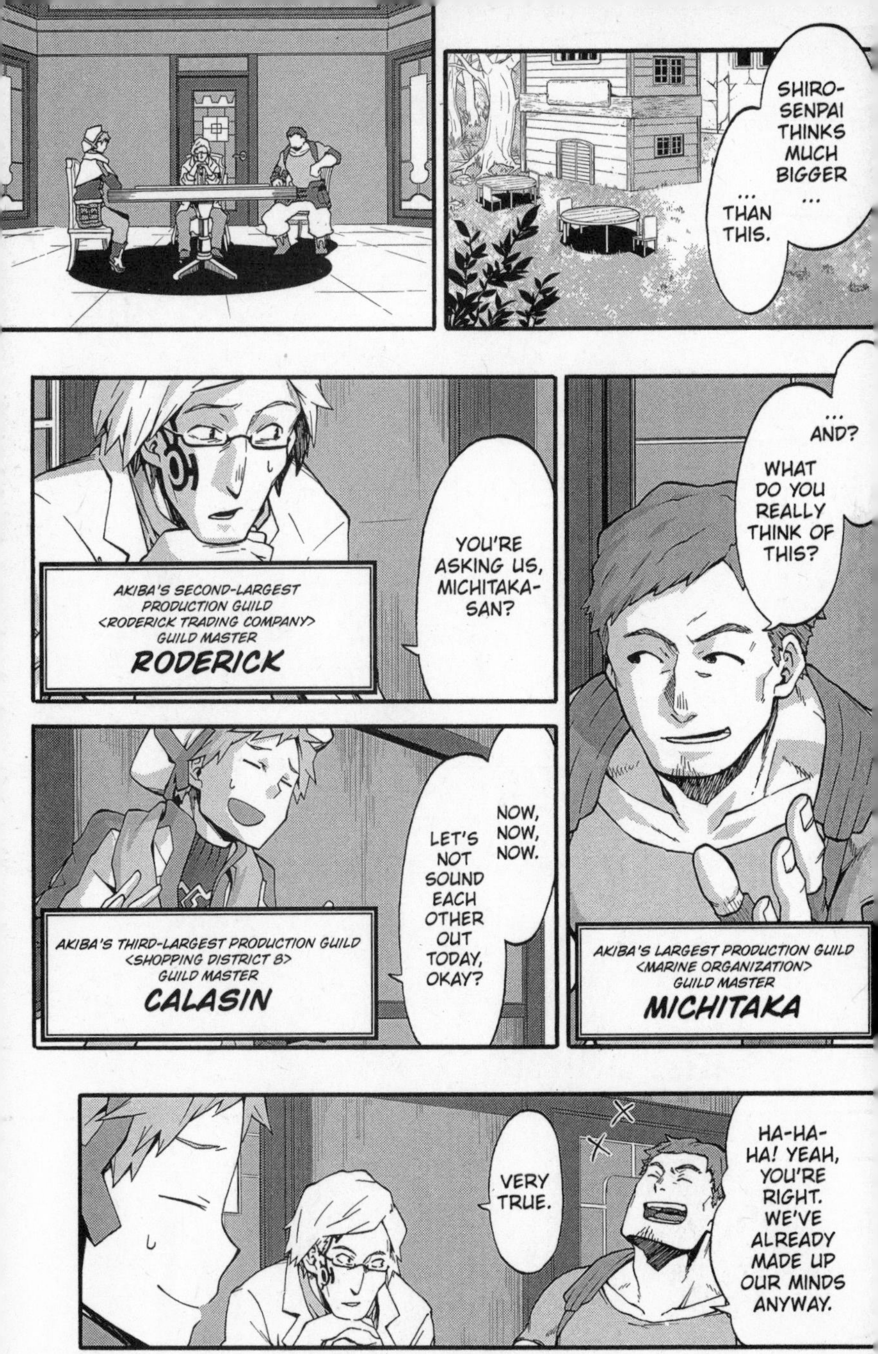
SHIRO-SENPAI THINKS MUCH BIGGER ... ... THAN THIS.
... AND?
WHAT DO YOU REALLY THINK OF THIS?
AKIBA'S LARGEST PRODUCTION GUILD <MARINE ORGANIZATION> GUILD MASTER MICHITAKA
YOU'RE ASKING US, MICHITAKA-SAN?
AKIBA'S SECOND-LARGEST PRODUCTION GUILD <RODERICK TRADING COMPANY> GUILD MASTER RODERICK
NOW, NOW, NOW.
LET'S NOT SOUND EACH OTHER OUT TODAY, OKAY?
AKIBA'S THIRD-LARGEST PRODUCTION GUILD <SHOPPING DISTRICT 8> GUILD MASTER CALASIN
HA-HA-HA! YEAH, YOU'RE RIGHT. WE'VE ALREADY MADE UP OUR MINDS ANYWAY.
VERY TRUE.

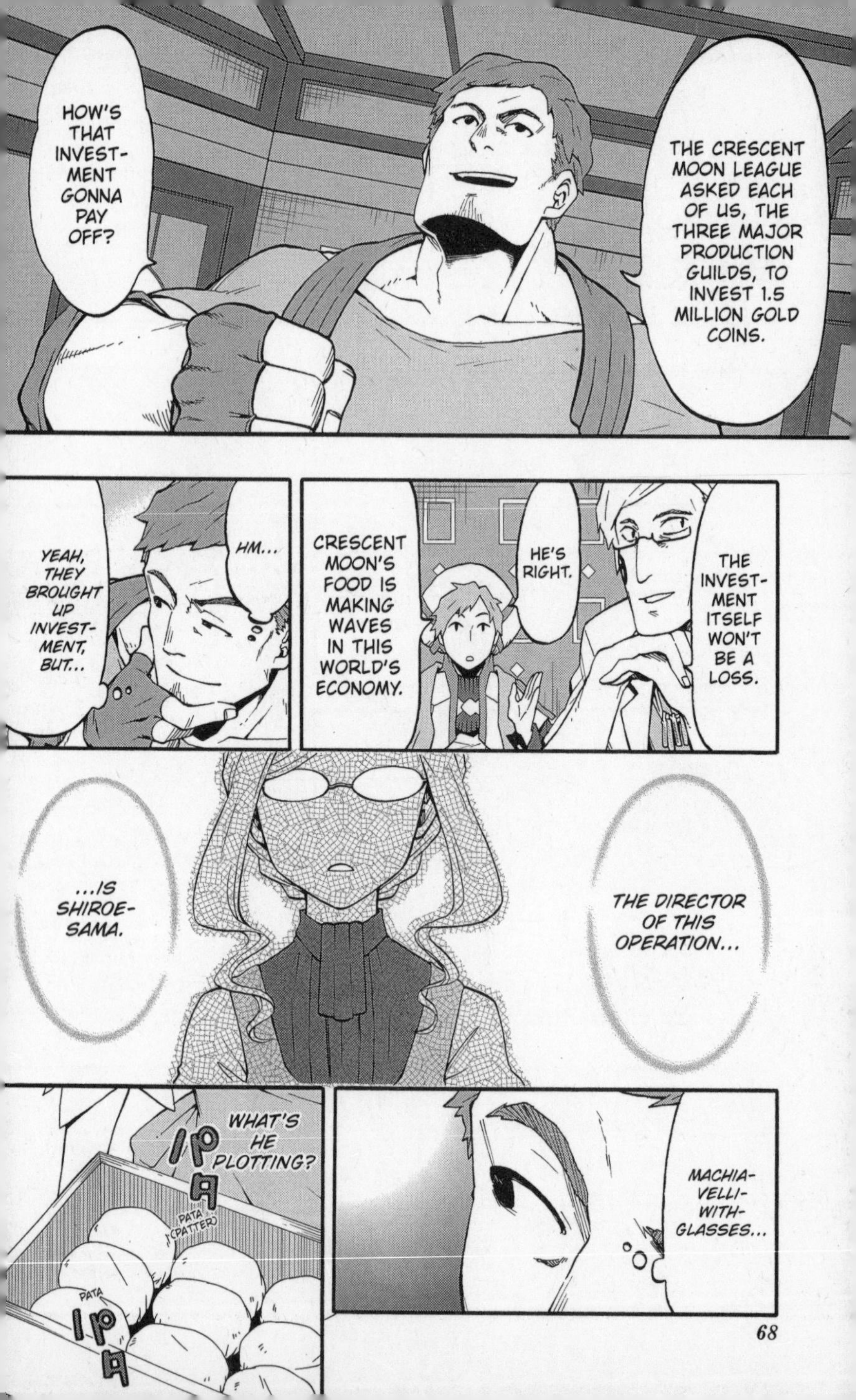
THE CRESCENT MOON LEAGUE ASKED EACH OF US, THE THREE MAJOR PRODUCTION GUILDS, TO INVEST 1.5 MILLION GOLD COINS.
HOW'S THAT INVESTMENT GONNA PAY OFF?
THE INVESTMENT ITSELF WON'T BE A LOSS.
HE'S RIGHT.
CRESCENT MOON'S FOOD IS MAKING WAVES IN THIS WORLD'S ECONOMY.
HM...
YEAH, THEY BROUGHT UP INVESTMENT, BUT...
THE DIRECTOR OF THIS OPERATION...
...IS SHIROE-SAMA.
MACHIAVELLI-WITH-GLASSES...
WHAT'S HE PLOTTING?
PATA (PATTER)
PATA

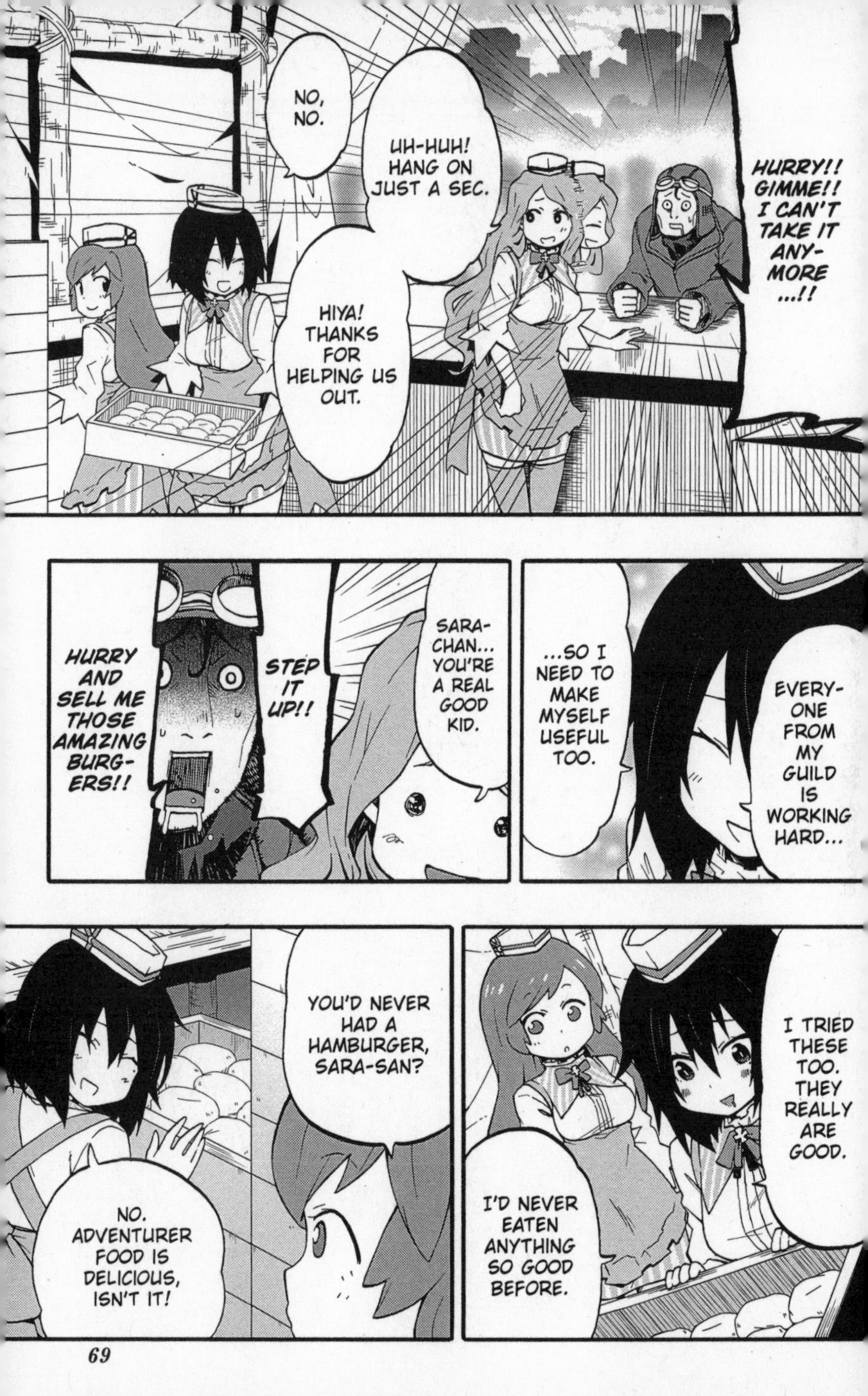
HURRY!! GIMME!! I CAN'T TAKE IT ANY-MORE...!!
UH-HUH! HANG ON JUST A SEC.
NO, NO.
HIYA! THANKS FOR HELPING US OUT.
EVERY-ONE FROM MY GUILD IS WORKING HARD...
...SO I NEED TO MAKE MYSELF USEFUL TOO.
SARA-CHAN... YOU'RE A REAL GOOD KID.
STEP IT UP!!
HURRY AND SELL ME THOSE AMAZING BURG-ERS!!
I TRIED THESE TOO. THEY REALLY ARE GOOD.
I'D NEVER EATEN ANYTHING SO GOOD BEFORE.
YOU'D NEVER HAD A HAMBURGER, SARA-SAN?
NO. ADVENTURER FOOD IS DELICIOUS, ISN'T IT!

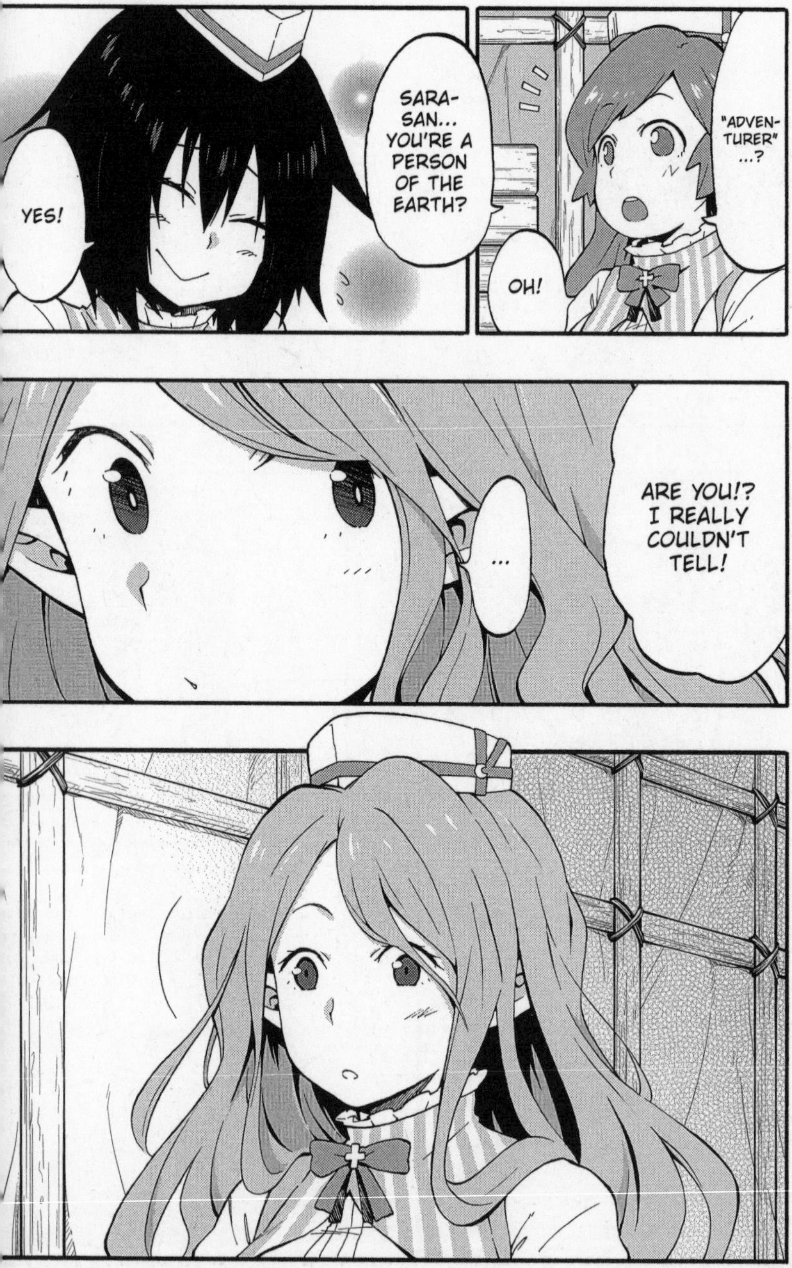
"ADVENTURER" ...?
OH!
SARA-SAN... YOU'RE A PERSON OF THE EARTH?
YES!
ARE YOU!? I REALLY COULDN'T TELL!
...

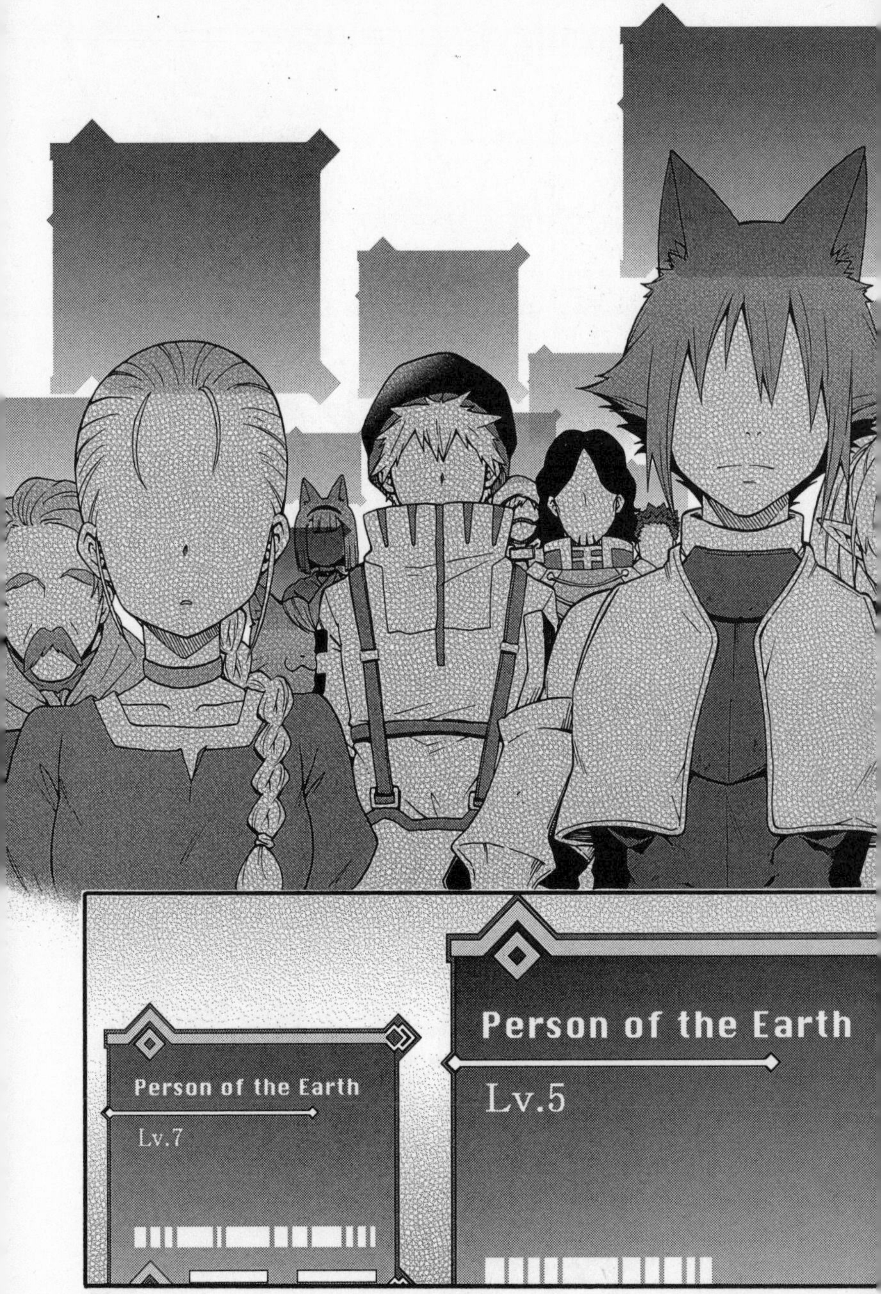
Person of the Earth
Lv.5
Person of the Earth
Lv.7

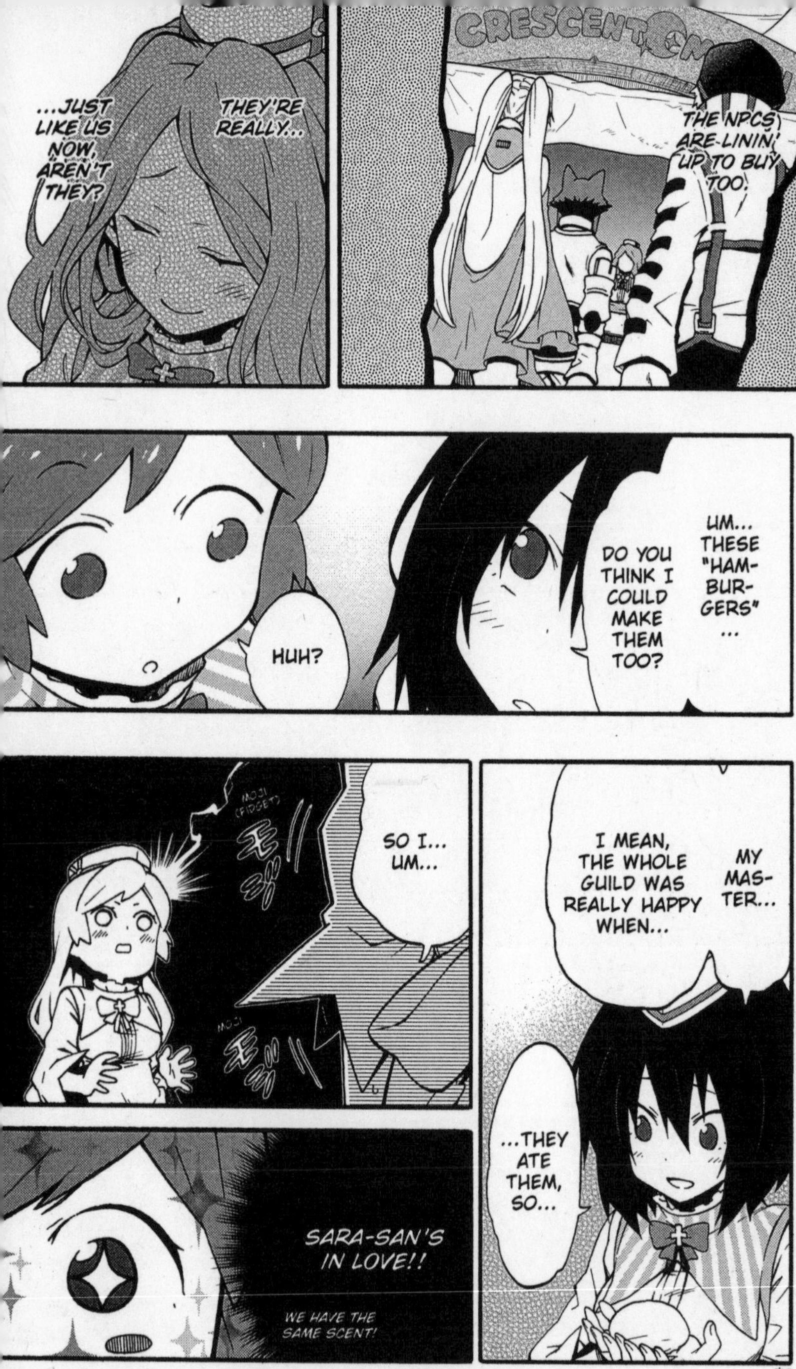
CRESCENT MOON
THE NPCS ARE LININ' UP TO BUY TOO.
THEY'RE REALLY...
...JUST LIKE US NOW, AREN'T THEY?
UM... THESE "HAMBURGERS"...
DO YOU THINK I COULD MAKE THEM TOO?
HUH?
MY MASTER...
I MEAN, THE WHOLE GUILD WAS REALLY HAPPY WHEN...
...THEY ATE THEM, SO...
SO I... UM...
MOJI (FIDGET)
MOJI
SARA-SAN'S IN LOVE!!
WE HAVE THE SAME SCENT!

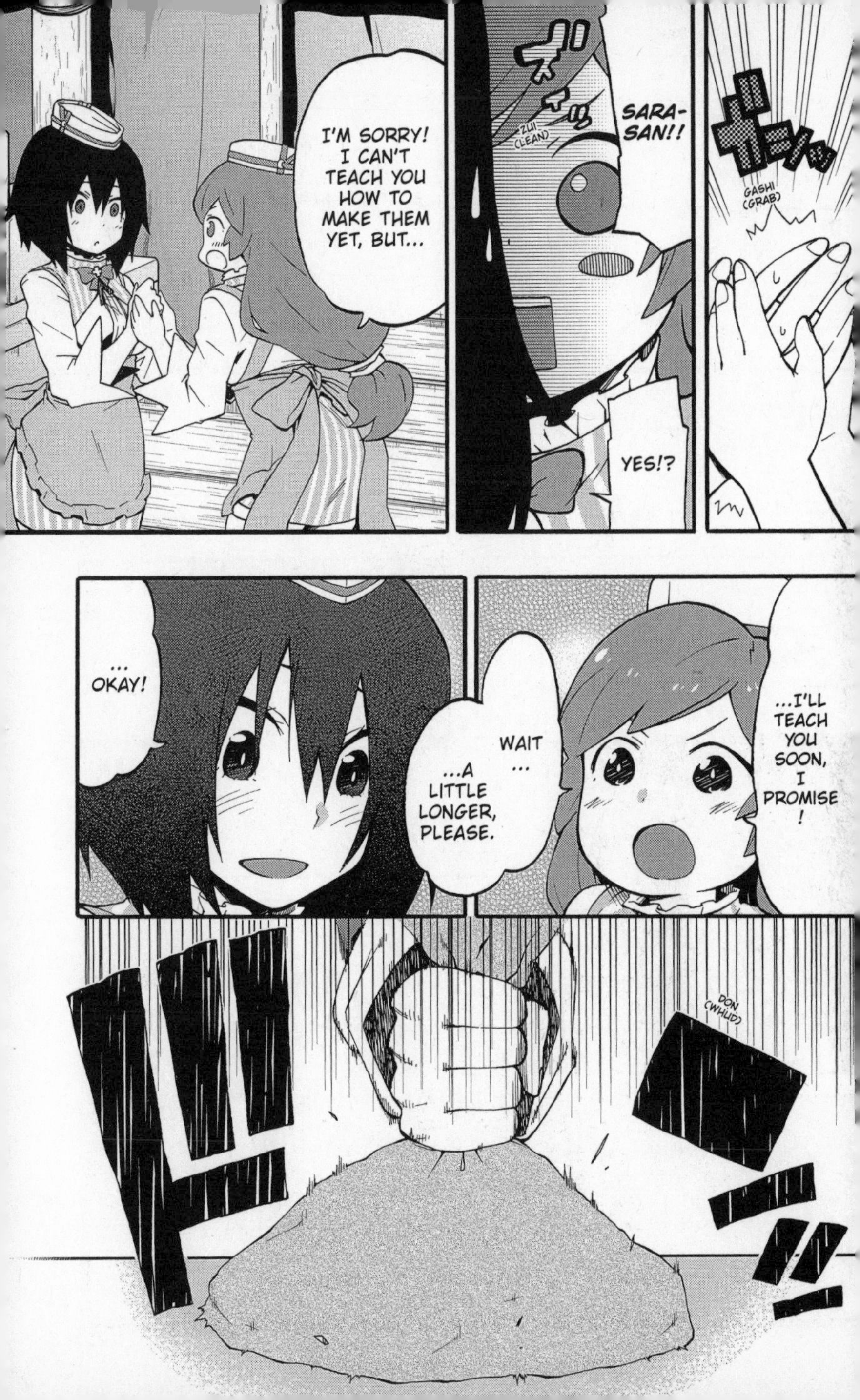
GASHI (GRAB)
SARA-SAN!!
ZUI (LEAN)
YES!?
I'M SORRY! I CAN'T TEACH YOU HOW TO MAKE THEM YET, BUT...
...I'LL TEACH YOU SOON, I PROMISE!
WAIT ...
...A LITTLE LONGER, PLEASE.
... OKAY!
DON (WHUD)

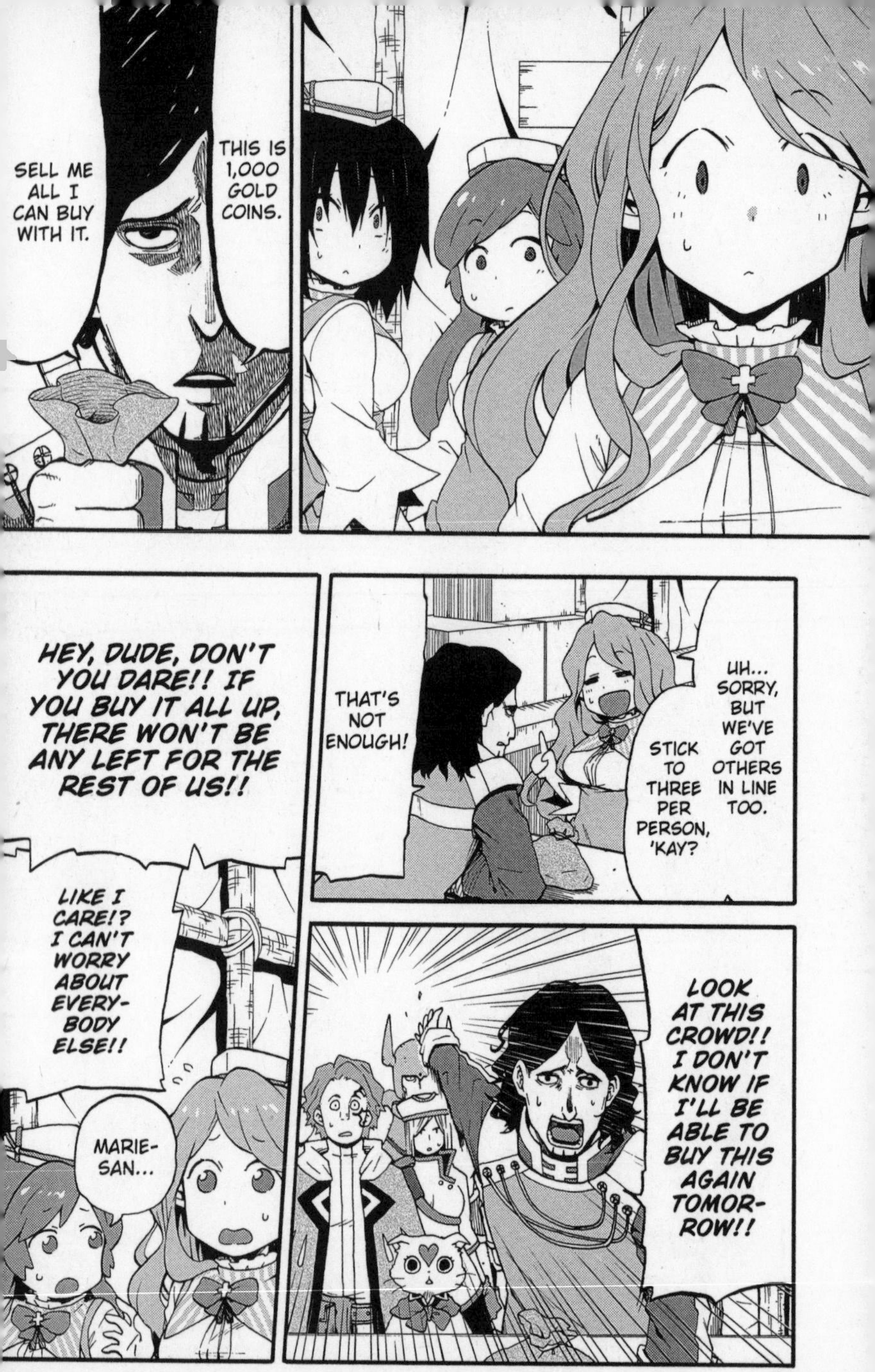
THIS IS 1,000 GOLD COINS.
SELL ME ALL I CAN BUY WITH IT.
UH... SORRY, BUT WE'VE GOT OTHERS IN LINE TOO.
STICK TO THREE PER PERSON, 'KAY?
THAT'S NOT ENOUGH!
LOOK AT THIS CROWD!! I DON'T KNOW IF I'LL BE ABLE TO BUY THIS AGAIN TOMOR-ROW!!
HEY, DUDE, DON'T YOU DARE!! IF YOU BUY IT ALL UP, THERE WON'T BE ANY LEFT FOR THE REST OF US!!
LIKE I CARE!? I CAN'T WORRY ABOUT EVERY-BODY ELSE!!
MARIE-SAN...

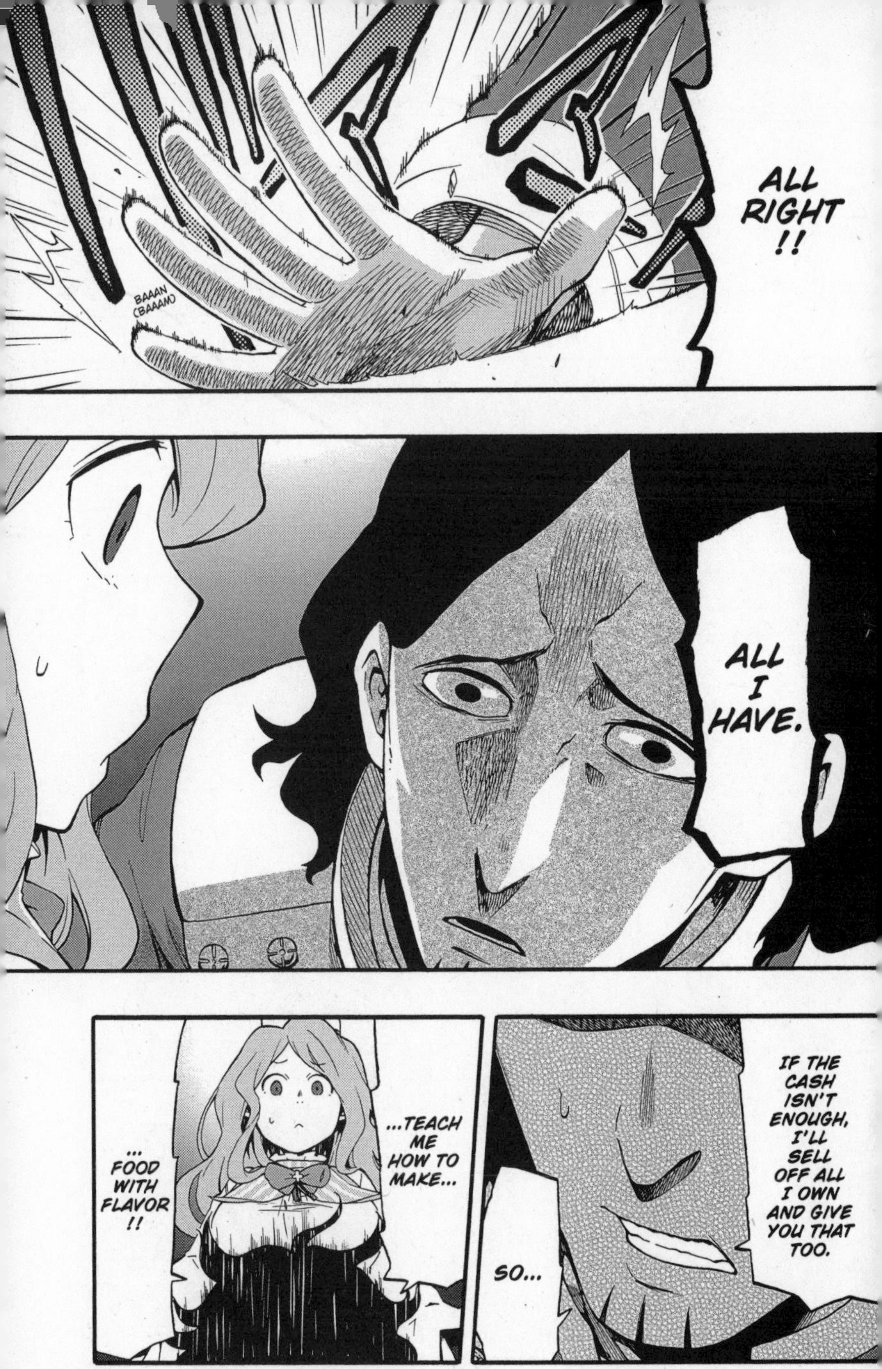
ALL RIGHT !!
BAAAN (BAAAM)
ALL I HAVE.
IF THE CASH ISN'T ENOUGH, I'LL SELL OFF ALL I OWN AND GIVE YOU THAT TOO.
SO...
...TEACH ME HOW TO MAKE...
...FOOD WITH FLAVOR !!

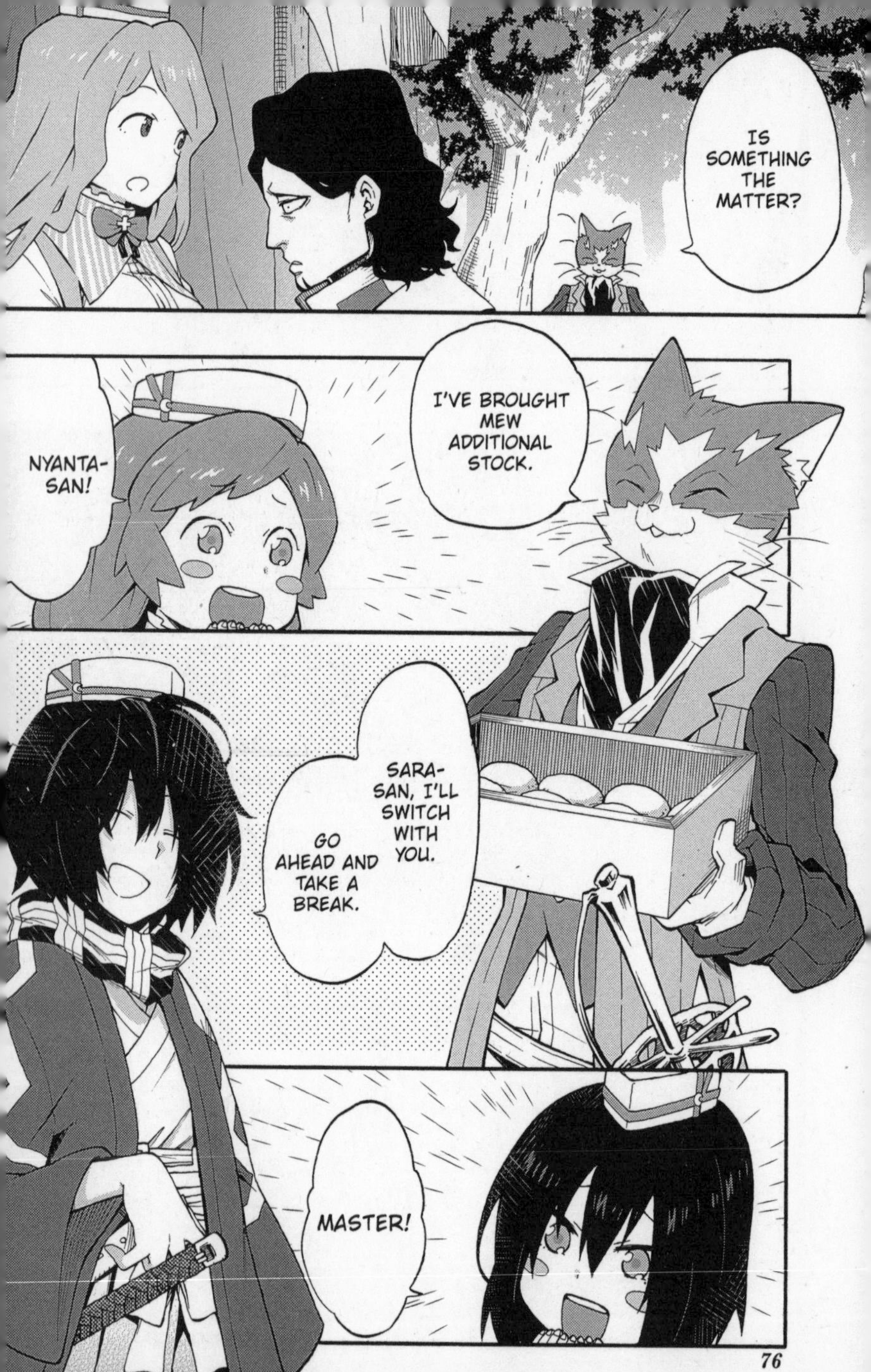
IS SOMETHING THE MATTER?
I'VE BROUGHT MEW ADDITIONAL STOCK.
NYANTA-SAN!
SARA-SAN, I'LL SWITCH WITH YOU.
GO AHEAD AND TAKE A BREAK.
MASTER!

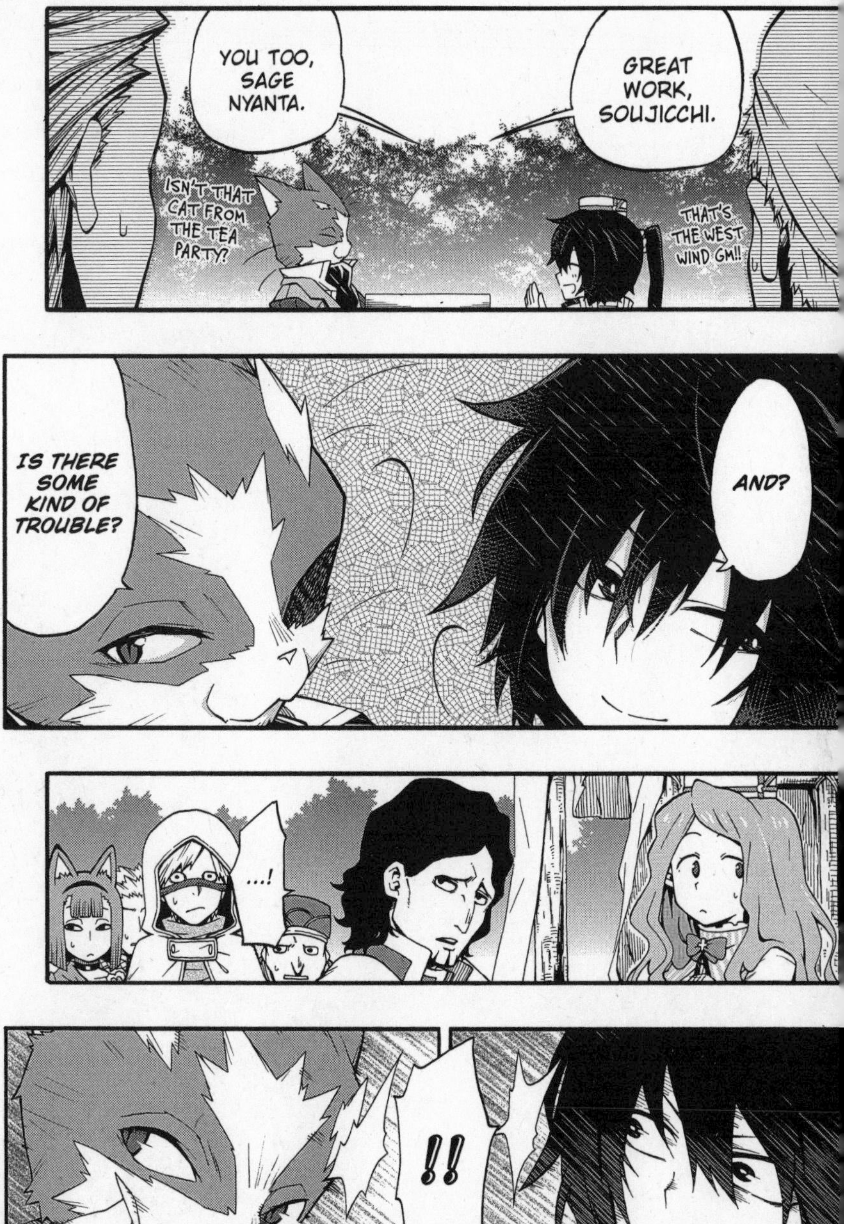
GREAT WORK, SOUJICCHI.
YOU TOO, SAGE NYANTA.
THAT'S THE WEST WIND GM!!
ISN'T THAT CAT FROM THE TEA PARTY?
AND?
IS THERE SOME KIND OF TROUBLE?
...!
!!

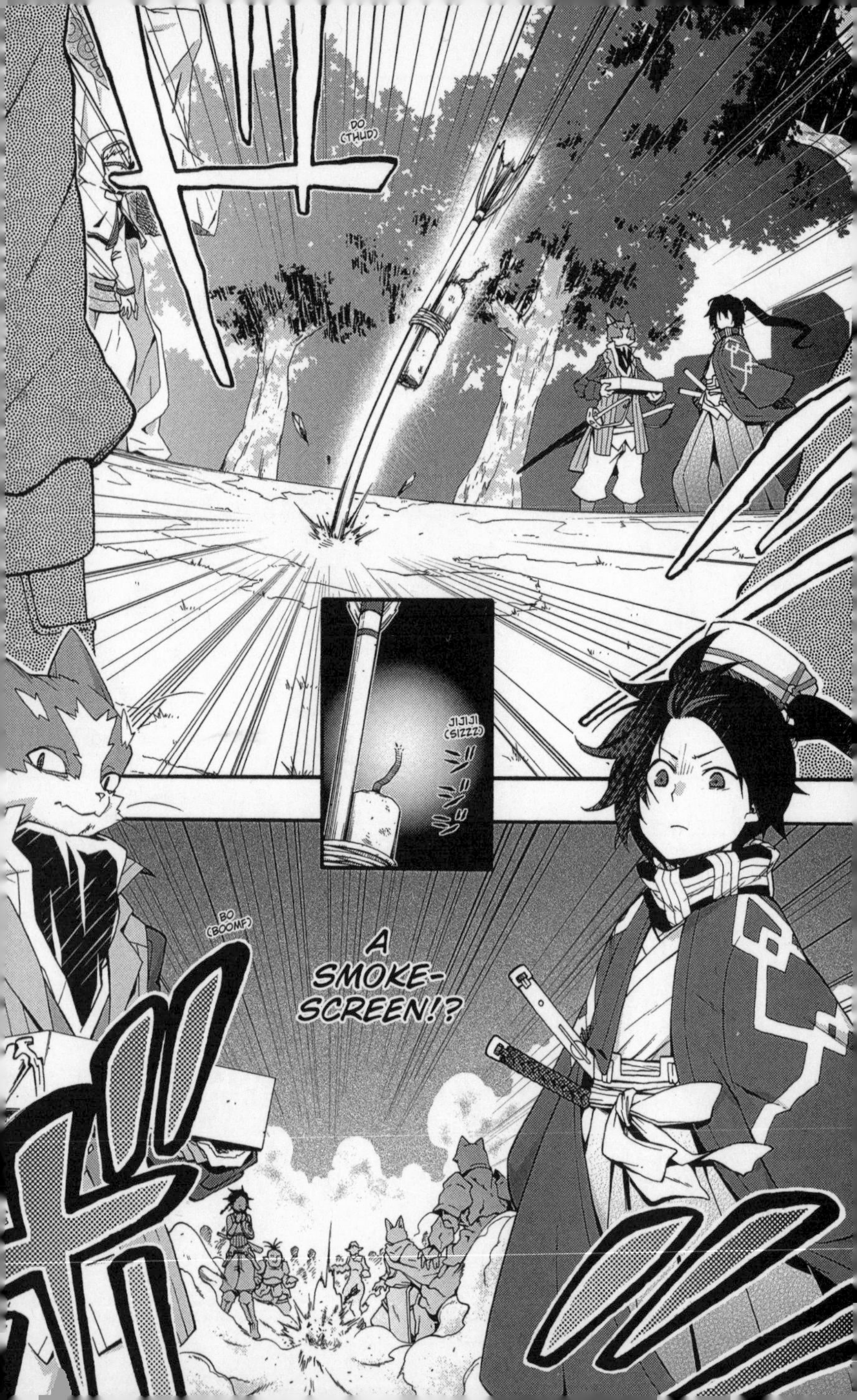
DO
(THUD)
JIJIJI
(SIZZZ)
BO
(BOOMF)
A SMOKE-SCREEN!?

LOG HORIZON
THE WEST WIND BRIGADE

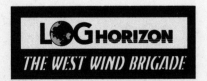

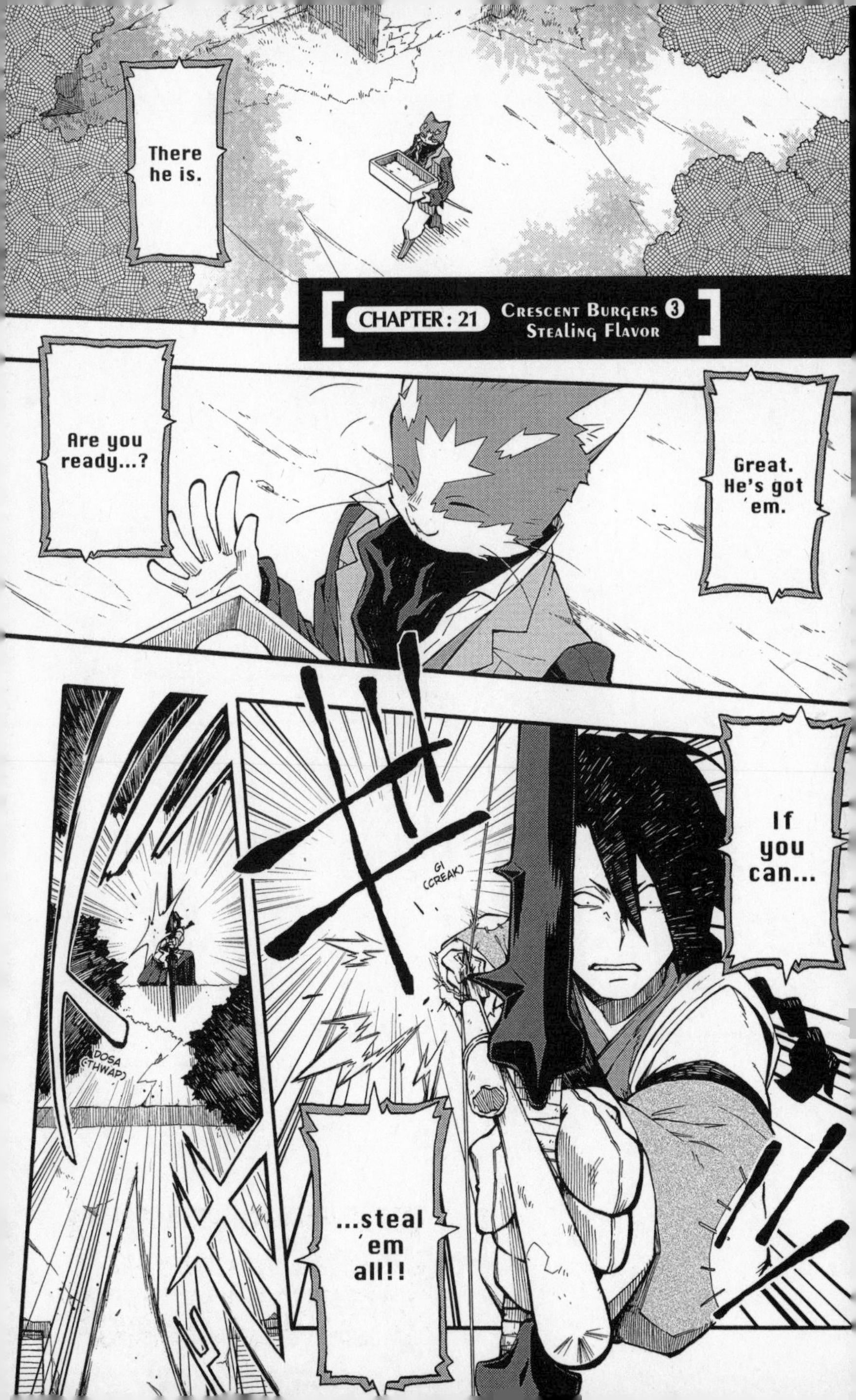

There he is.
CHAPTER : 21
Crescent Burgers 3
Stealing Flavor
Great. He's got 'em.
Are you ready...?
If you can...
GI (CREAK)
DOSA (THWAP)
...steal 'em all!!

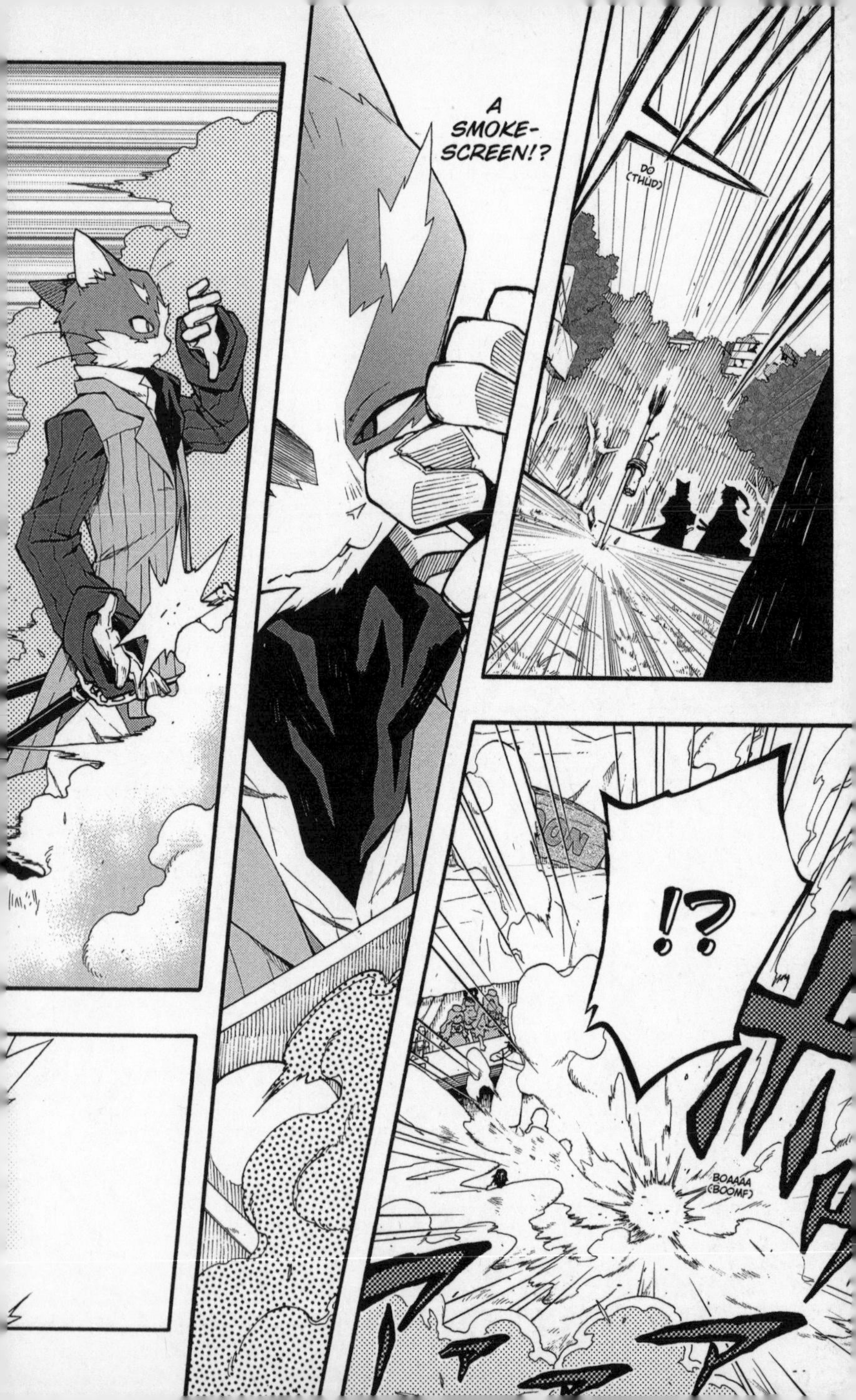
DO
(THUD)
A SMOKE-SCREEN!?
!?
BOAAAA
(BOOMF)

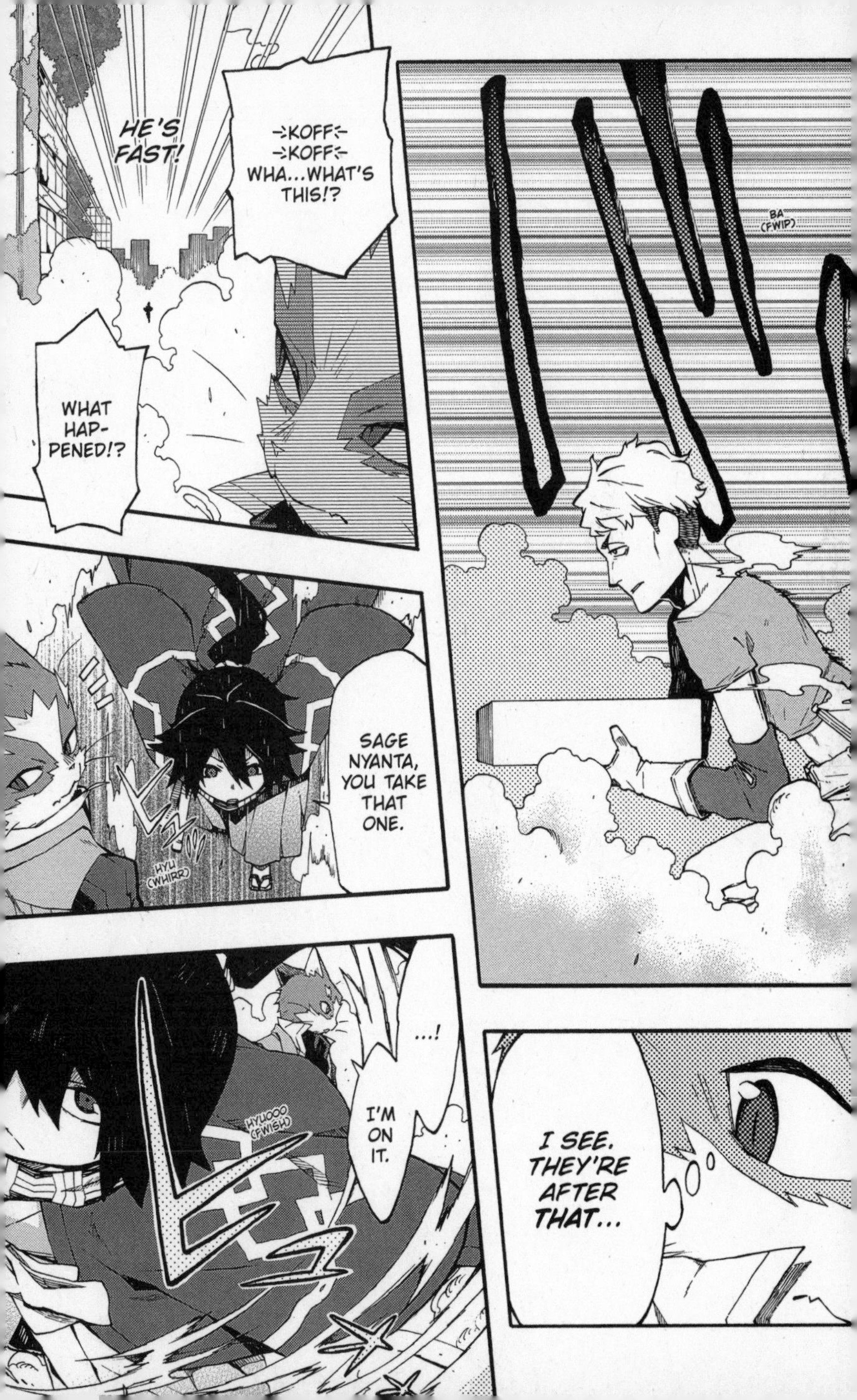
BA (FWIP)
-KOFF- -KOFF- WHA...WHAT'S THIS!?
HE'S FAST!
WHAT HAP-PENED!?
SAGE NYANTA, YOU TAKE THAT ONE.
HYU (WHIRR)
I SEE. THEY'RE AFTER THAT...
...!
I'M ON IT.
HYUOOO (FWISH)

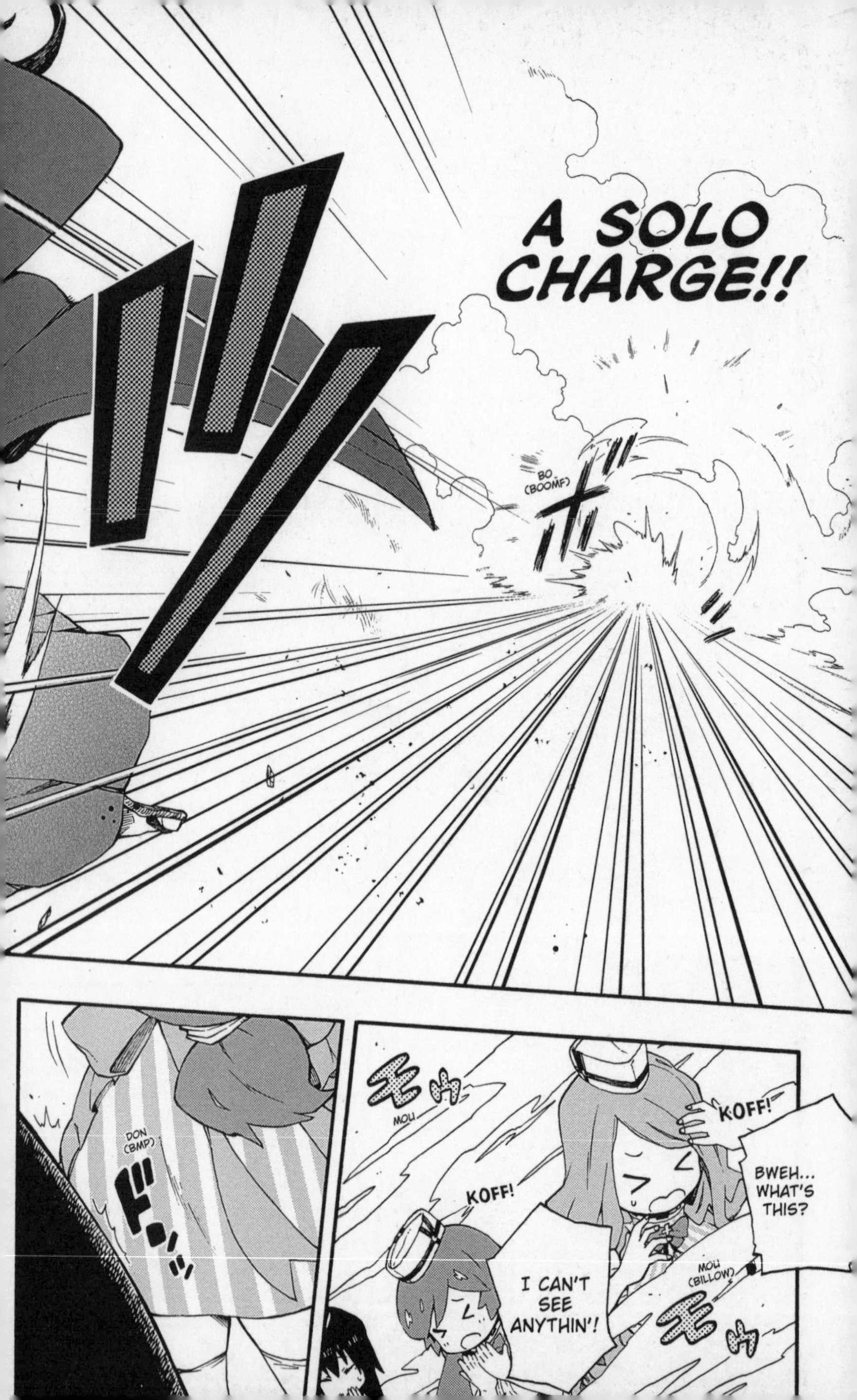
A SOLO CHARGE!!
BO (BOOMF)
MOU
KOFF!
BWEH... WHAT'S THIS?
KOFF!
I CAN'T SEE ANYTHIN'!
MOU (BILLOW)
DON (BMP)

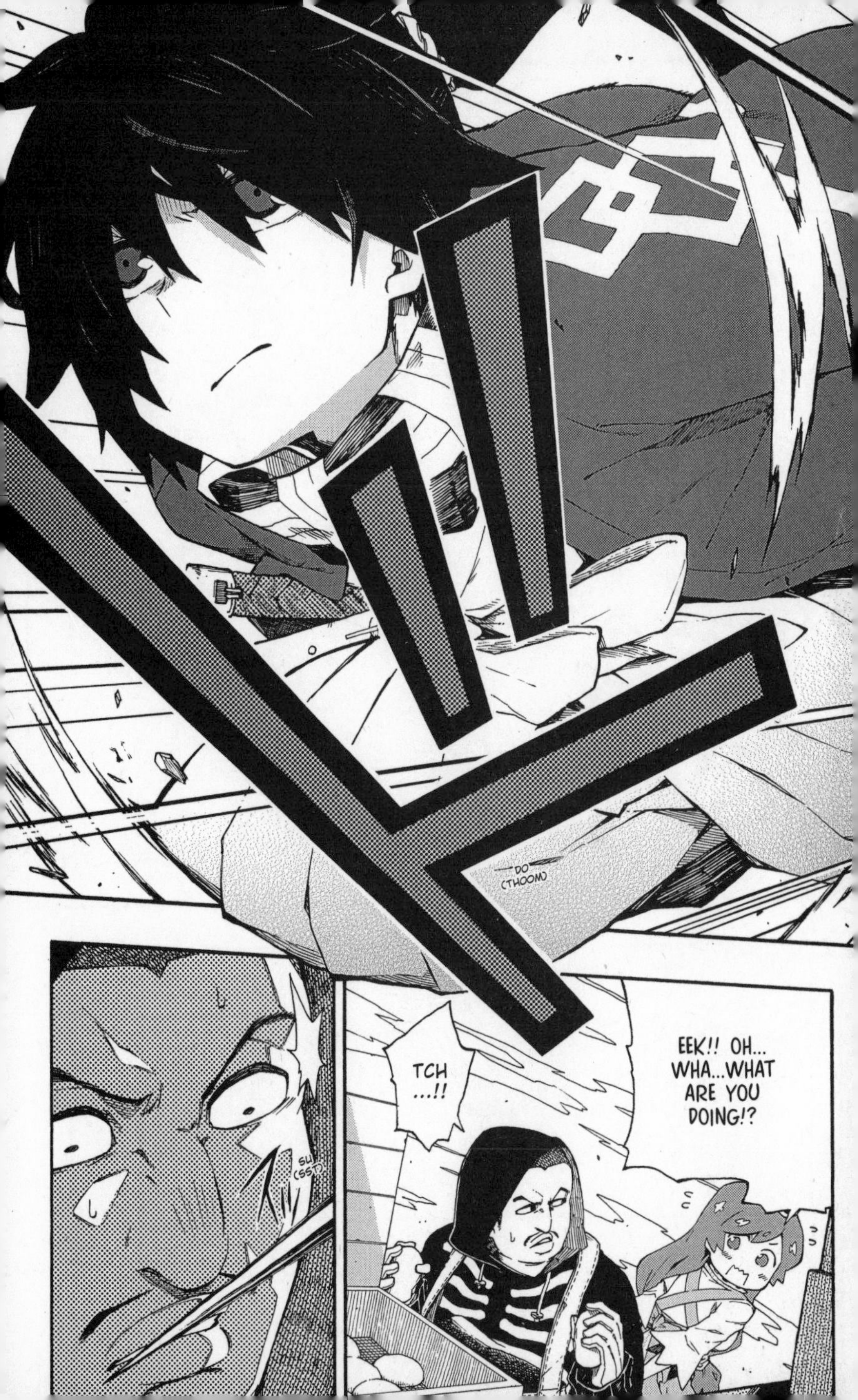
DO
(THOOM)
EEK!! OH... WHA...WHAT ARE YOU DOING!?
TCH ...!!
SU
(SST)

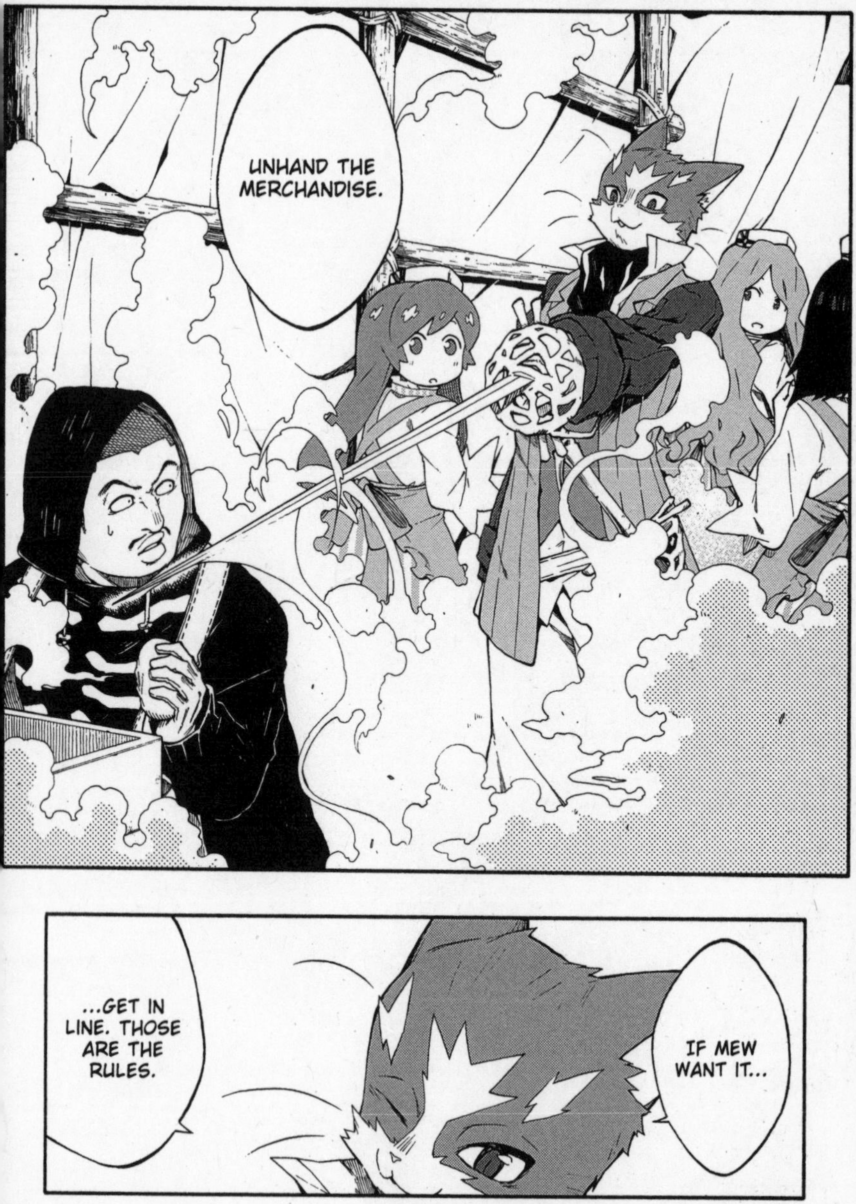
UNHAND THE MERCHANDISE.
IF MEW WANT IT...
...GET IN LINE. THOSE ARE THE RULES.

[CHAPTER: 21 Crescent Burgers 3 Stealing Flavor]

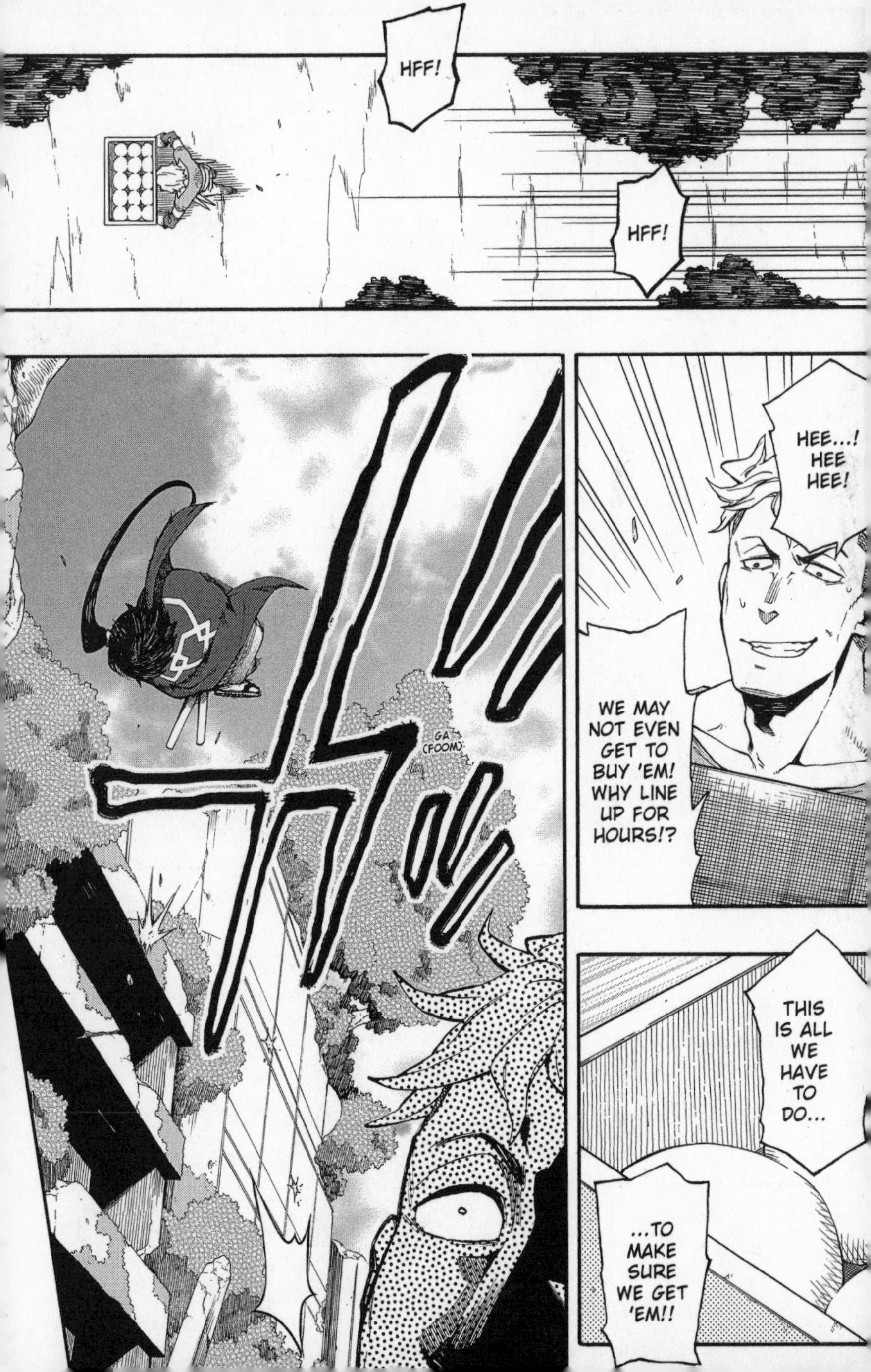
HFF!
HFF!
HEE...! HEE HEE!
WE MAY NOT EVEN GET TO BUY 'EM! WHY LINE UP FOR HOURS!?
THIS IS ALL WE HAVE TO DO...
...TO MAKE SURE WE GET 'EM!!
GA (FOOM)

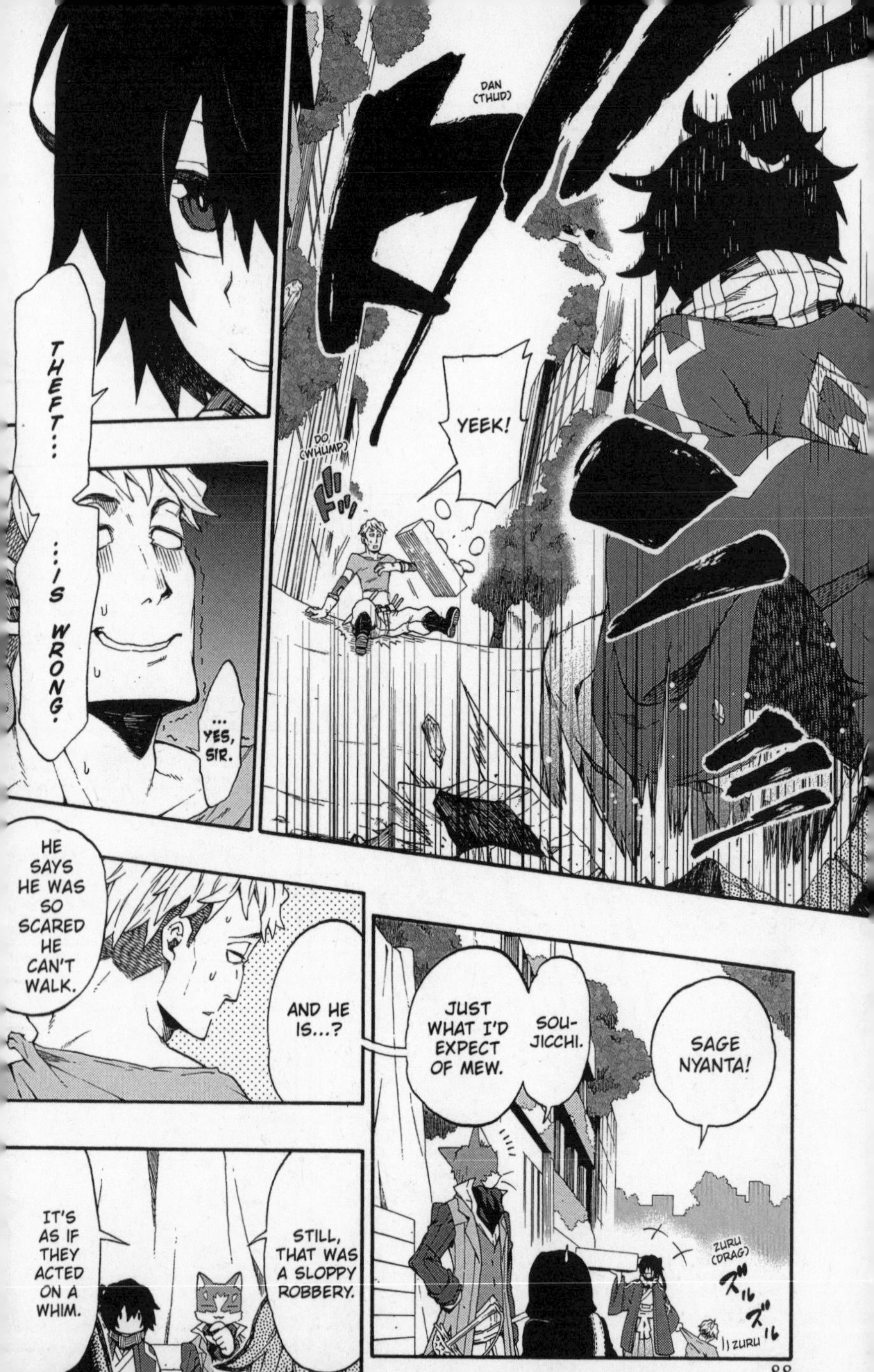
DAN (THUD)
DO (WHUMP)
YEEK!
THEFT...
...IS WRONG.
...YES, SIR.
SAGE NYANTA!
SOU-JICCHI.
JUST WHAT I'D EXPECT OF MEW.
ZURU (DRAG)
ZURU
AND HE IS...?
HE SAYS HE WAS SO SCARED HE CAN'T WALK.
STILL, THAT WAS A SLOPPY ROBBERY.
IT'S AS IF THEY ACTED ON A WHIM.

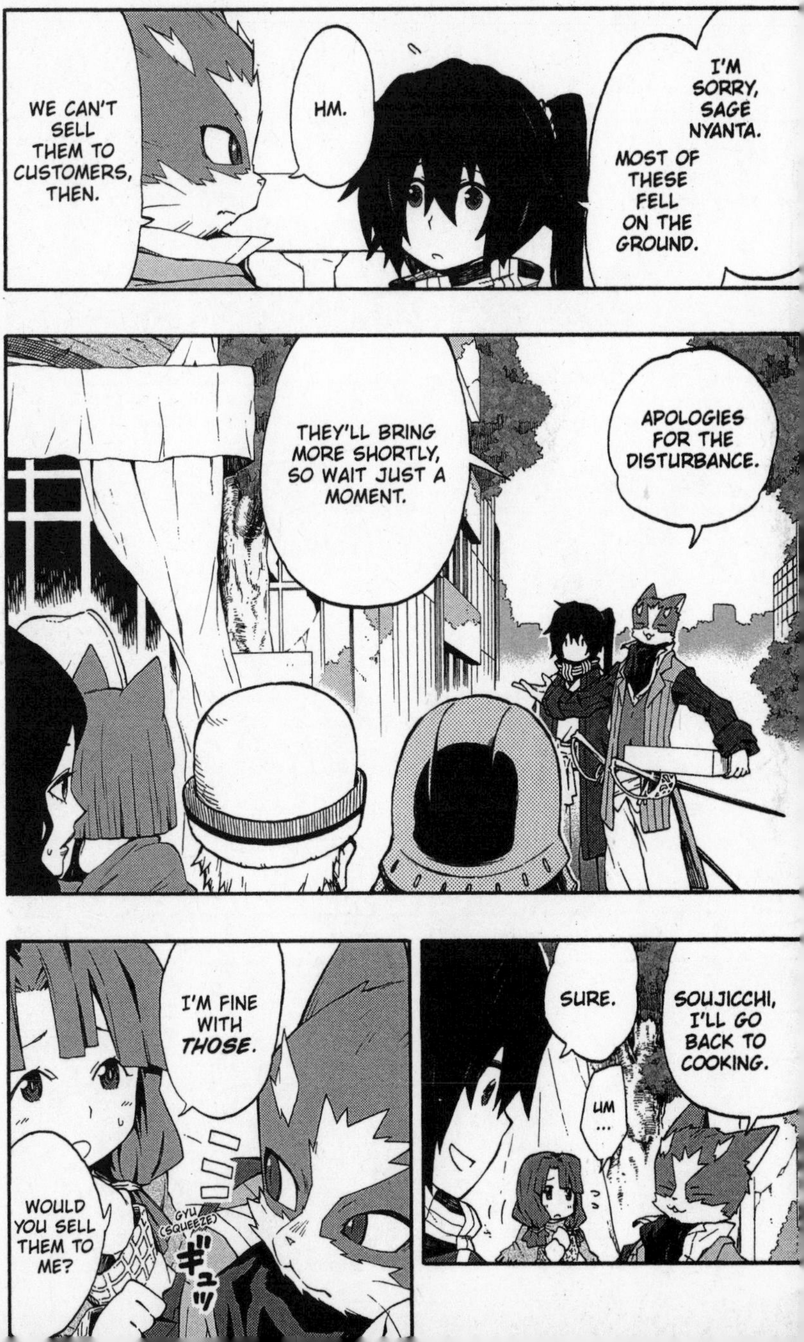
I'M SORRY, SAGE NYANTA.
MOST OF THESE FELL ON THE GROUND.
HM.
WE CAN'T SELL THEM TO CUSTOMERS, THEN.
APOLOGIES FOR THE DISTURBANCE.
THEY'LL BRING MORE SHORTLY, SO WAIT JUST A MOMENT.
SOUJICCHI, I'LL GO BACK TO COOKING.
SURE.
UM ...
I'M FINE WITH *THOSE*.
WOULD YOU SELL THEM TO ME?
GYU (SQUEEZE)
ギュッ

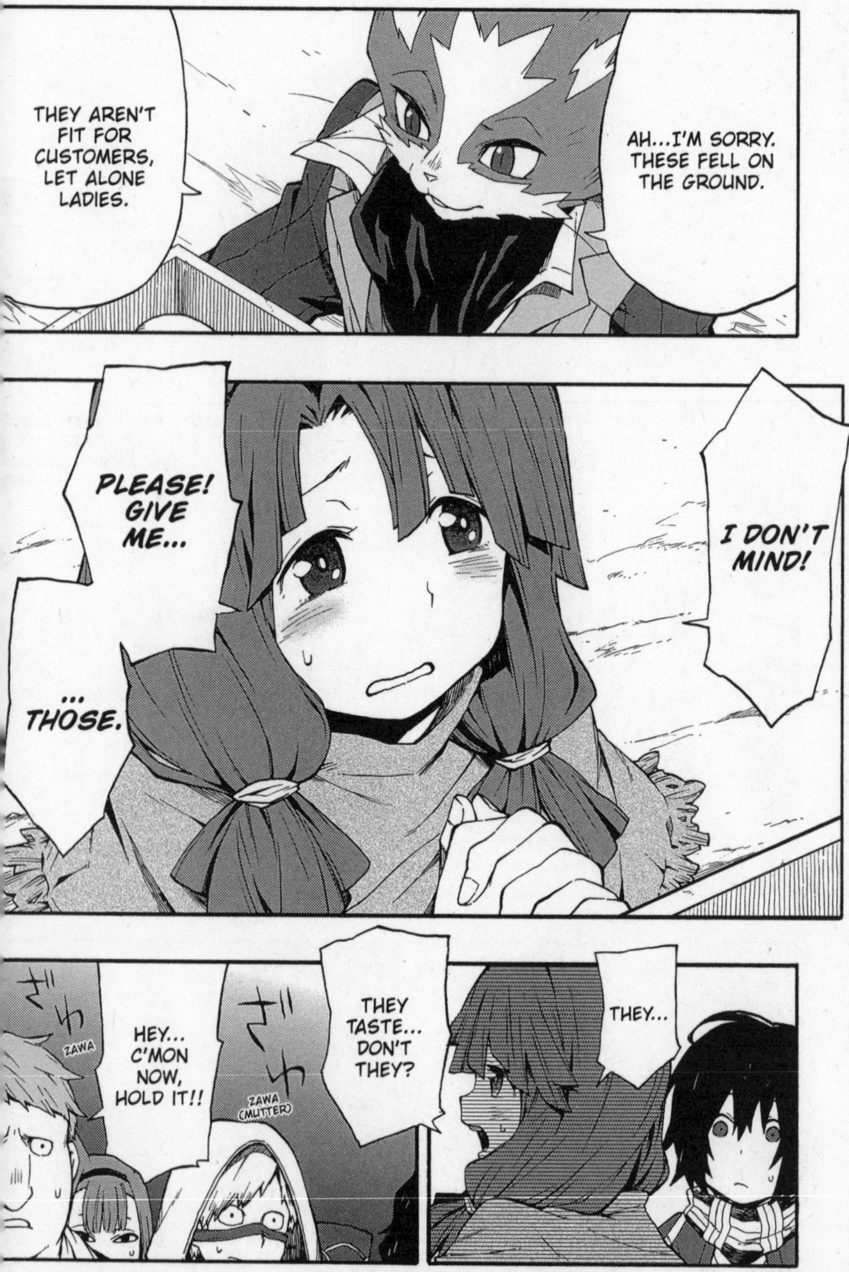
AH...I'M SORRY. THESE FELL ON THE GROUND.
THEY AREN'T FIT FOR CUSTOMERS, LET ALONE LADIES.
I DON'T MIND!
PLEASE! GIVE ME...
...THOSE.
THEY...
THEY TASTE... DON'T THEY?
ざわ
ZAWA (MUTTER)
HEY... C'MON NOW, HOLD IT!!
ざわ
ZAWA

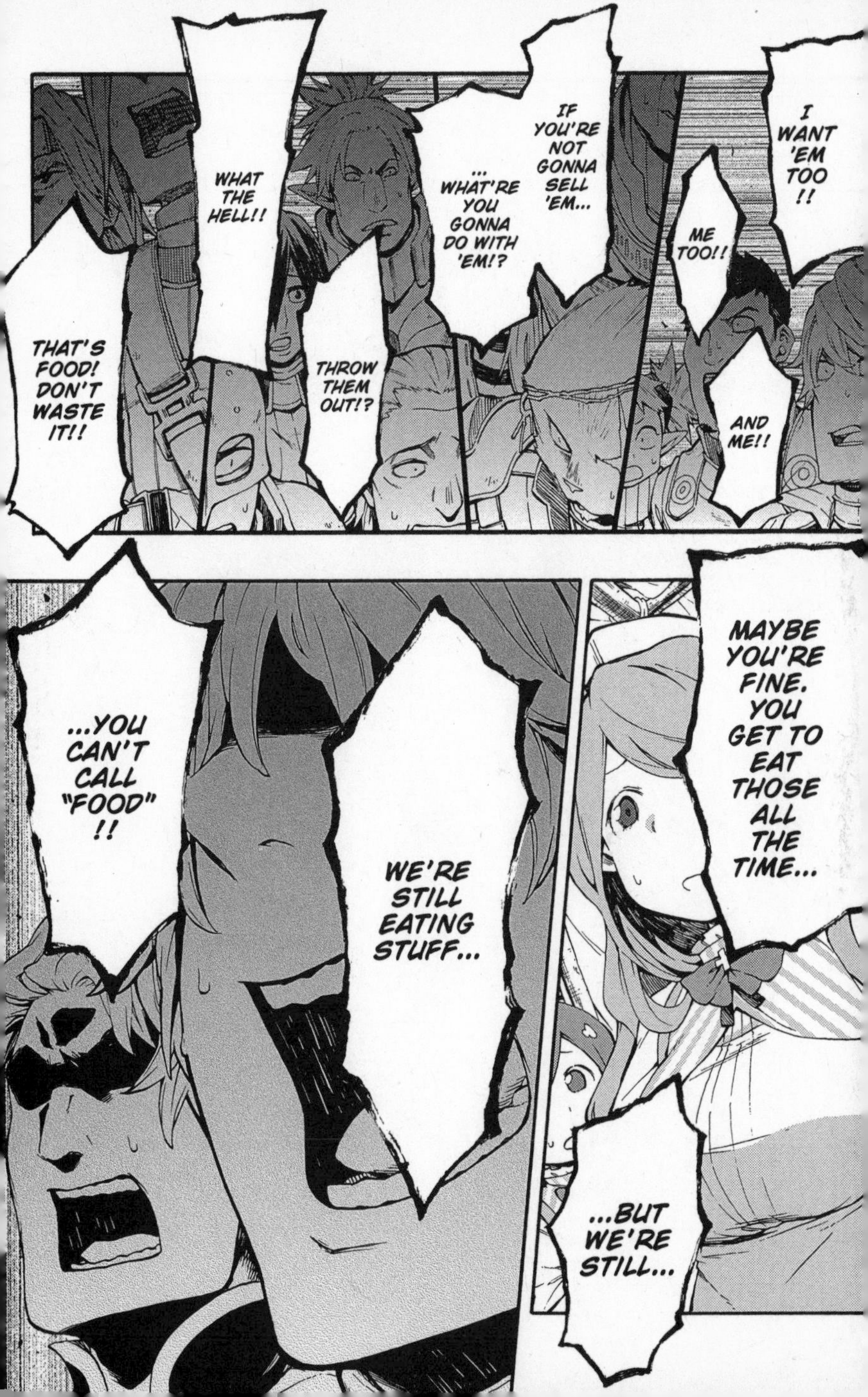
I WANT 'EM TOO!!
ME TOO!!
AND ME!!
IF YOU'RE NOT GONNA SELL 'EM...
...WHAT'RE YOU GONNA DO WITH 'EM!?
WHAT THE HELL!!
THROW THEM OUT!?
THAT'S FOOD! DON'T WASTE IT!!
MAYBE YOU'RE FINE. YOU GET TO EAT THOSE ALL THE TIME...
...BUT WE'RE STILL...
WE'RE STILL EATING STUFF...
...YOU CAN'T CALL "FOOD"!!

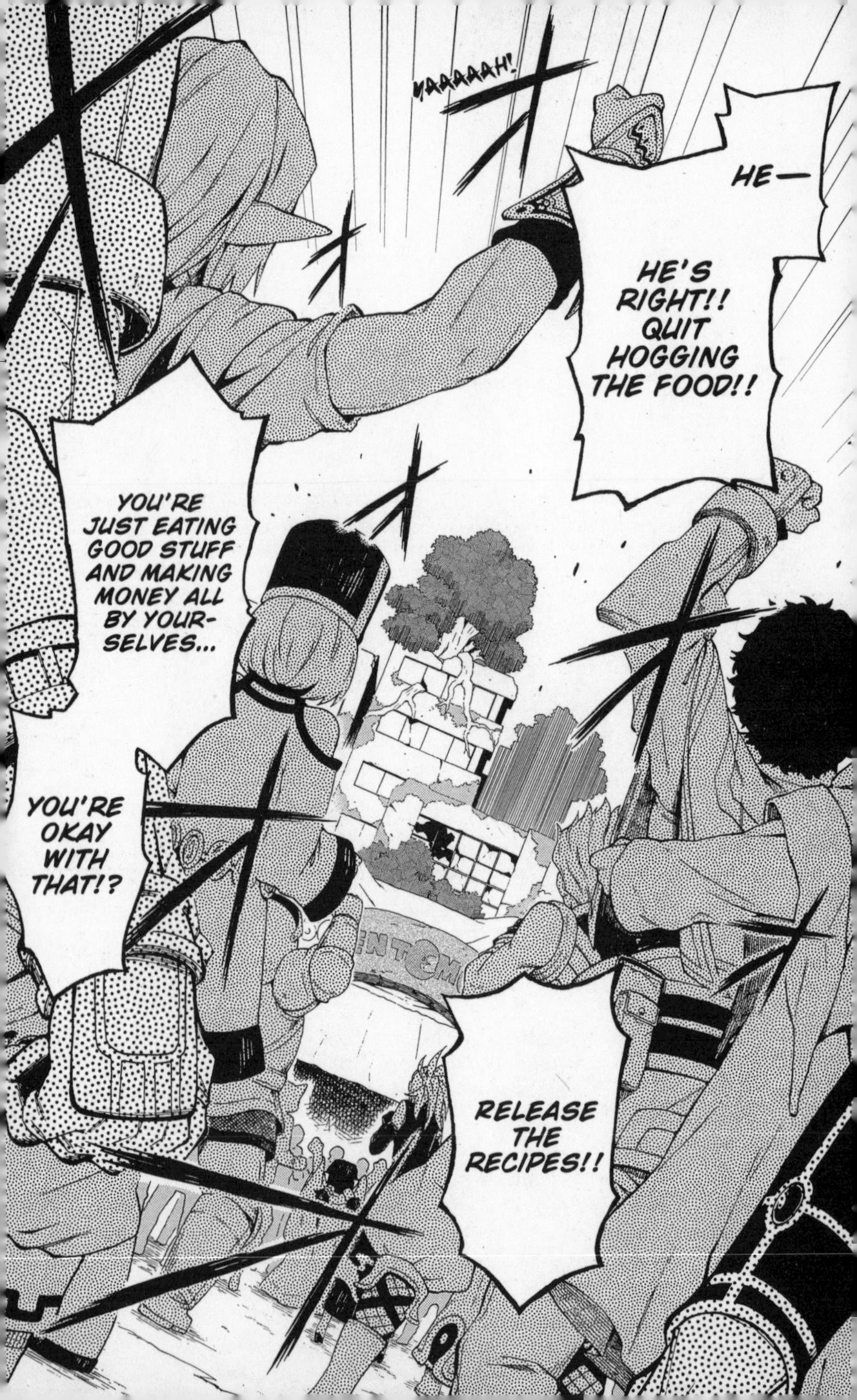
YAAAAAH!
HE—
HE'S RIGHT!! QUIT HOGGING THE FOOD!!
YOU'RE JUST EATING GOOD STUFF AND MAKING MONEY ALL BY YOUR-SELVES...
YOU'RE OKAY WITH THAT!?
RELEASE THE RECIPES!!

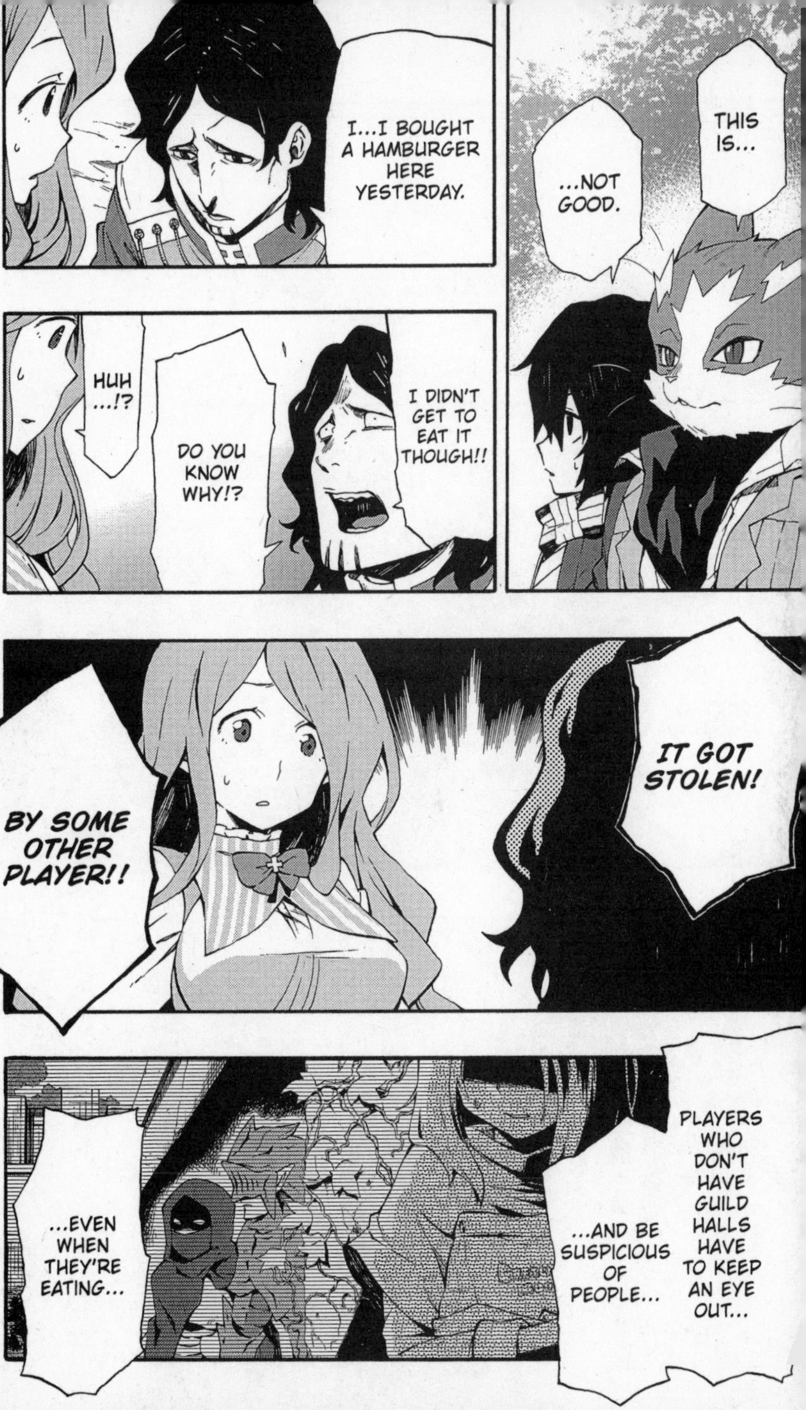
THIS IS...
...NOT GOOD.
I...I BOUGHT A HAMBURGER HERE YESTERDAY.
I DIDN'T GET TO EAT IT THOUGH!!
DO YOU KNOW WHY!?
HUH ...!?
IT GOT STOLEN!
BY SOME OTHER PLAYER!!
PLAYERS WHO DON'T HAVE GUILD HALLS HAVE TO KEEP AN EYE OUT...
...AND BE SUSPICIOUS OF PEOPLE...
...EVEN WHEN THEY'RE EATING...

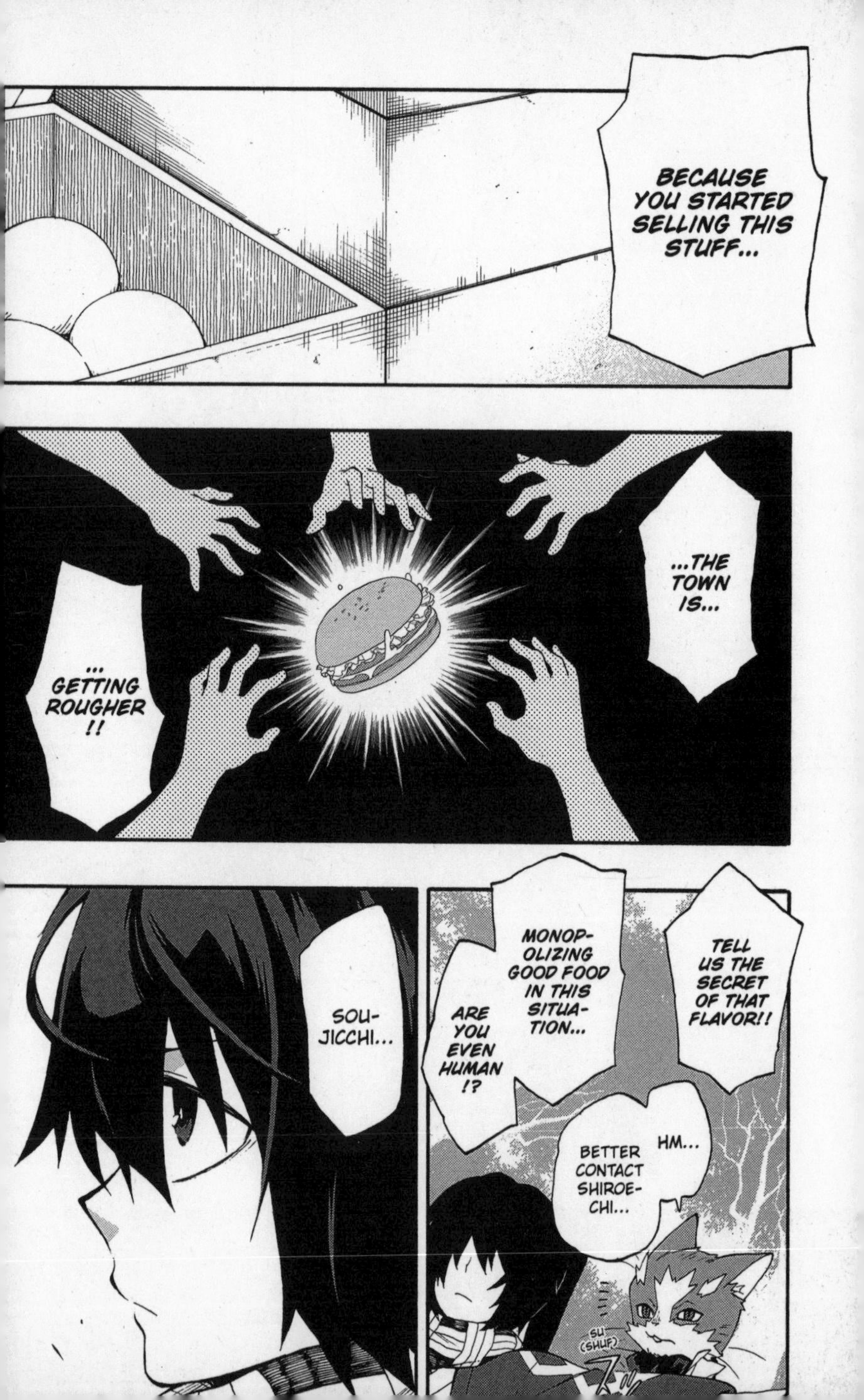
BECAUSE YOU STARTED SELLING THIS STUFF...
...THE TOWN IS...
...GETTING ROUGHER!!
TELL US THE SECRET OF THAT FLAVOR!!
MONOPOLIZING GOOD FOOD IN THIS SITUATION...
ARE YOU EVEN HUMAN!?
HM...
BETTER CONTACT SHIROE-CHI...
SU (SHUF)
SOUJICCHI...

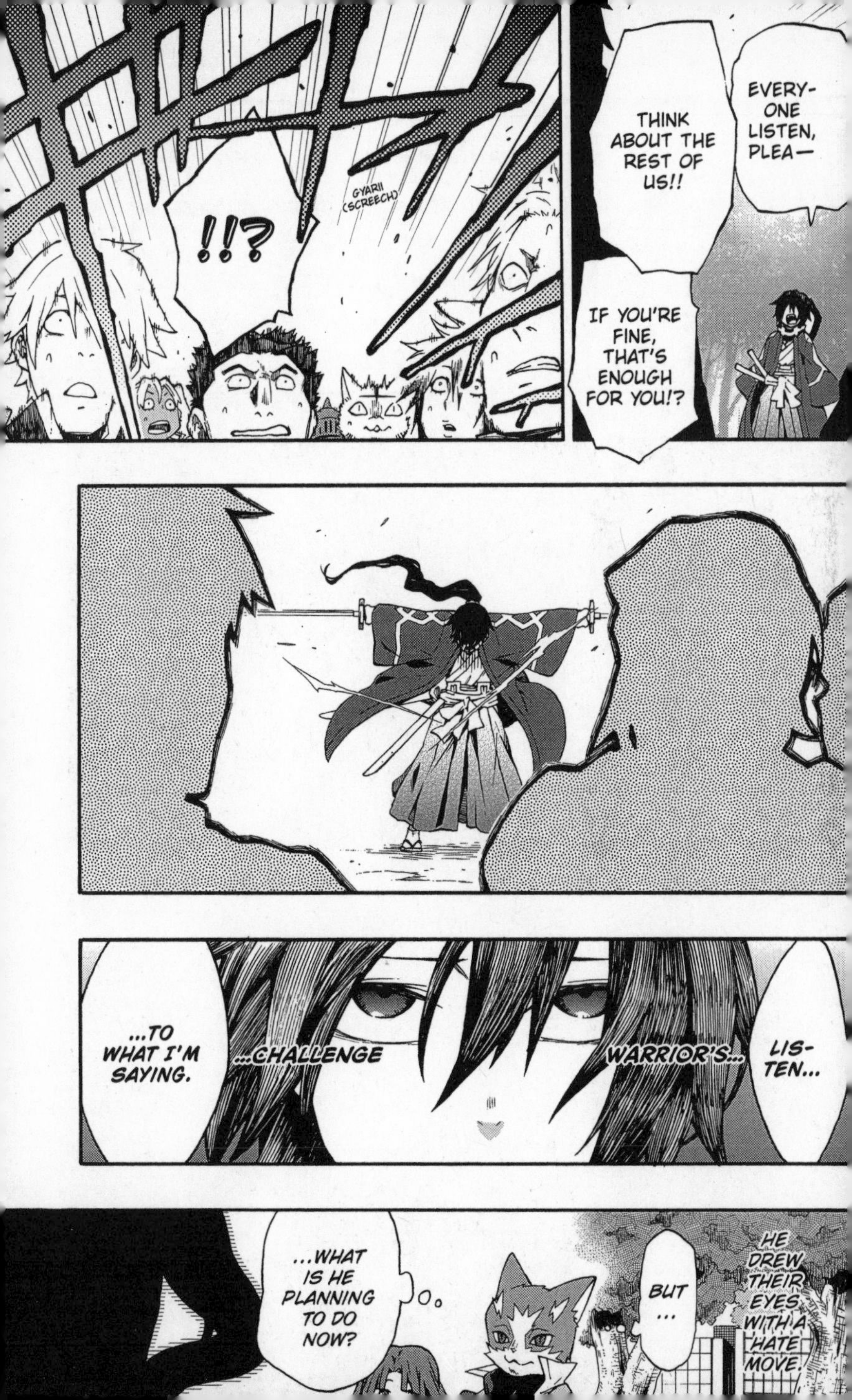
EVERY-ONE LISTEN, PLEA—
THINK ABOUT THE REST OF US!!
IF YOU'RE FINE, THAT'S ENOUGH FOR YOU!?
GYARII (SCREECH)
!!?
LIS-TEN...
WARRIOR'S...
...CHALLENGE
...TO WHAT I'M SAYING.
HE DREW THEIR EYES WITH A HATE MOVE
BUT ...
...WHAT IS HE PLANNING TO DO NOW?

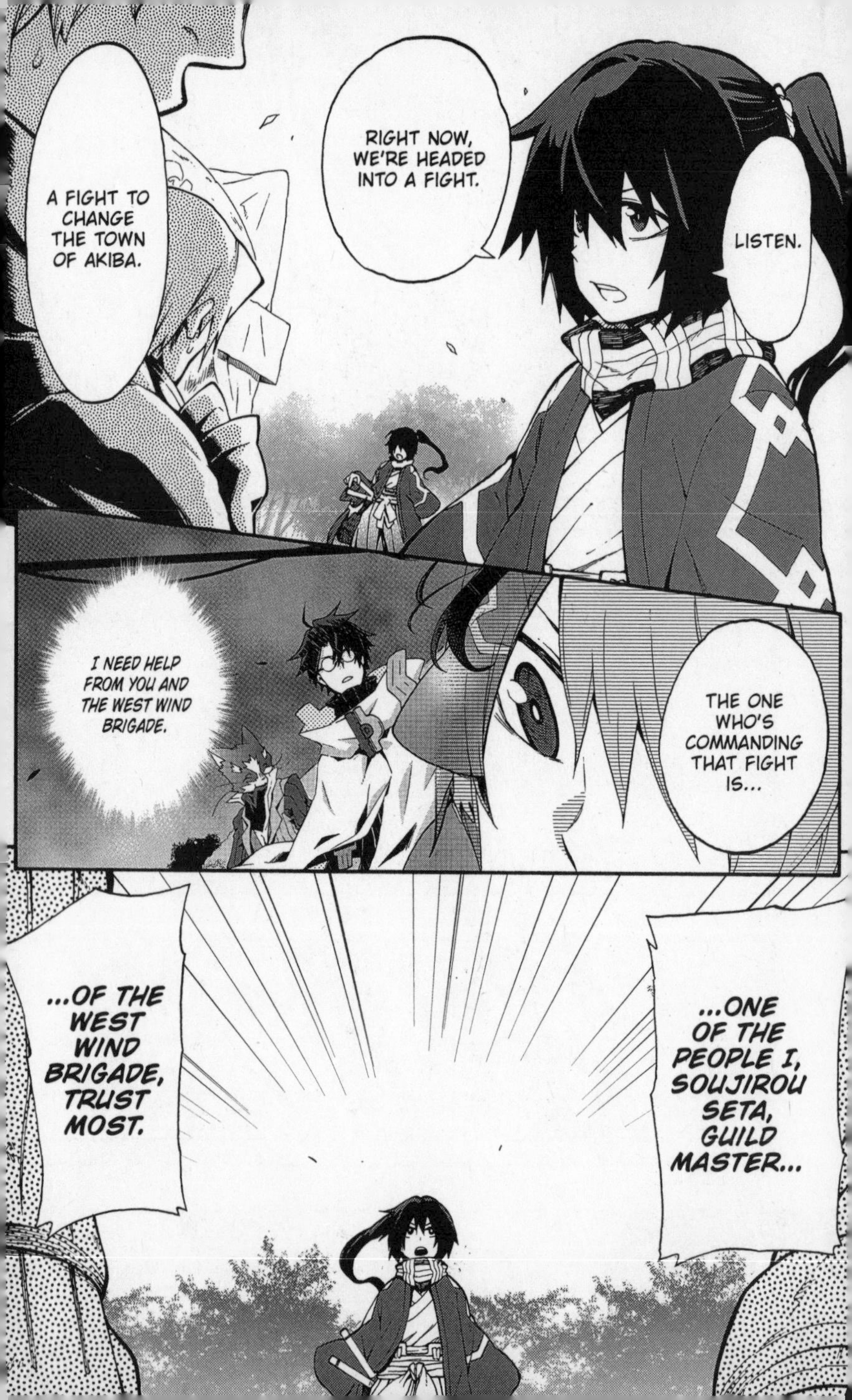
LISTEN.
RIGHT NOW, WE'RE HEADED INTO A FIGHT.
A FIGHT TO CHANGE THE TOWN OF AKIBA.
THE ONE WHO'S COMMANDING THAT FIGHT IS...
I NEED HELP FROM YOU AND THE WEST WIND BRIGADE.
...ONE OF THE PEOPLE I, SOUJIROU SETA, GUILD MASTER...
...OF THE WEST WIND BRIGADE, TRUST MOST.

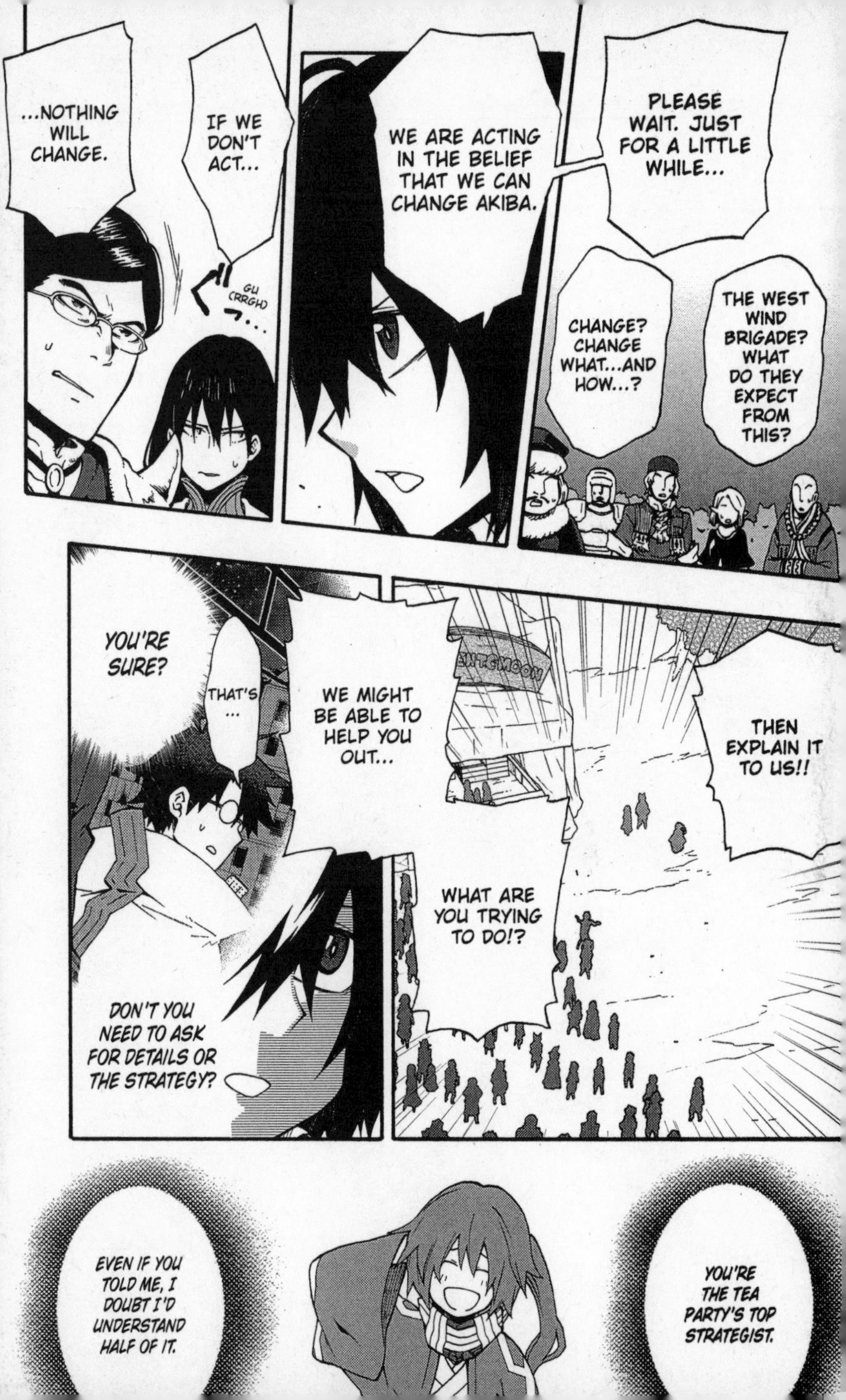
PLEASE WAIT. JUST FOR A LITTLE WHILE...
THE WEST WIND BRIGADE? WHAT DO THEY EXPECT FROM THIS?
CHANGE? CHANGE WHAT...AND HOW...?
WE ARE ACTING IN THE BELIEF THAT WE CAN CHANGE AKIBA.
IF WE DON'T ACT...
GU (RRGH)
...NOTHING WILL CHANGE.
THEN EXPLAIN IT TO US!!
WHAT ARE YOU TRYING TO DO!?
WE MIGHT BE ABLE TO HELP YOU OUT...
THAT'S...
YOU'RE SURE?
DON'T YOU NEED TO ASK FOR DETAILS OR THE STRATEGY?
YOU'RE THE TEA PARTY'S TOP STRATEGIST.
EVEN IF YOU TOLD ME, I DOUBT I'D UNDERSTAND HALF OF IT.

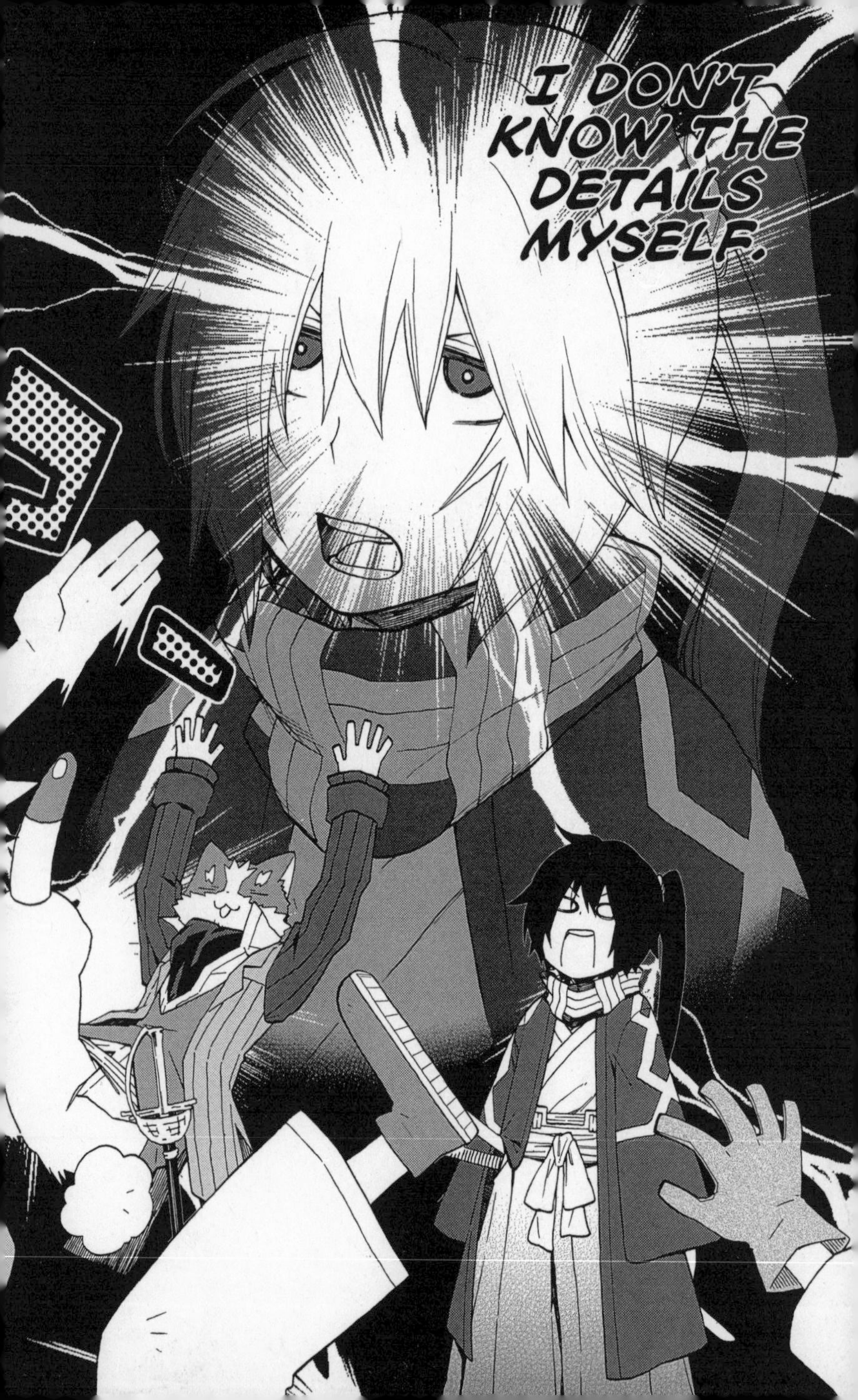
I DON'T KNOW THE DETAILS MYSELF.

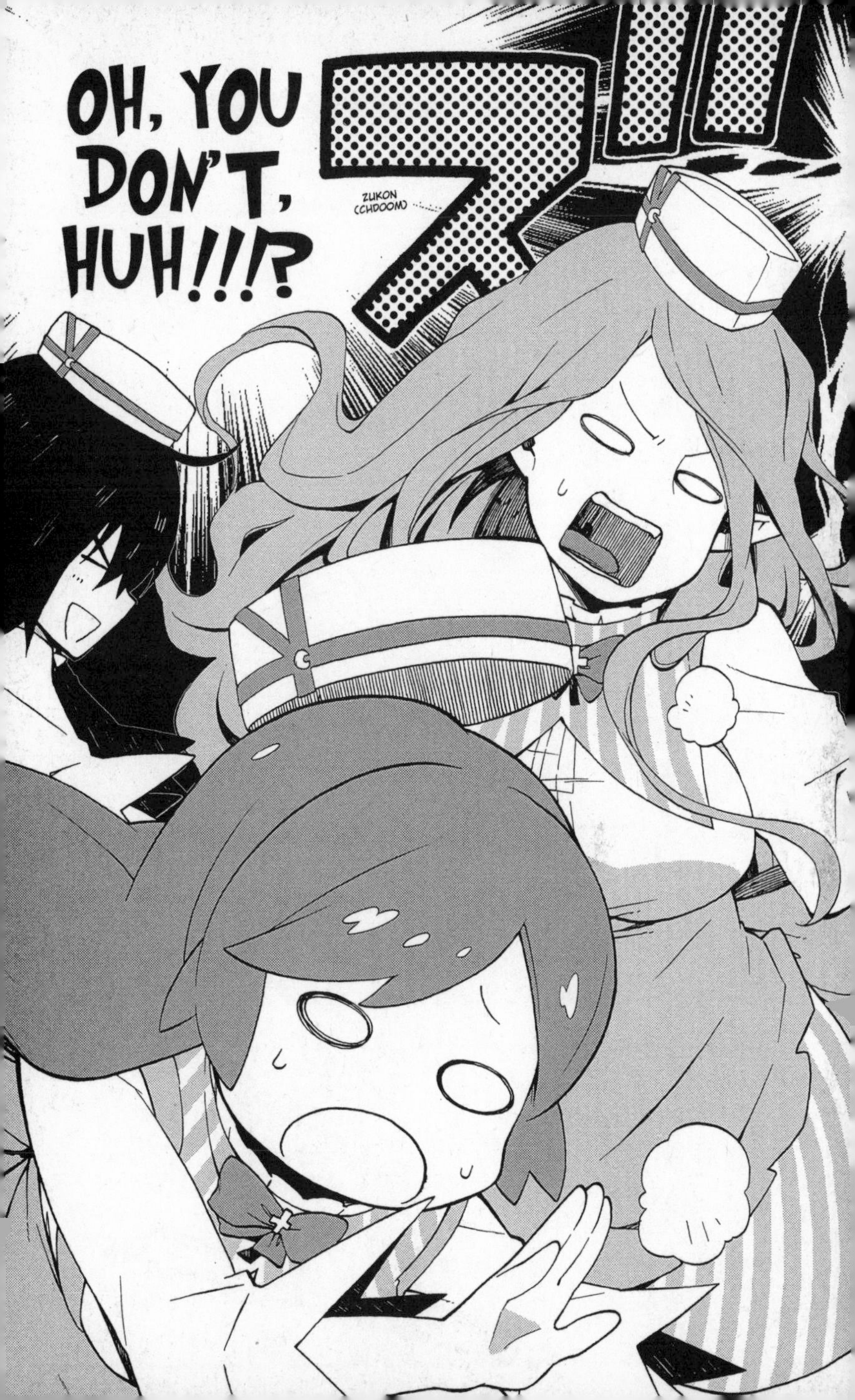
OH, YOU DON'T, HUH!!!?
ZUKON (CHDOOM)

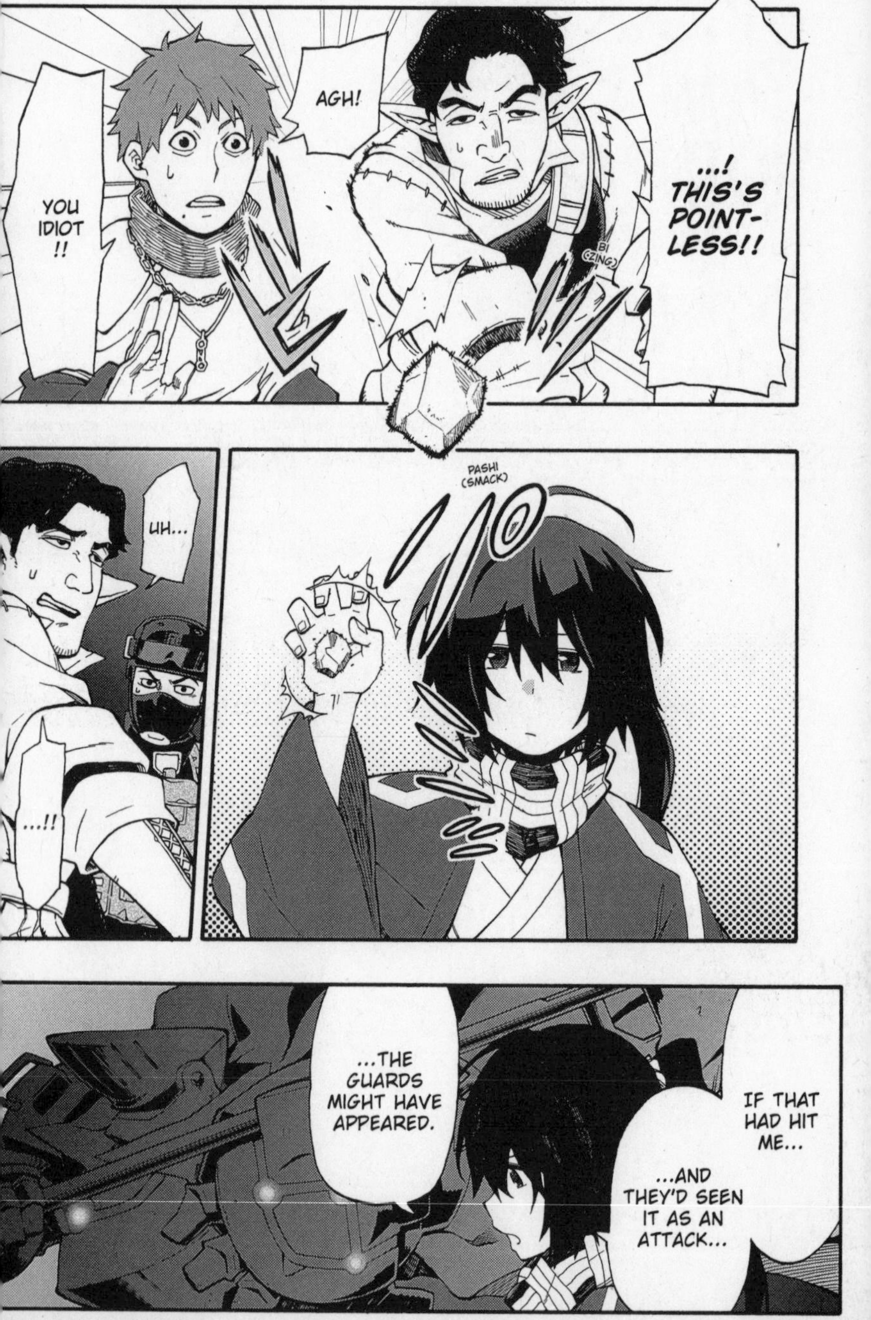
...! THIS'S POINT-LESS!!
AGH!
BI (ZING)
YOU IDIOT !!
PASHI (SMACK)
UH...
...!!
IF THAT HAD HIT ME...
...AND THEY'D SEEN IT AS AN ATTACK...
...THE GUARDS MIGHT HAVE APPEARED.

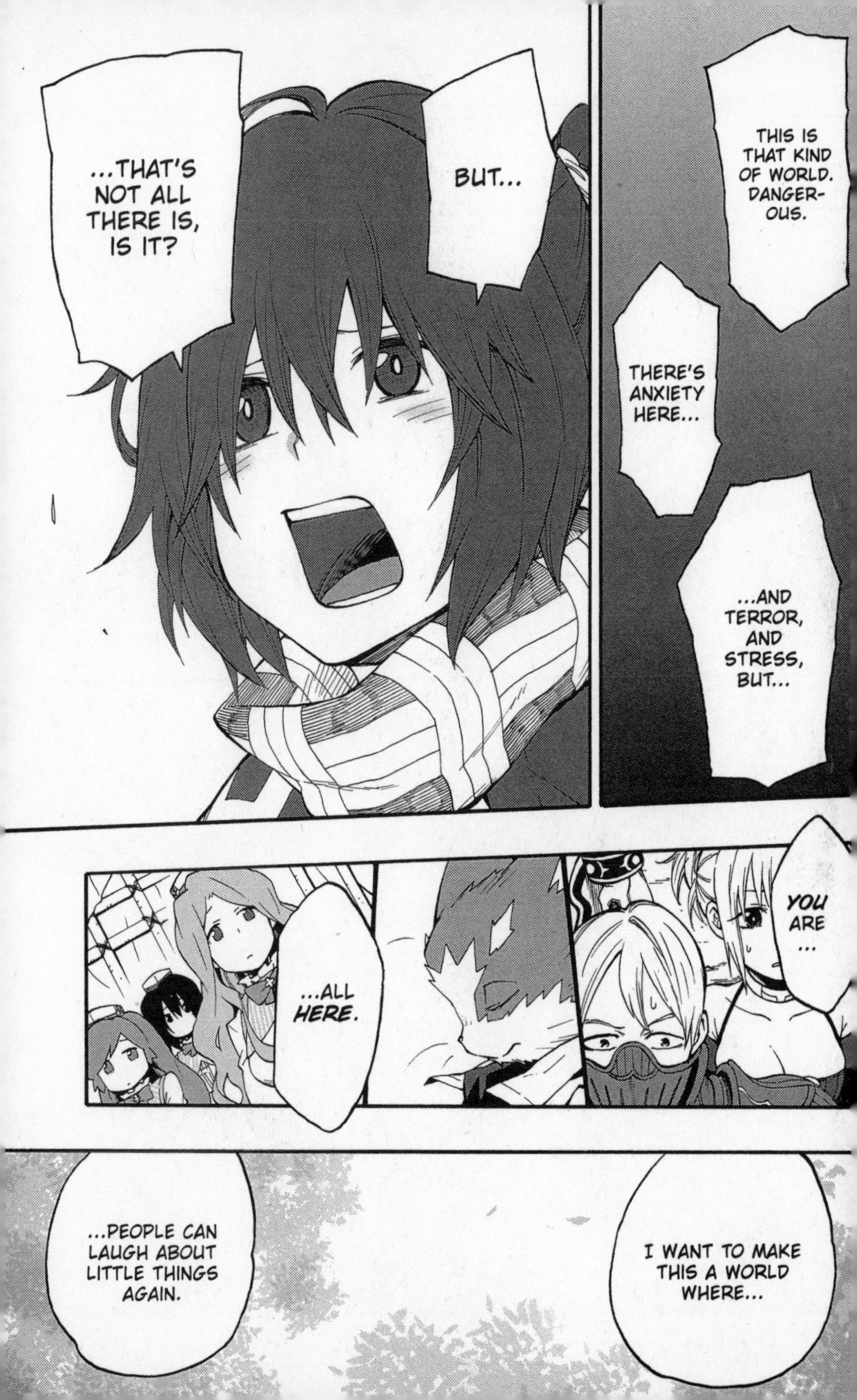
THIS IS THAT KIND OF WORLD. DANGER-OUS.
THERE'S ANXIETY HERE...
...AND TERROR, AND STRESS, BUT...
BUT...
...THAT'S NOT ALL THERE IS, IS IT?
YOU ARE ...
...ALL *HERE*.
I WANT TO MAKE THIS A WORLD WHERE...
...PEOPLE CAN LAUGH ABOUT LITTLE THINGS AGAIN.

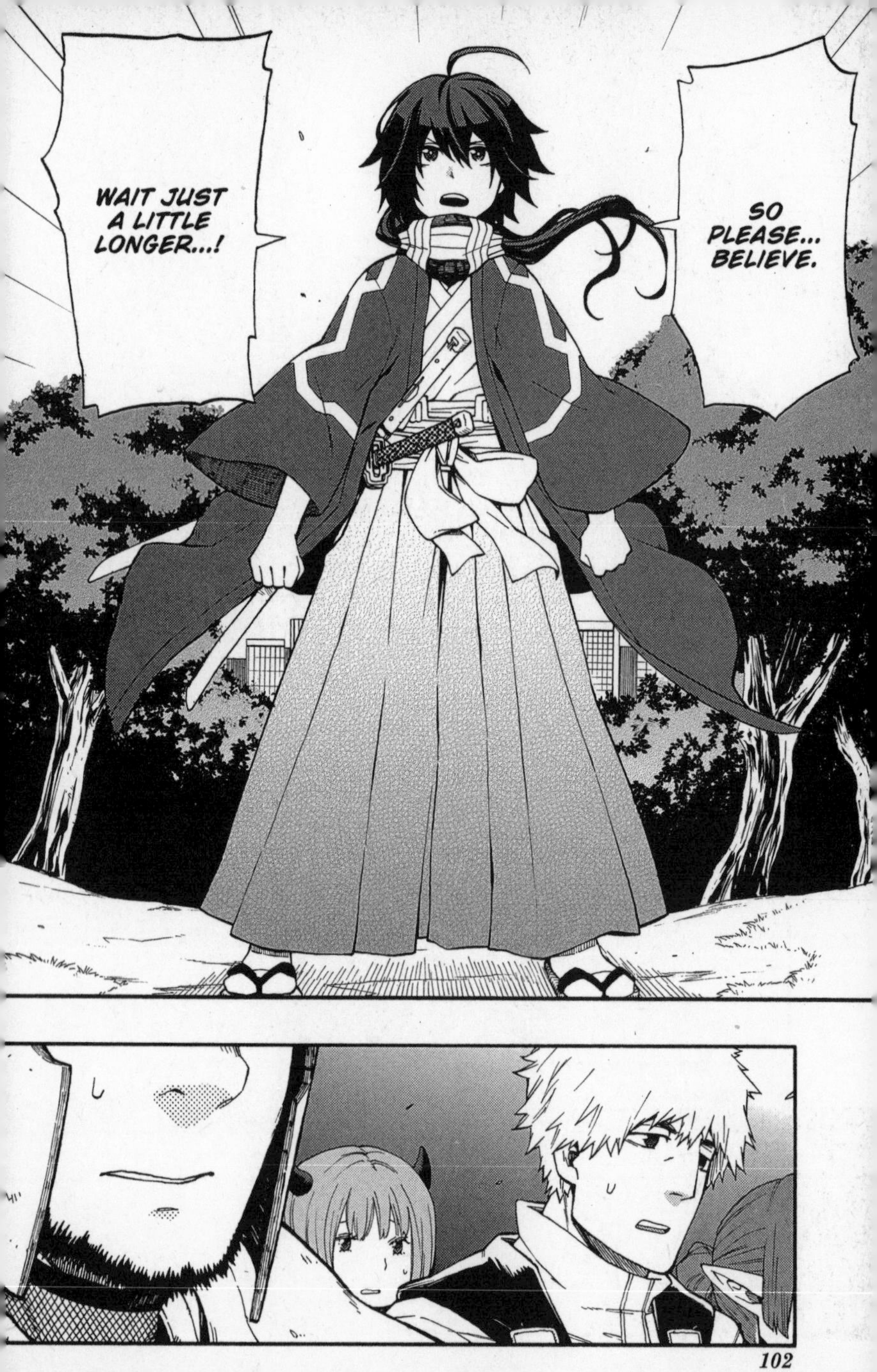
SO PLEASE... BELIEVE.
WAIT JUST A LITTLE LONGER...!

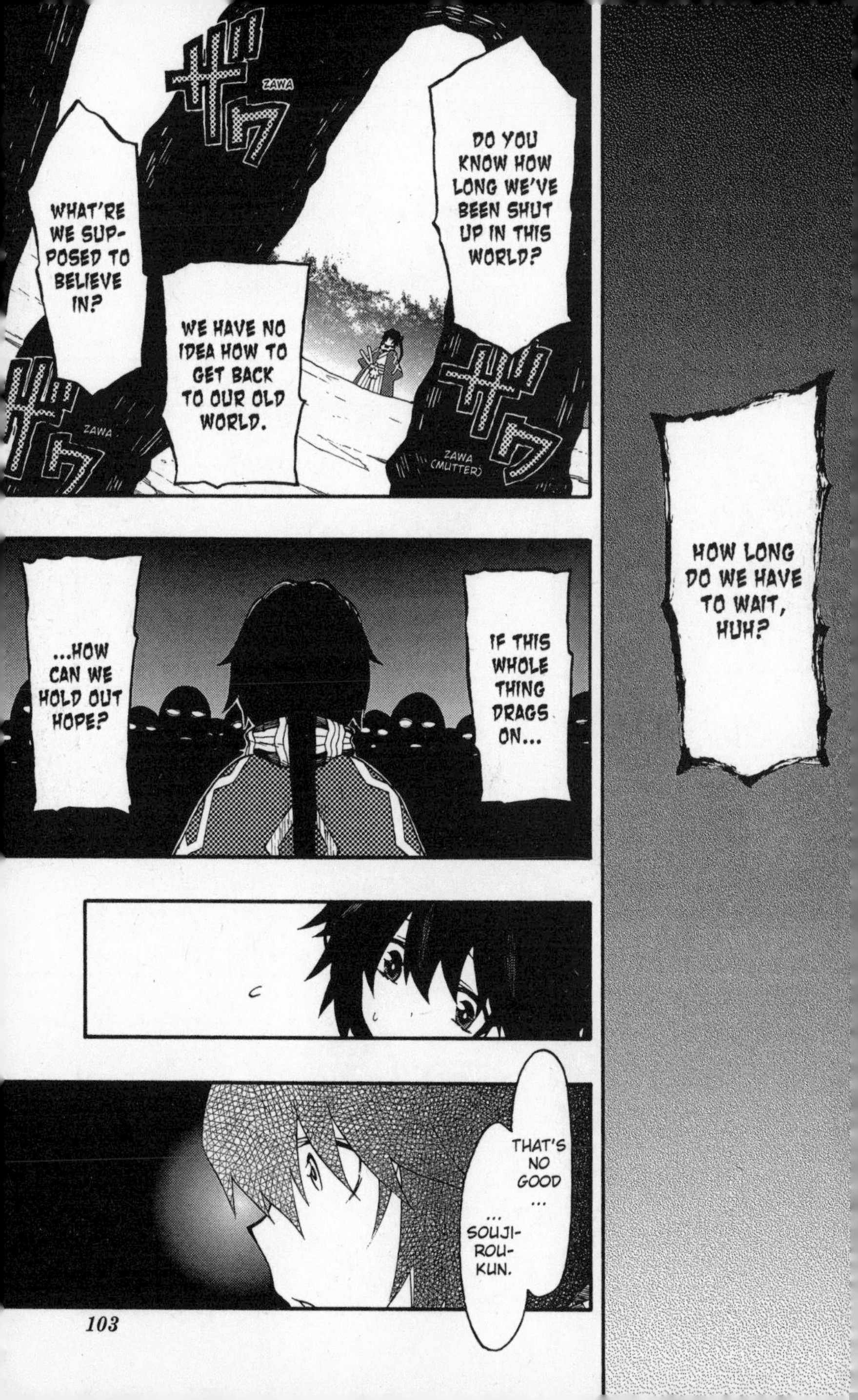
HOW LONG DO WE HAVE TO WAIT, HUH?
ZAWA
DO YOU KNOW HOW LONG WE'VE BEEN SHUT UP IN THIS WORLD?
WHAT'RE WE SUP-POSED TO BELIEVE IN?
WE HAVE NO IDEA HOW TO GET BACK TO OUR OLD WORLD.
ZAWA (MUTTER)
ZAWA
IF THIS WHOLE THING DRAGS ON...
...HOW CAN WE HOLD OUT HOPE?
THAT'S NO GOOD ...
... SOUJI-ROU-KUN.

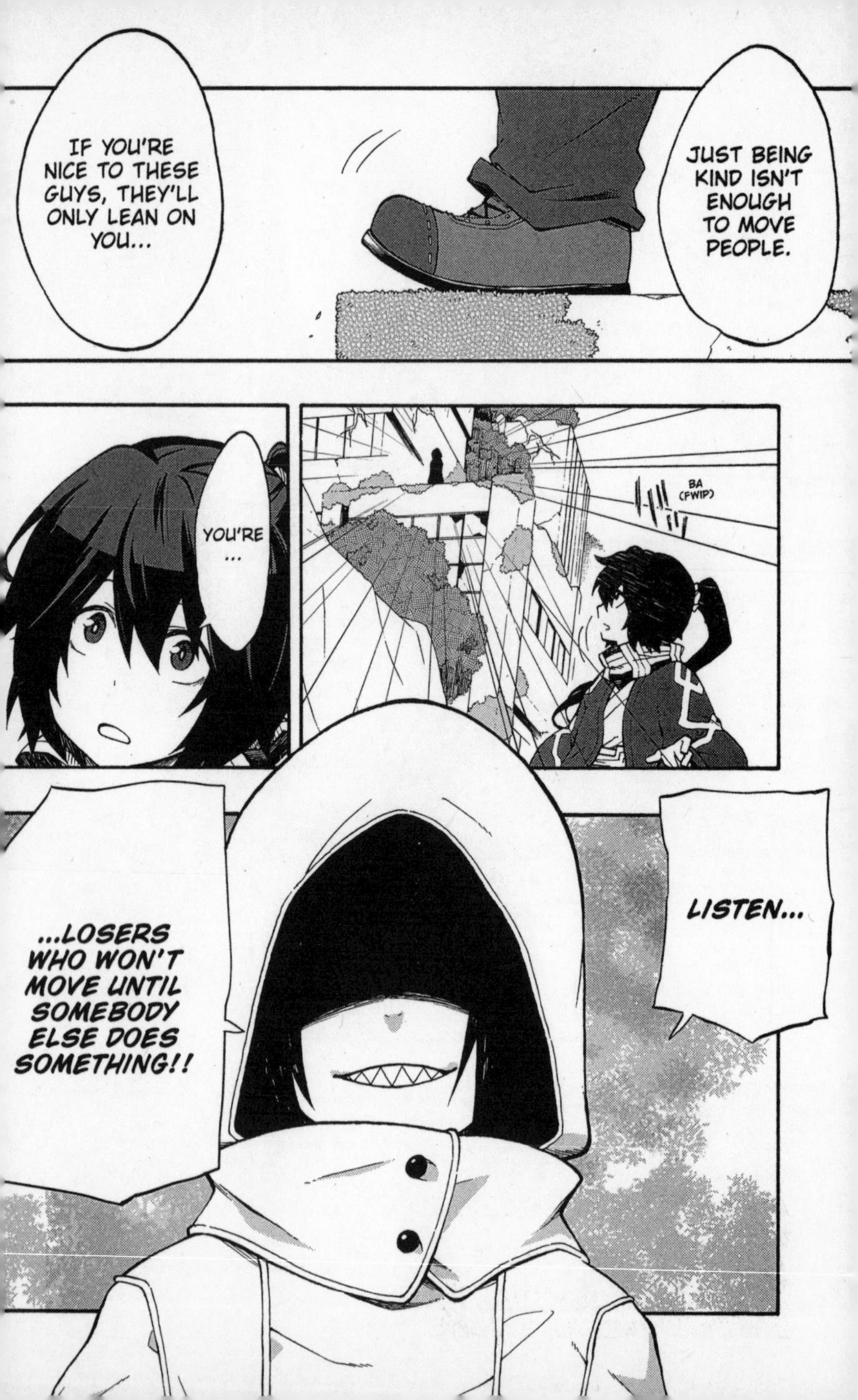
JUST BEING KIND ISN'T ENOUGH TO MOVE PEOPLE.
IF YOU'RE NICE TO THESE GUYS, THEY'LL ONLY LEAN ON YOU...
BA (FWIP)
YOU'RE ...
LISTEN...
...LOSERS WHO WON'T MOVE UNTIL SOMEBODY ELSE DOES SOMETHING!!

LOG HORIZON
THE WEST WIND BRIGADE

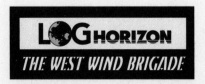

LOG HORIZON

THE WEST WIND BRIGADE

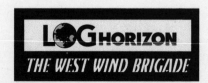

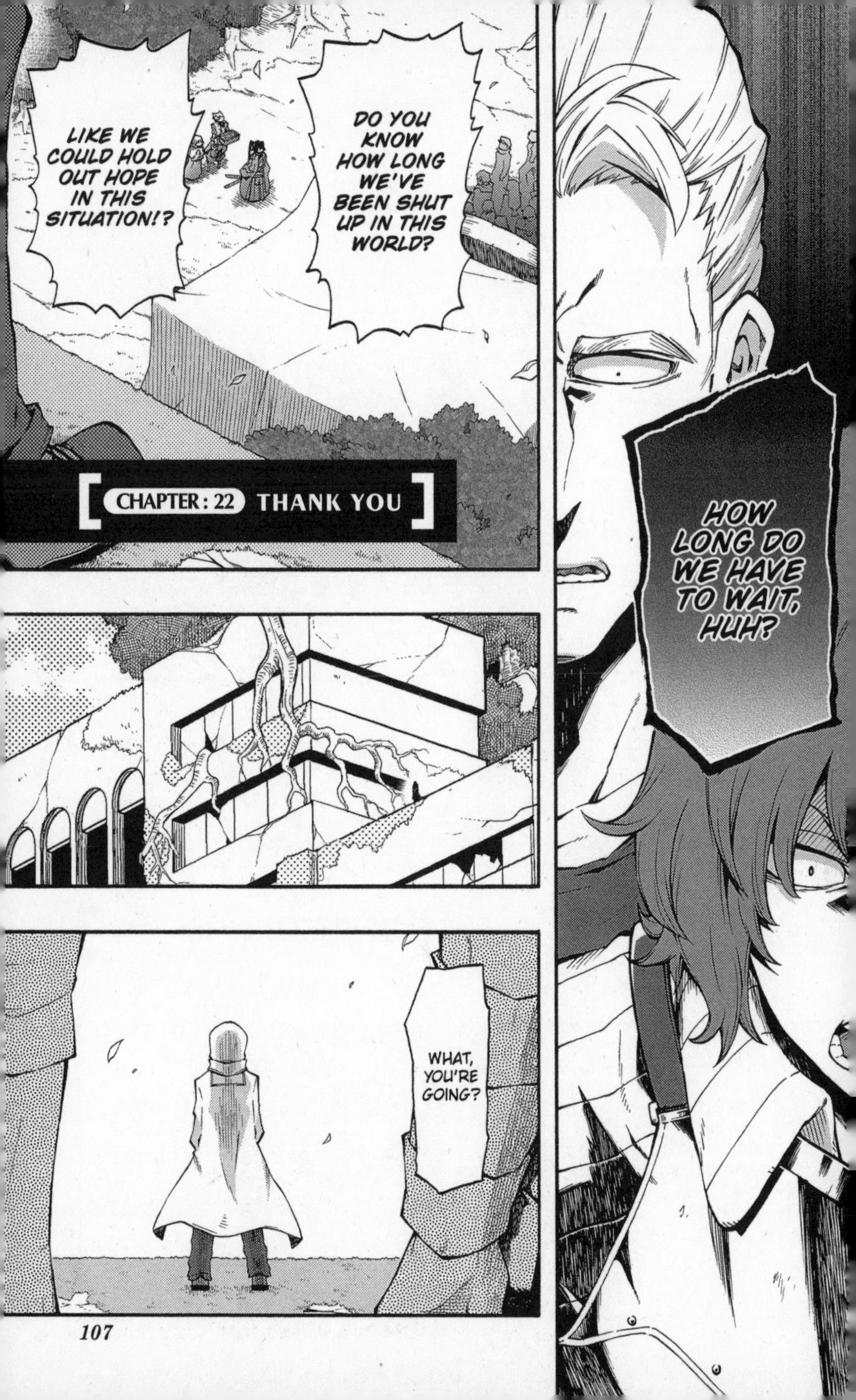
HOW LONG DO WE HAVE TO WAIT, HUH?
DO YOU KNOW HOW LONG WE'VE BEEN SHUT UP IN THIS WORLD?
LIKE WE COULD HOLD OUT HOPE IN THIS SITUATION!?
[CHAPTER : 22 THANK YOU]
WHAT, YOU'RE GOING?

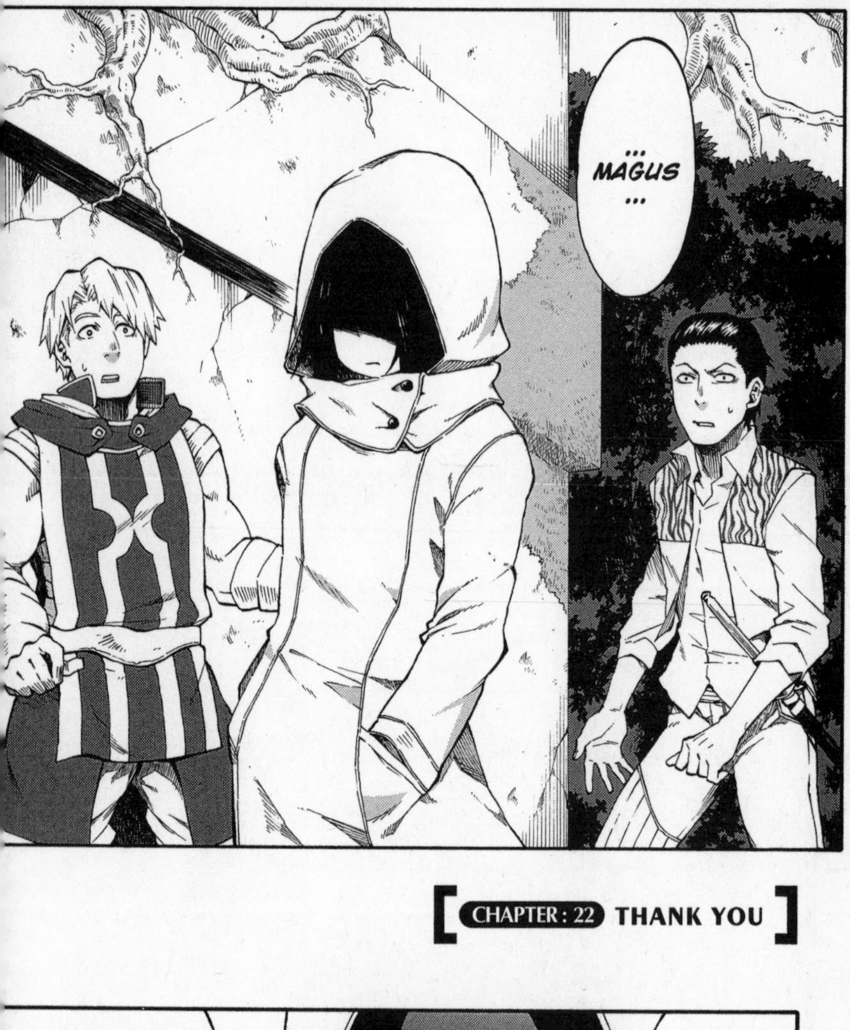
... MAGUS ...

[CHAPTER : 22 THANK YOU]

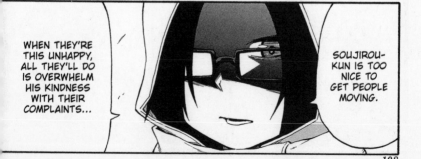

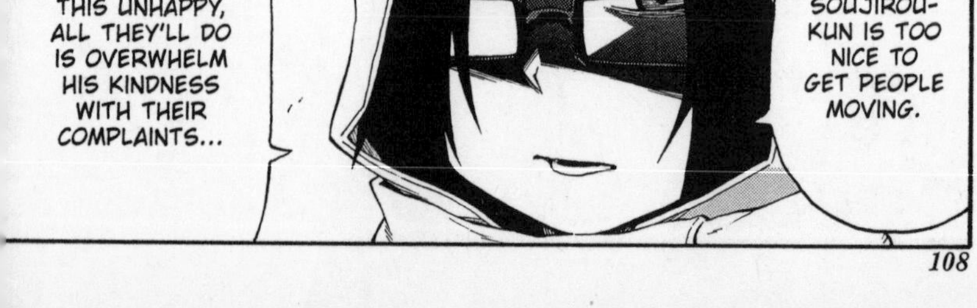
SOUJIROU-KUN IS TOO NICE TO GET PEOPLE MOVING.
WHEN THEY'RE THIS UNHAPPY, ALL THEY'LL DO IS OVERWHELM HIS KINDNESS WITH THEIR COMPLAINTS...

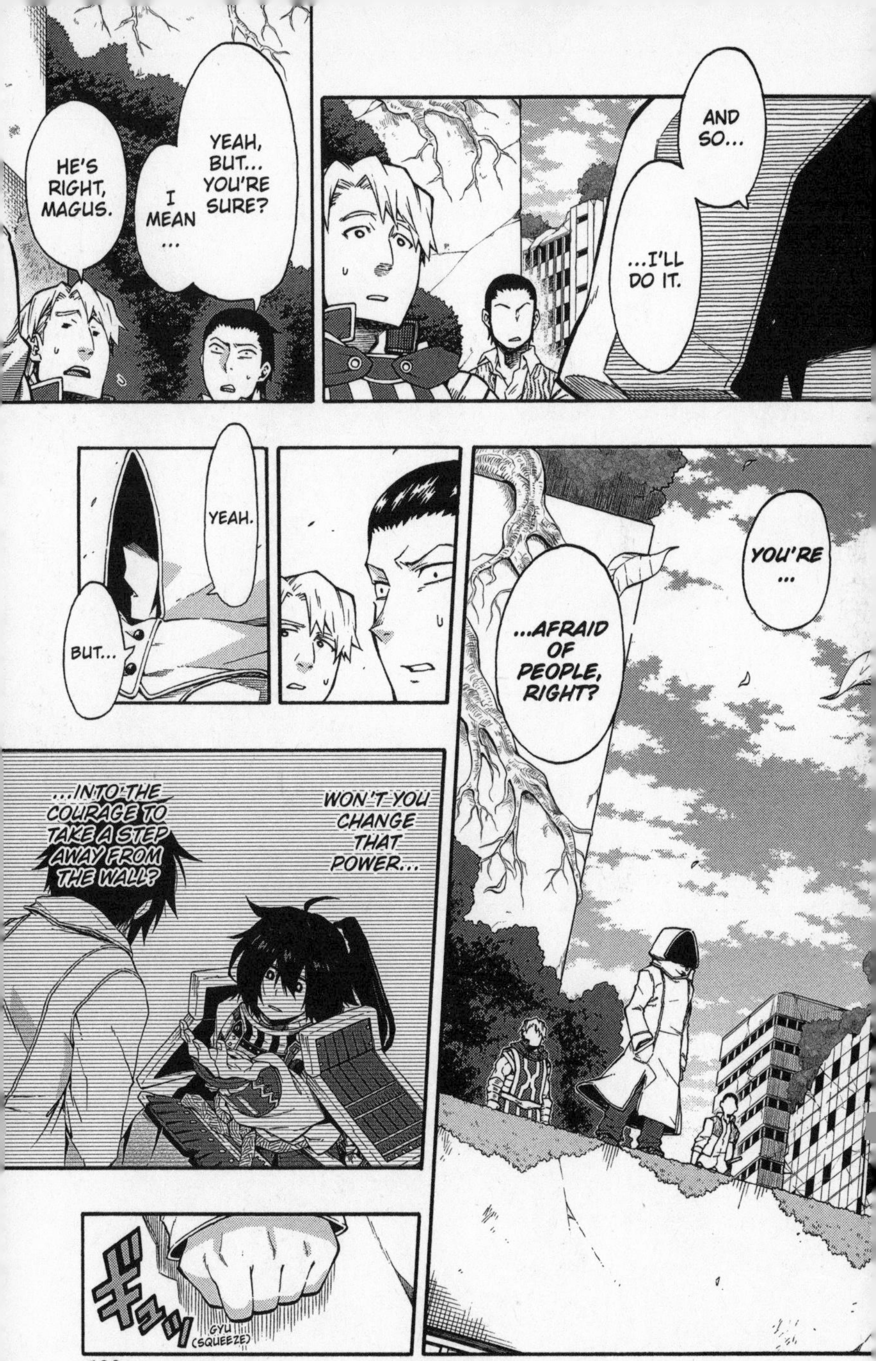
AND SO...
...I'LL DO IT.
YEAH, BUT... YOU'RE SURE?
I MEAN ...
HE'S RIGHT, MAGUS.
YOU'RE ...
...AFRAID OF PEOPLE, RIGHT?
YEAH.
BUT...
WON'T YOU CHANGE THAT POWER...
...INTO THE COURAGE TO TAKE A STEP AWAY FROM THE WALL?
ギュッ
GYU (SQUEEZE)

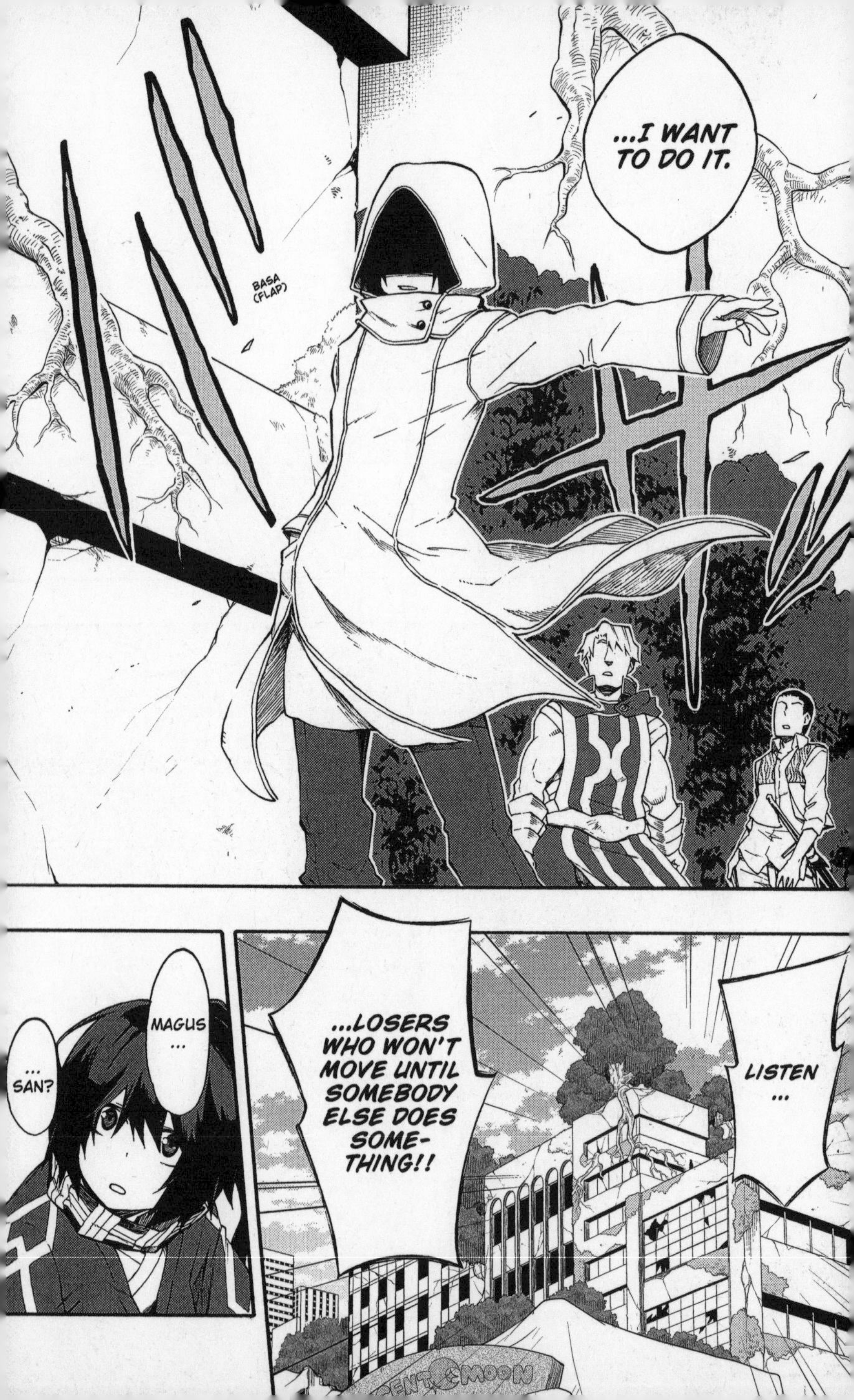
...I WANT TO DO IT.
BASA (FLAP)
LISTEN ...
...LOSERS WHO WON'T MOVE UNTIL SOMEBODY ELSE DOES SOME-THING!!
MAGUS ...
... SAN?

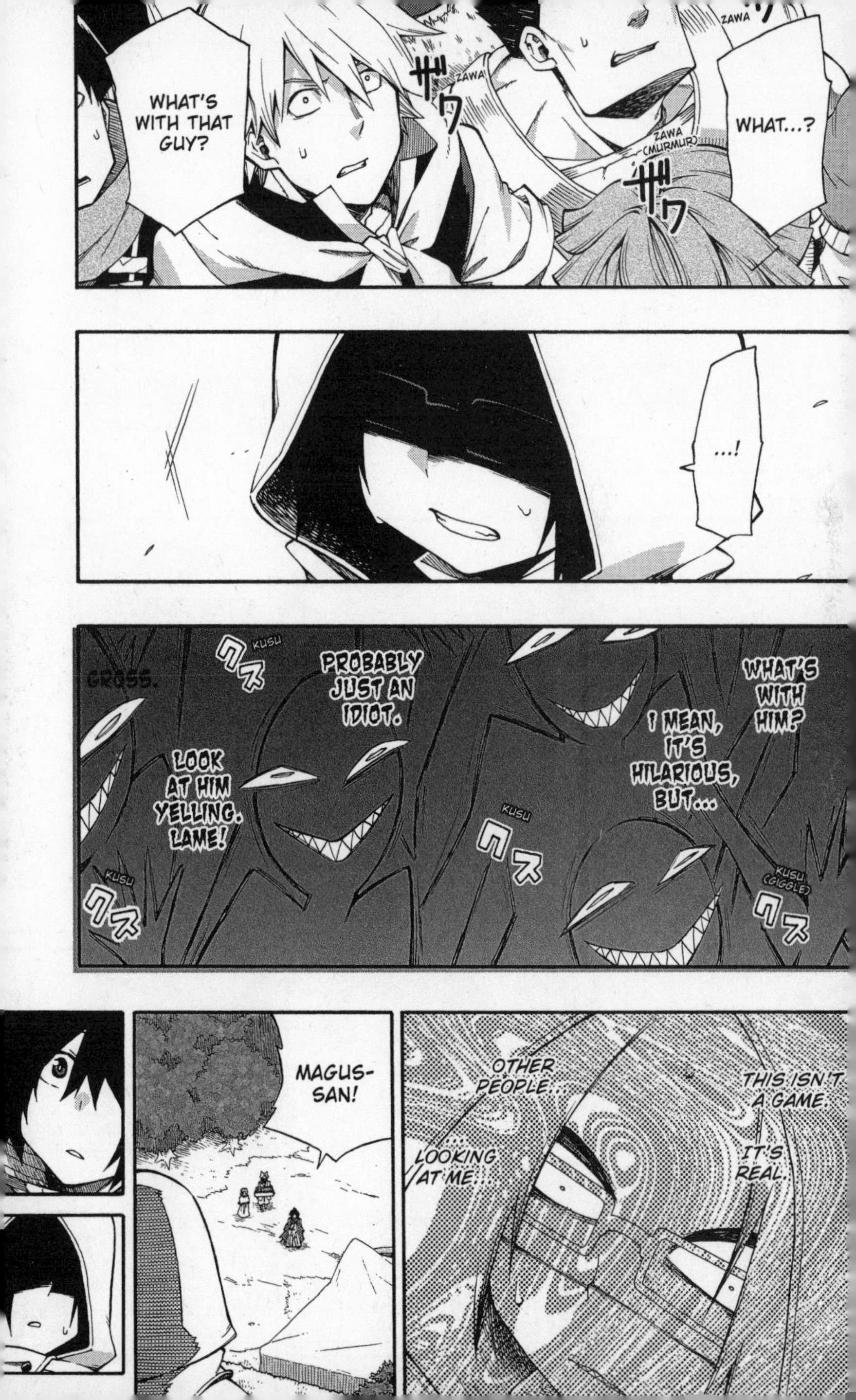
ZAWA
WHAT...?
ZAWA (MURMUR)
ZAWA
WHAT'S WITH THAT GUY?
...!
WHAT'S WITH HIM?
KUSU (GIGGLE)
I MEAN, IT'S HILARIOUS, BUT...
PROBABLY JUST AN IDIOT.
KUSU
LOOK AT HIM YELLING. LAME!
KUSU
GROSS.
KUSU
THIS ISN'T A GAME.
IT'S REAL.
OTHER PEOPLE...
...LOOKING AT ME...
MAGUS-SAN!

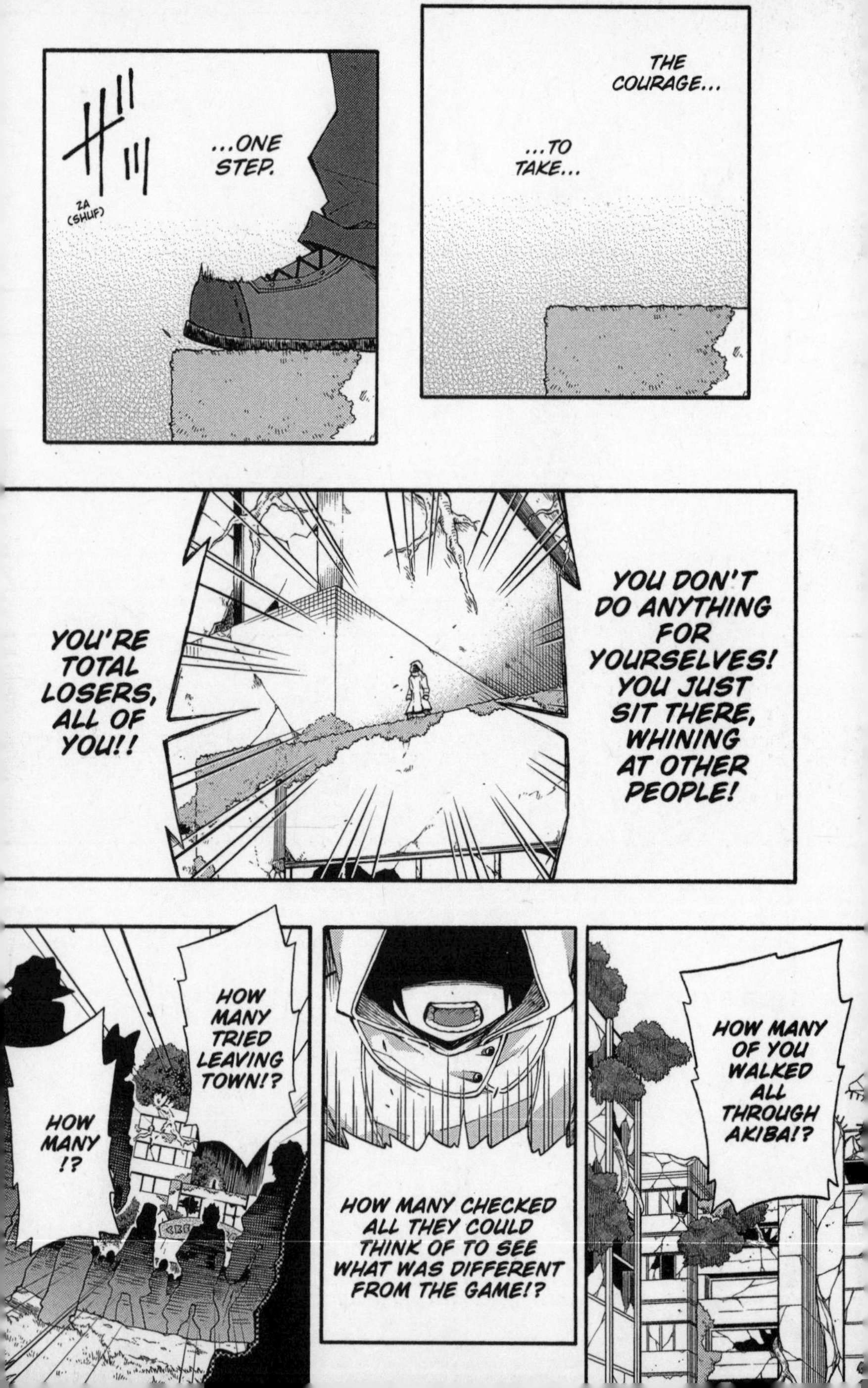
THE COURAGE...
...TO TAKE...
...ONE STEP.
ZA (SHUF)
YOU DON'T DO ANYTHING FOR YOURSELVES! YOU JUST SIT THERE, WHINING AT OTHER PEOPLE!
YOU'RE TOTAL LOSERS, ALL OF YOU!!
HOW MANY OF YOU WALKED ALL THROUGH AKIBA!?
HOW MANY CHECKED ALL THEY COULD THINK OF TO SEE WHAT WAS DIFFERENT FROM THE GAME!?
HOW MANY TRIED LEAVING TOWN!?
HOW MANY!?

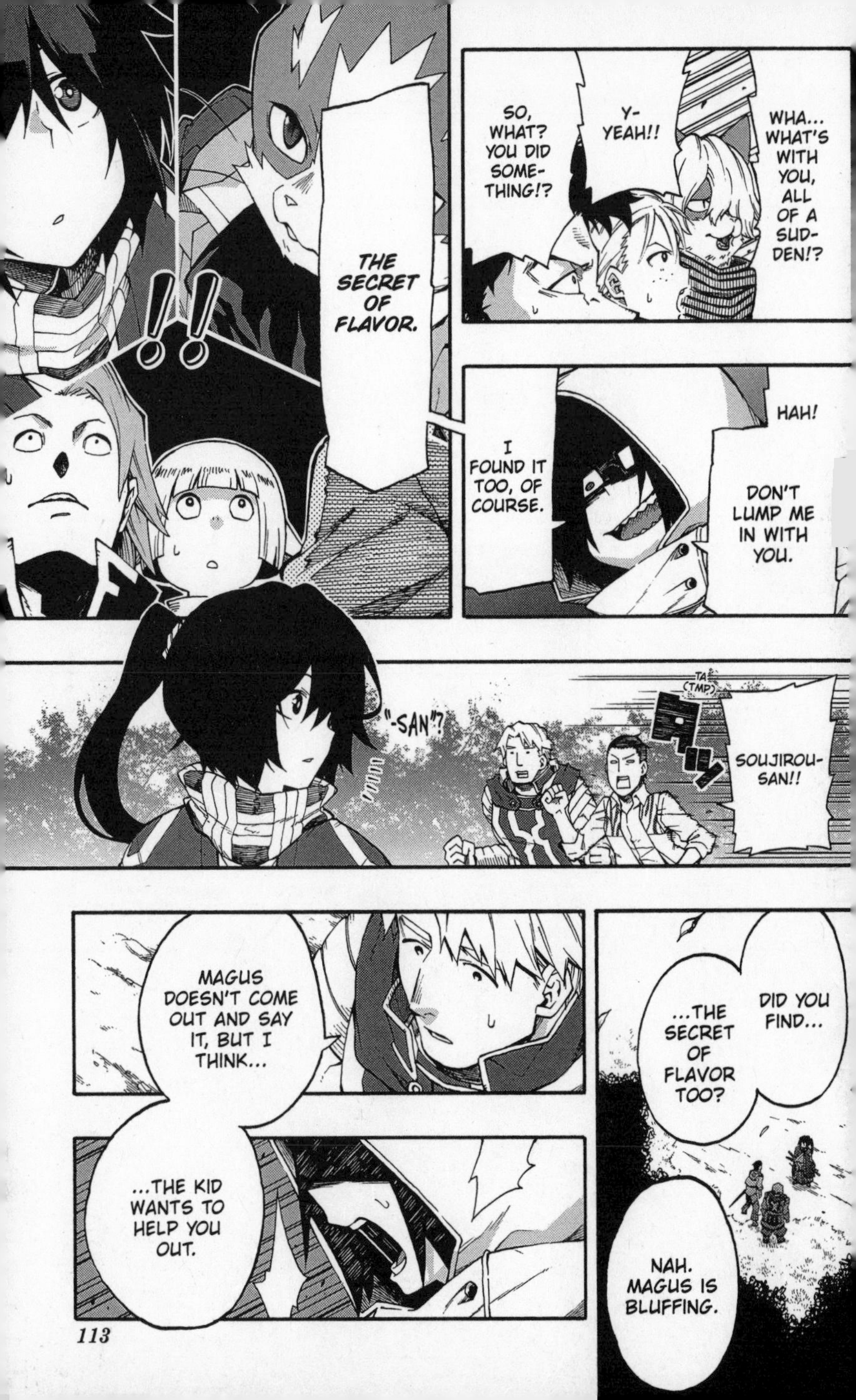
WHA... WHAT'S WITH YOU, ALL OF A SUDDEN!?
Y-YEAH!!
SO, WHAT? YOU DID SOMETHING!?
HAH!
DON'T LUMP ME IN WITH YOU.
I FOUND IT TOO, OF COURSE.
THE SECRET OF FLAVOR.
SOUJIROU-SAN!!
TA (TMP)
"-SAN"?
DID YOU FIND...
...THE SECRET OF FLAVOR TOO?
NAH. MAGUS IS BLUFFING.
MAGUS DOESN'T COME OUT AND SAY IT, BUT I THINK...
...THE KID WANTS TO HELP YOU OUT.

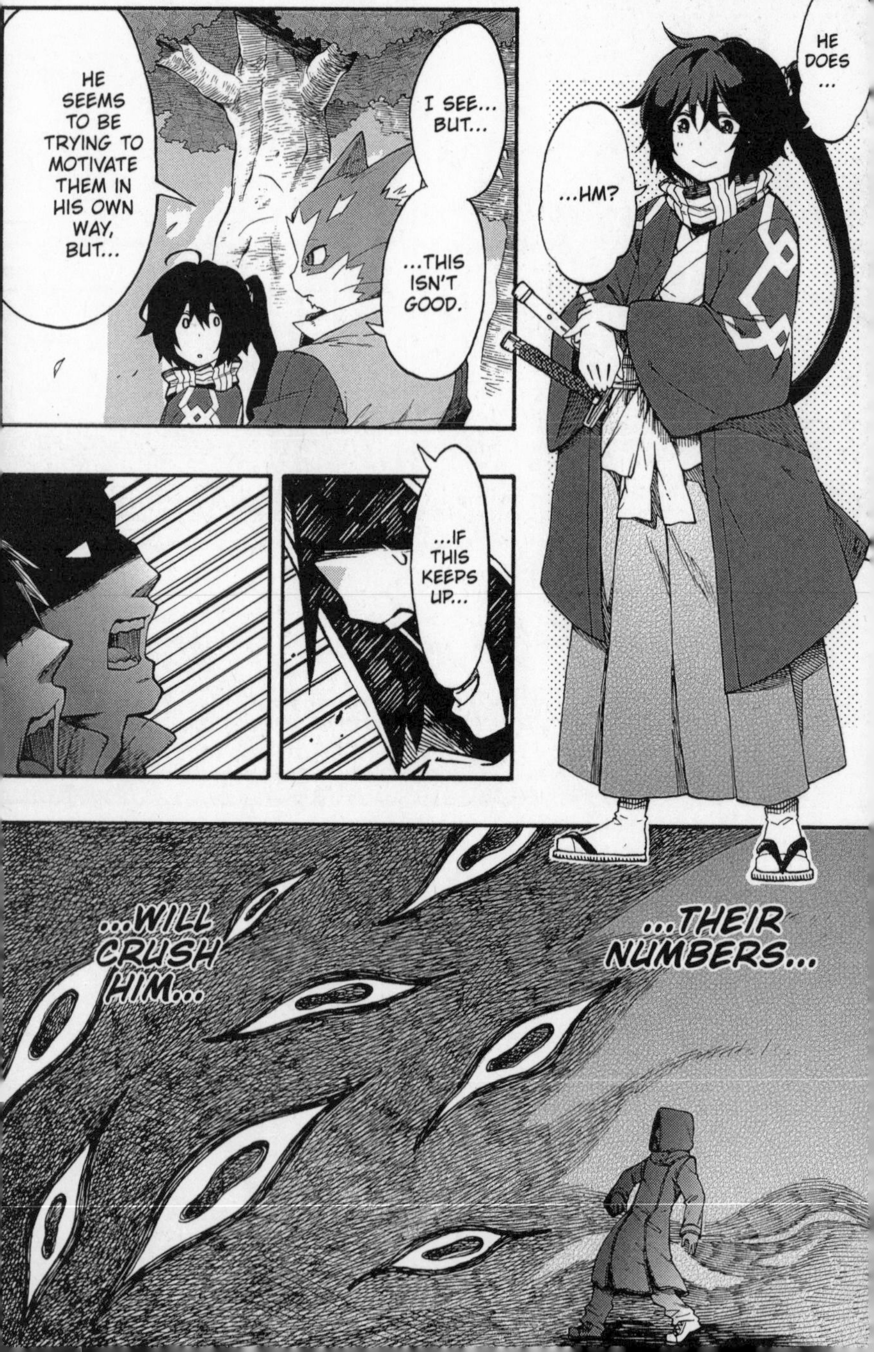
HE DOES ...
...HM?
HE SEEMS TO BE TRYING TO MOTIVATE THEM IN HIS OWN WAY, BUT...
I SEE... BUT...
...THIS ISN'T GOOD.
...IF THIS KEEPS UP...
...THEIR NUMBERS...
...WILL CRUSH HIM...

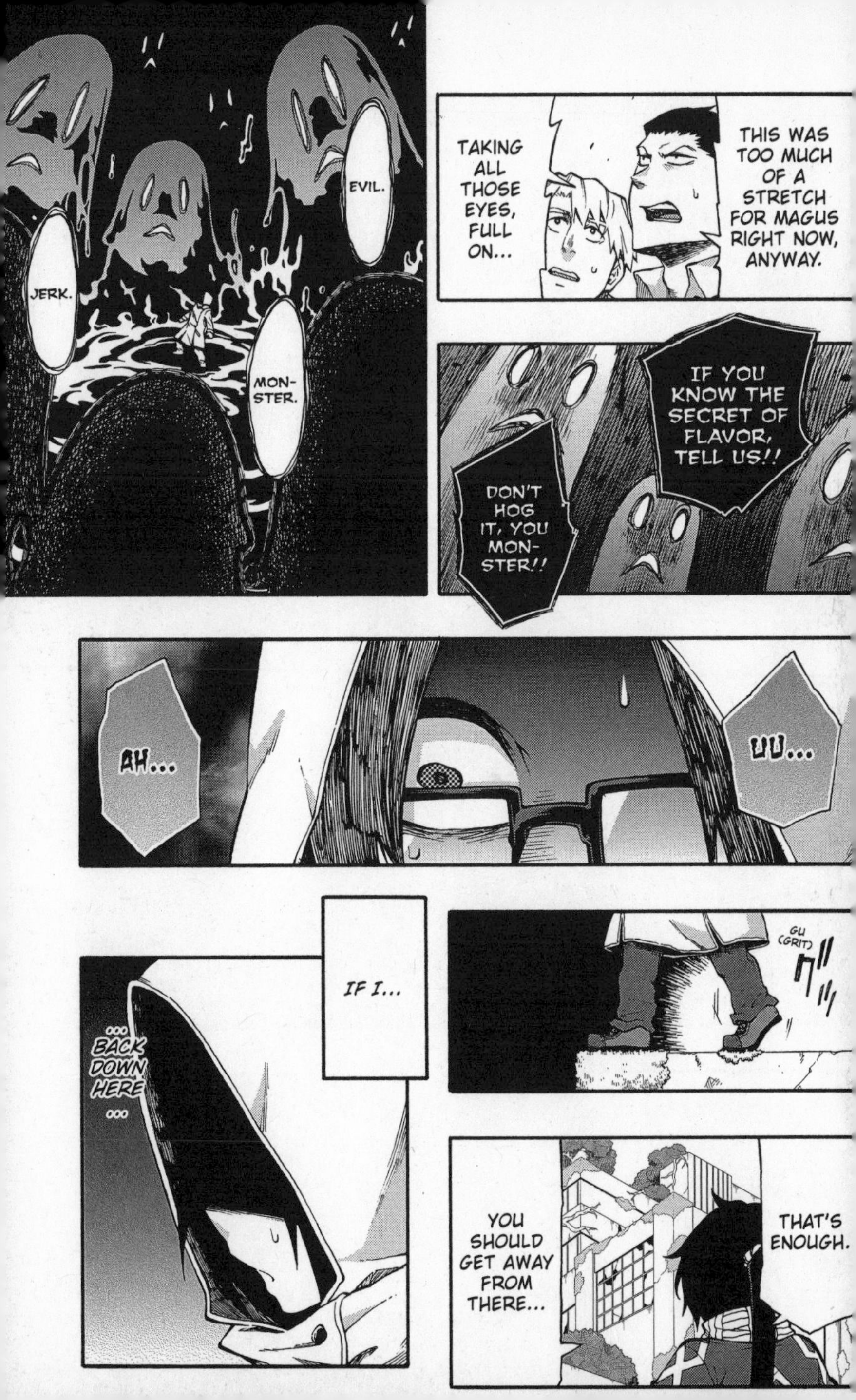

THIS WAS TOO MUCH OF A STRETCH FOR MAGUS RIGHT NOW, ANYWAY.
TAKING ALL THOSE EYES, FULL ON...
IF YOU KNOW THE SECRET OF FLAVOR, TELL US!!
DON'T HOG IT, YOU MONSTER!!
EVIL.
MONSTER.
JERK.
UU...
AH...
GU (GRIT)
IF I...
...BACK DOWN HERE...
THAT'S ENOUGH.
YOU SHOULD GET AWAY FROM THERE...

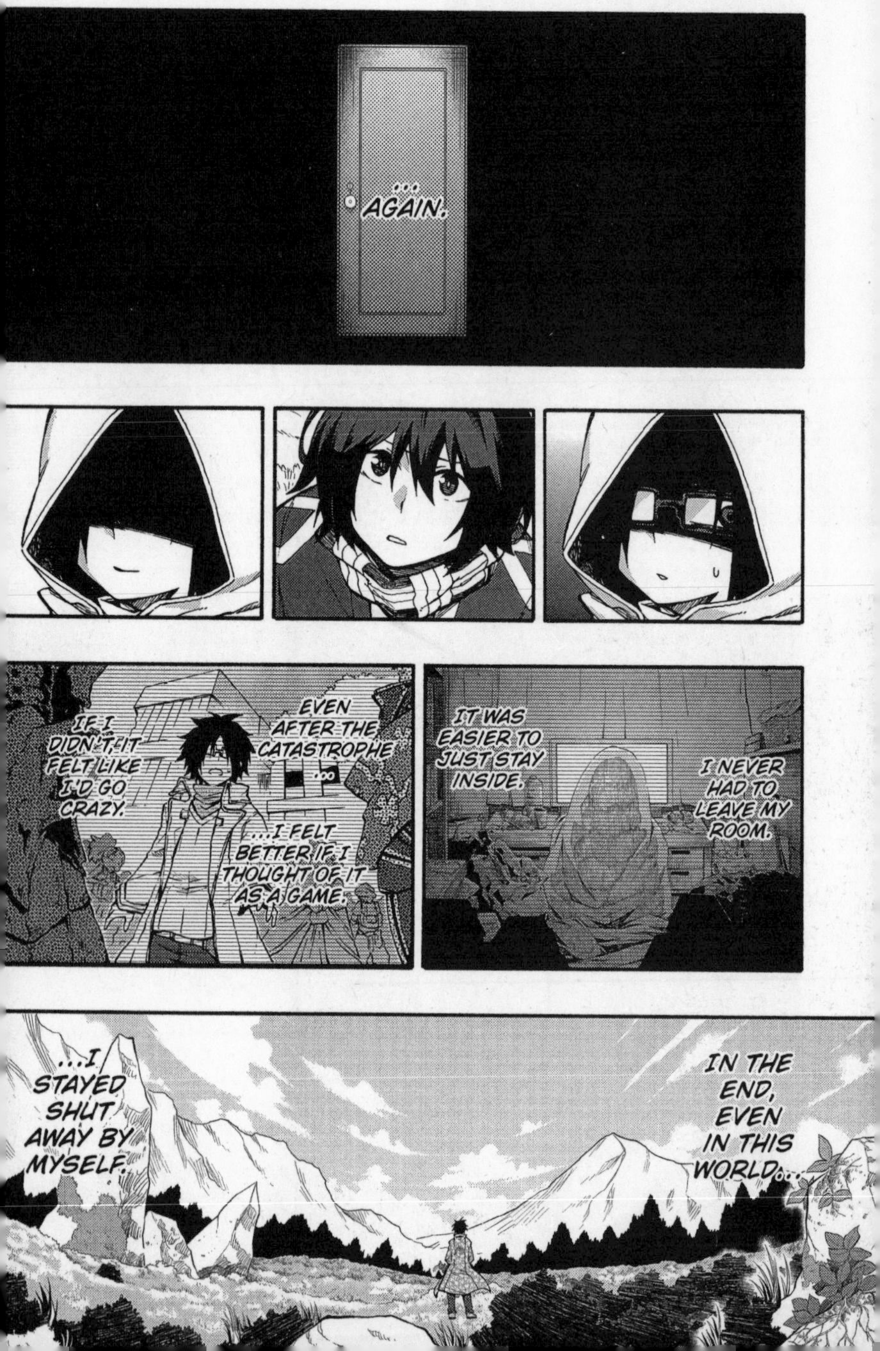
...AGAIN.
I NEVER HAD TO LEAVE MY ROOM.
IT WAS EASIER TO JUST STAY INSIDE.
EVEN AFTER THE CATASTROPHE...
...I FELT BETTER IF I THOUGHT OF IT AS A GAME.
IF I DIDN'T, IT FELT LIKE I'D GO CRAZY.
IN THE END, EVEN IN THIS WORLD...
...I STAYED SHUT AWAY BY MYSELF.

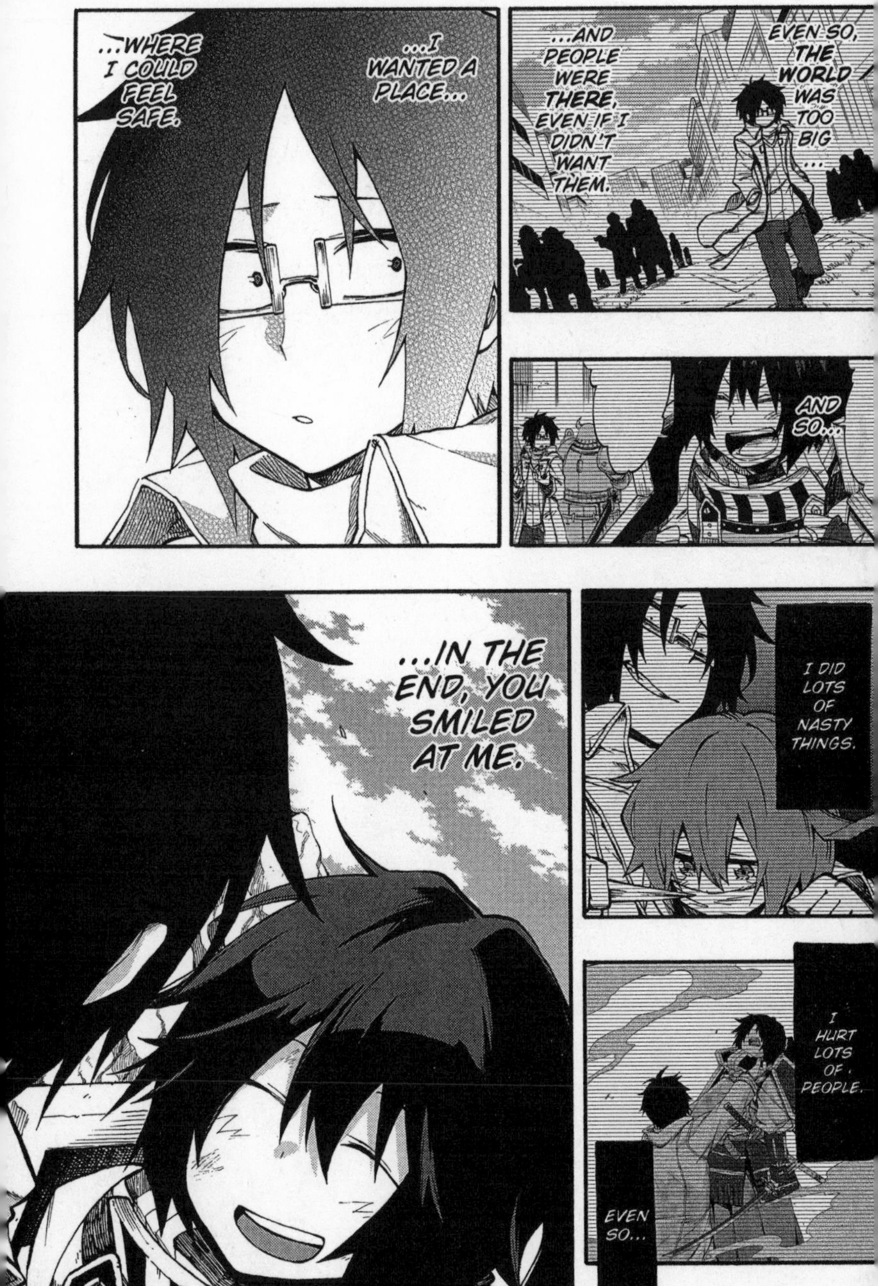
EVEN SO, THE WORLD WAS TOO BIG...
...AND PEOPLE WERE THERE, EVEN IF I DIDN'T WANT THEM.
AND SO...
...I WANTED A PLACE...
...WHERE I COULD FEEL SAFE.
I DID LOTS OF NASTY THINGS.
I HURT LOTS OF PEOPLE.
EVEN SO...
...IN THE END, YOU SMILED AT ME.

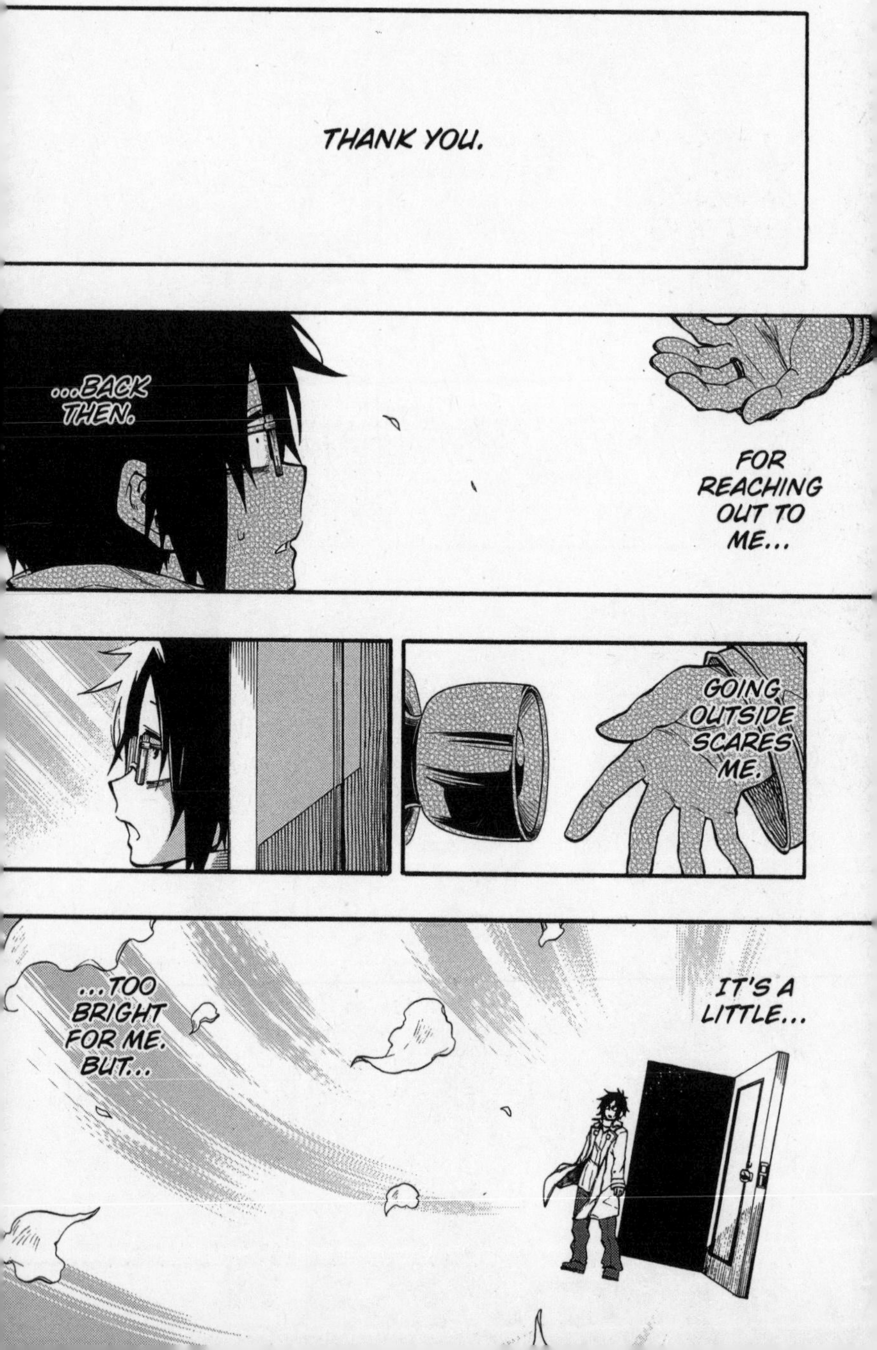
THANK YOU.
FOR REACHING OUT TO ME...
...BACK THEN.
GOING OUTSIDE SCARES ME.
IT'S A LITTLE...
...TOO BRIGHT FOR ME. BUT...

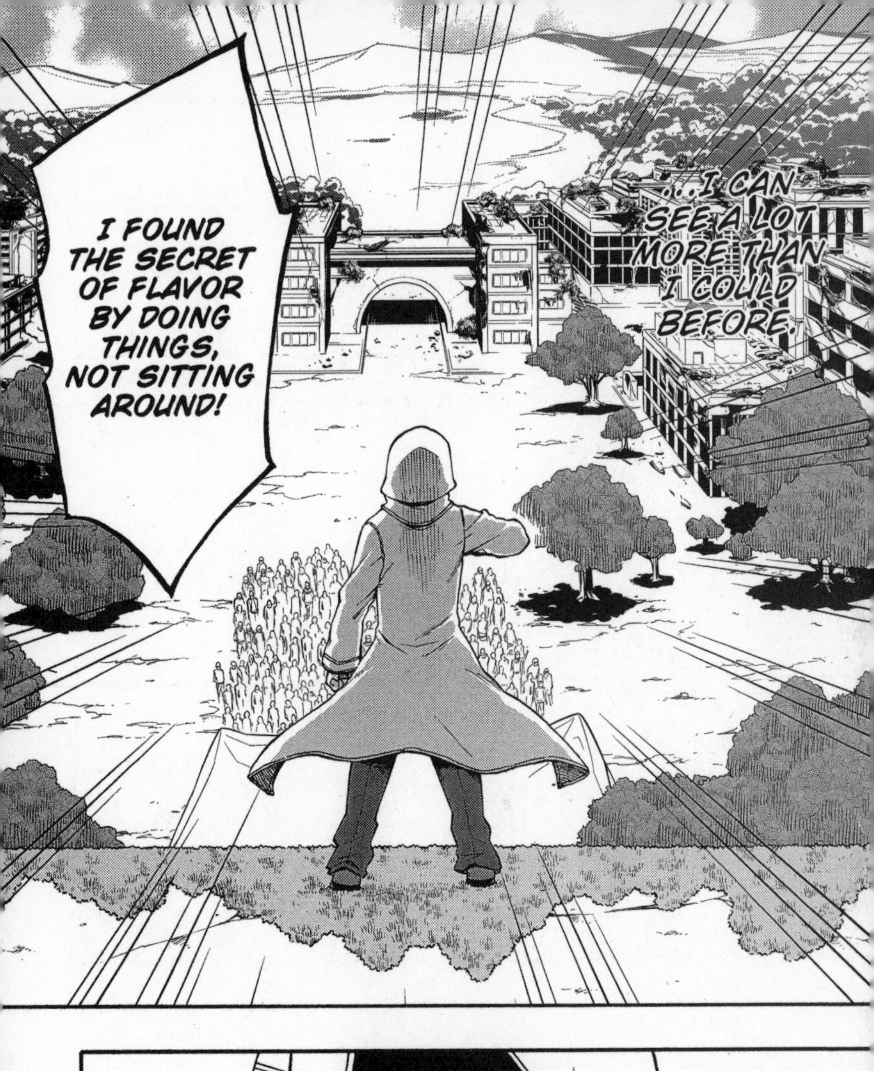
...I CAN SEE A LOT MORE THAN I COULD BEFORE.
I FOUND THE SECRET OF FLAVOR BY DOING THINGS, NOT SITTING AROUND!

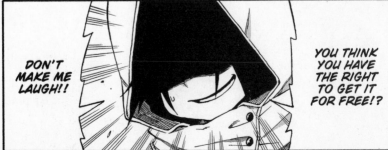

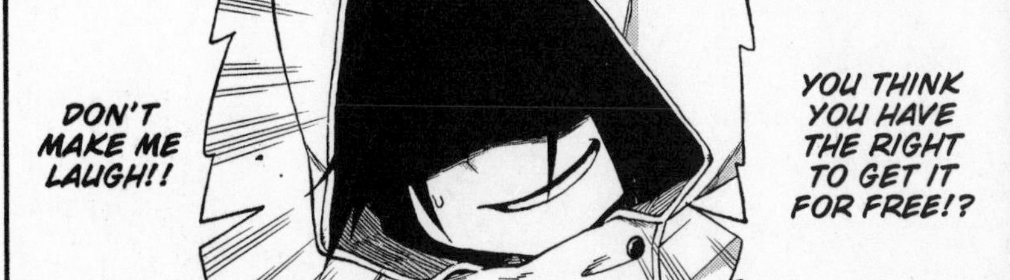
YOU THINK YOU HAVE THE RIGHT TO GET IT FOR FREE!?
DON'T MAKE ME LAUGH!!

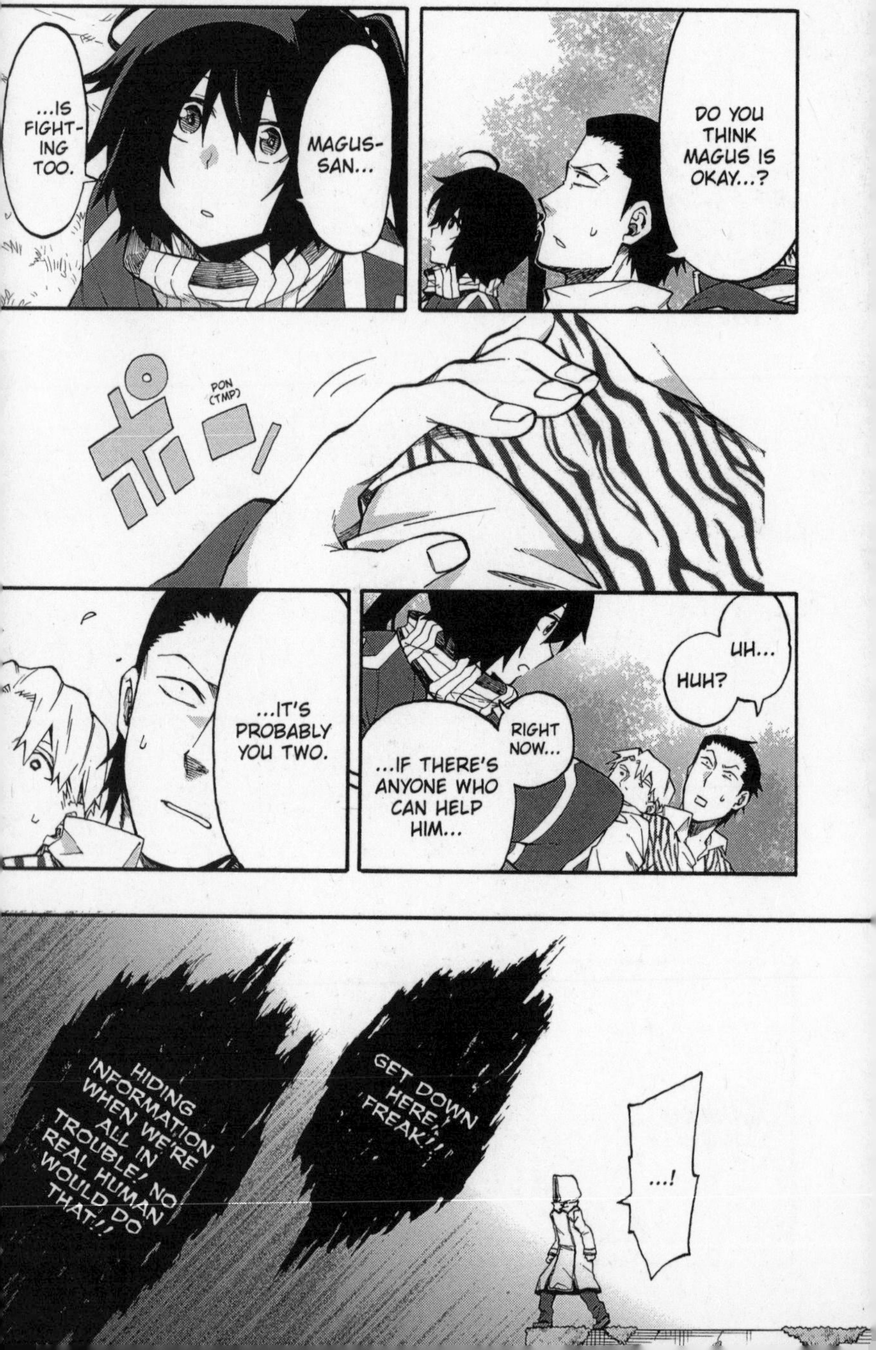
DO YOU THINK MAGUS IS OKAY...?
MAGUS-SAN...
...IS FIGHTING TOO.
PON (TMP)
UH... HUH?
RIGHT NOW...
...IF THERE'S ANYONE WHO CAN HELP HIM...
...IT'S PROBABLY YOU TWO.
...!
GET DOWN HERE, FREAK!!
HIDING INFORMATION WHEN WE'RE ALL IN TROUBLE! NO REAL HUMAN WOULD DO THAT!!

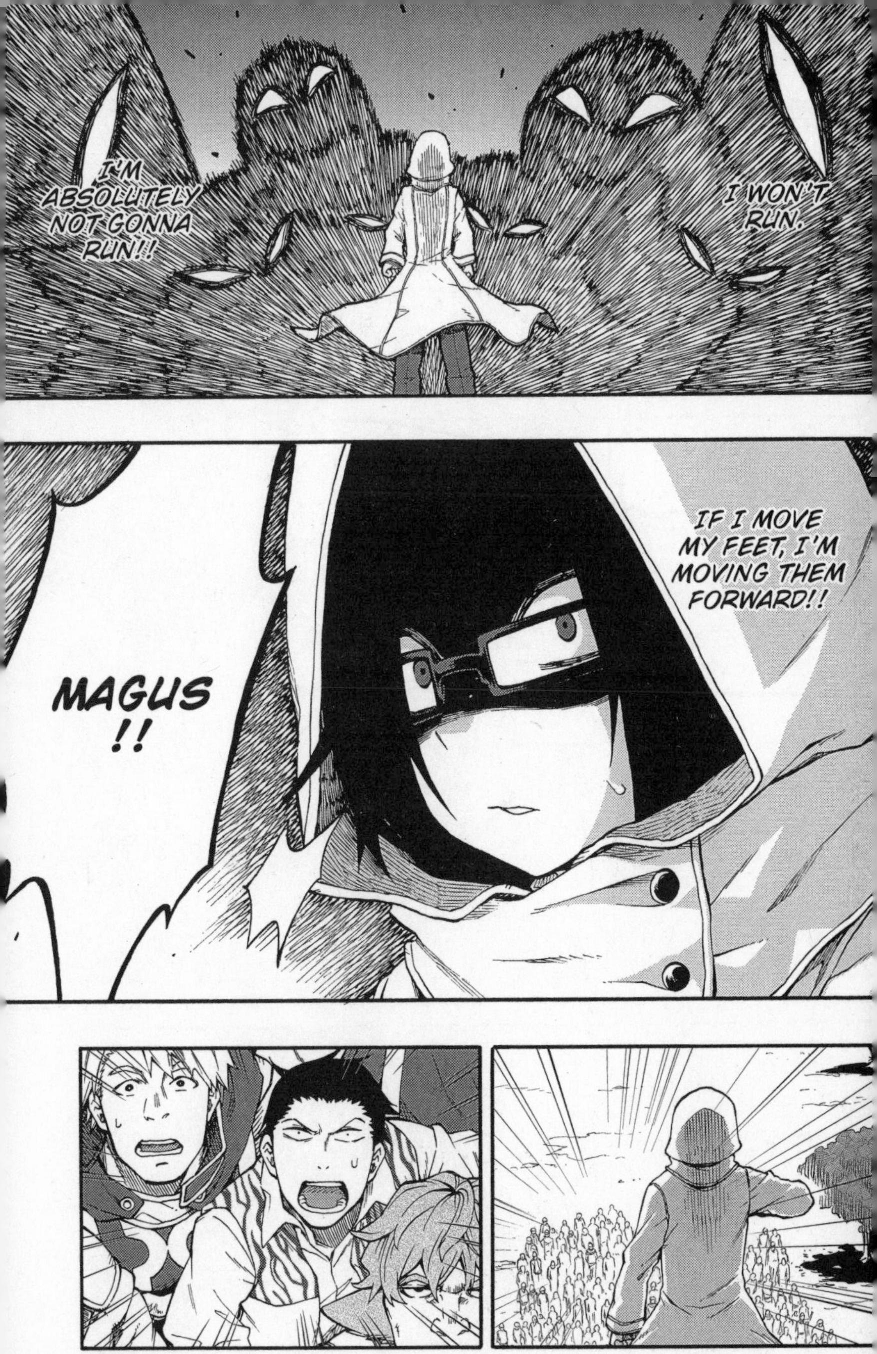
I WON'T RUN.
I'M ABSOLUTELY NOT GONNA RUN!!
IF I MOVE MY FEET, I'M MOVING THEM FORWARD!!
MAGUS!!

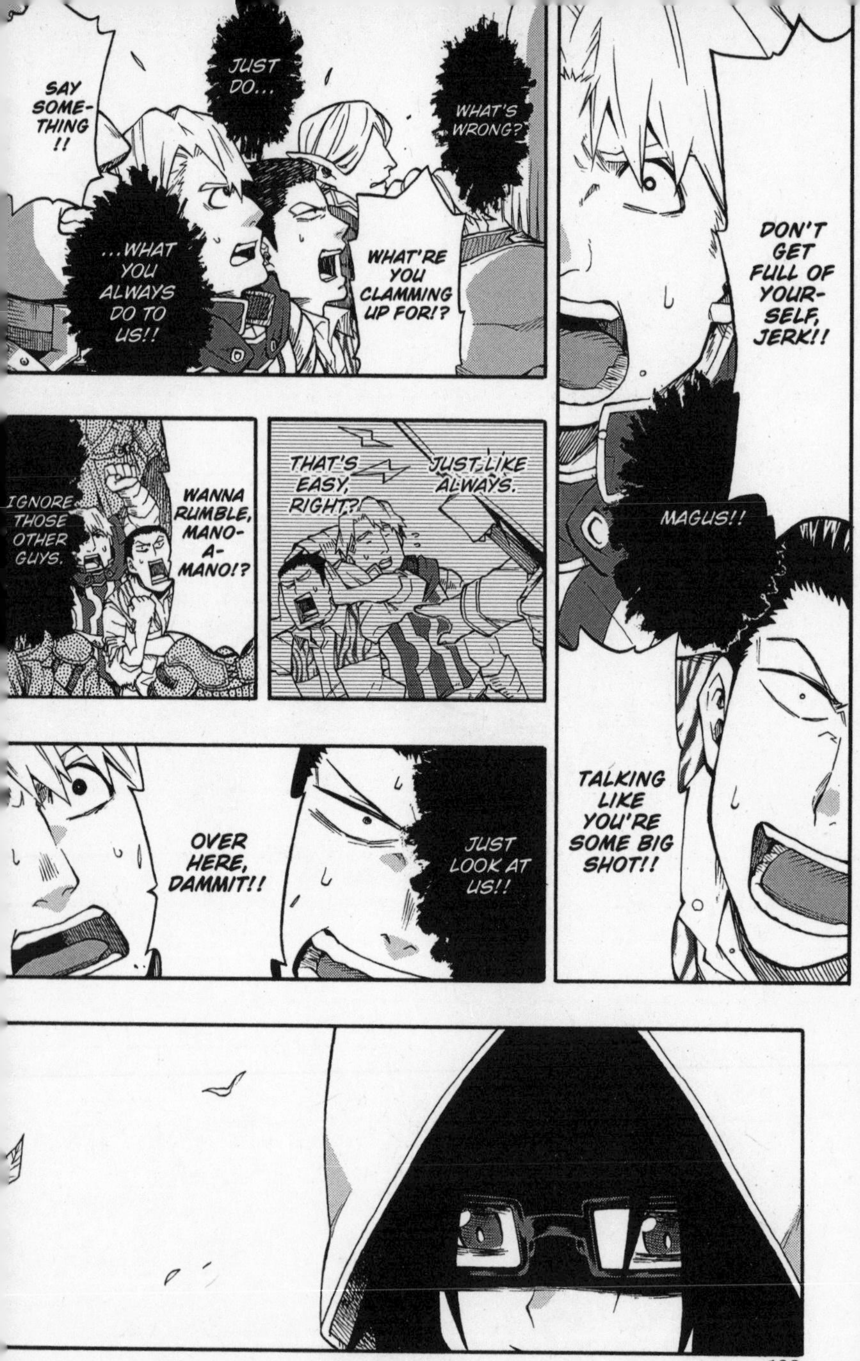
DON'T GET FULL OF YOUR-SELF, JERK!!
MAGUS!!
TALKING LIKE YOU'RE SOME BIG SHOT!!
WHAT'S WRONG?
WHAT'RE YOU CLAMMING UP FOR!?
JUST DO...
...WHAT YOU ALWAYS DO TO US!!
SAY SOME-THING!!
JUST LIKE ALWAYS.
THAT'S EASY, RIGHT?
WANNA RUMBLE, MANO-A-MANO!?
IGNORE THOSE OTHER GUYS.
JUST LOOK AT US!!
OVER HERE, DAMMIT!!

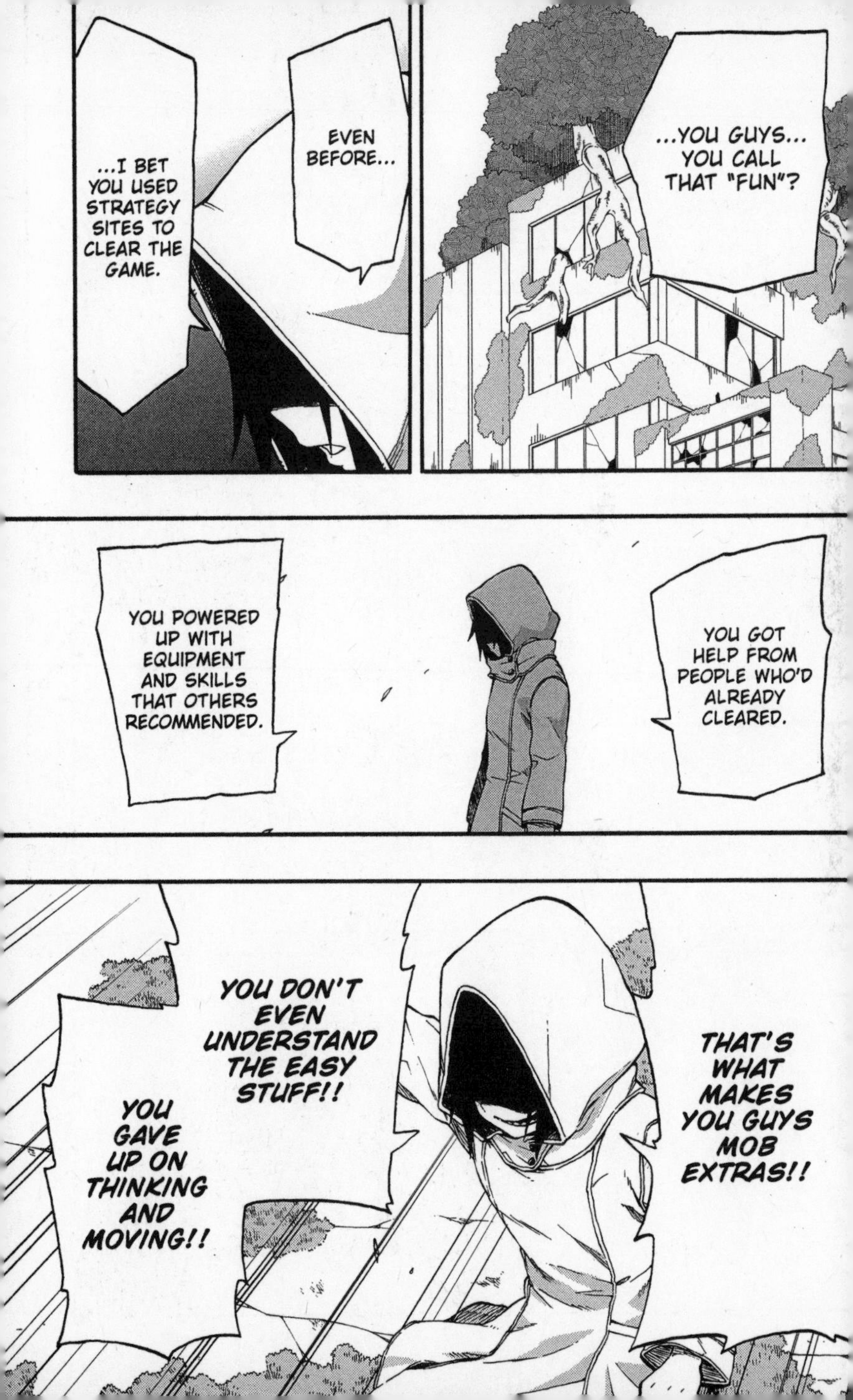
...YOU GUYS... YOU CALL THAT "FUN"?
EVEN BEFORE...
...I BET YOU USED STRATEGY SITES TO CLEAR THE GAME.
YOU GOT HELP FROM PEOPLE WHO'D ALREADY CLEARED.
YOU POWERED UP WITH EQUIPMENT AND SKILLS THAT OTHERS RECOMMENDED.
THAT'S WHAT MAKES YOU GUYS MOB EXTRAS!!
YOU DON'T EVEN UNDERSTAND THE EASY STUFF!!
YOU GAVE UP ON THINKING AND MOVING!!

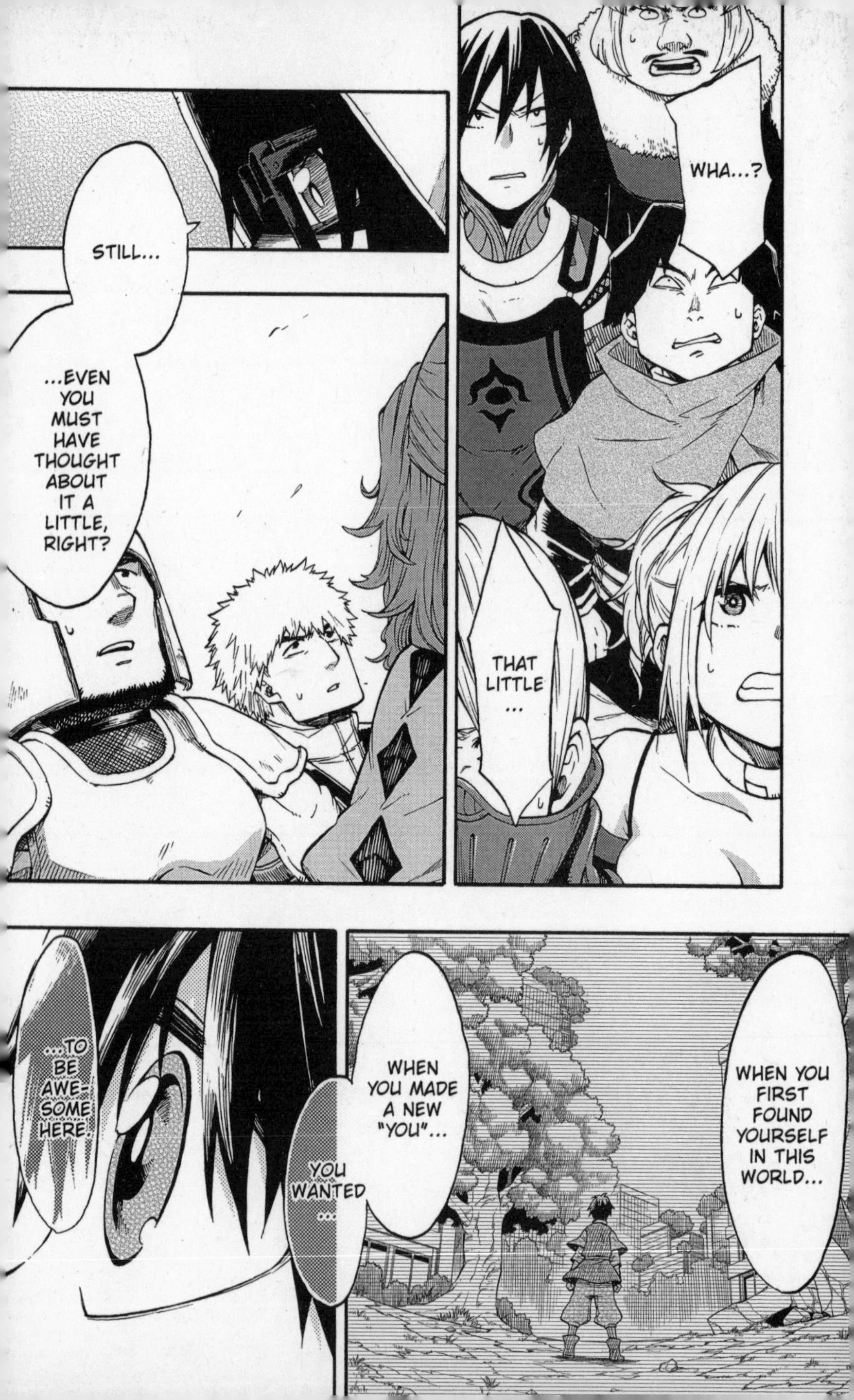
WHA...?
THAT LITTLE ...
STILL...
...EVEN YOU MUST HAVE THOUGHT ABOUT IT A LITTLE, RIGHT?
WHEN YOU FIRST FOUND YOURSELF IN THIS WORLD...
WHEN YOU MADE A NEW "YOU"...
YOU WANTED ...
...TO BE AWE-SOME HERE.

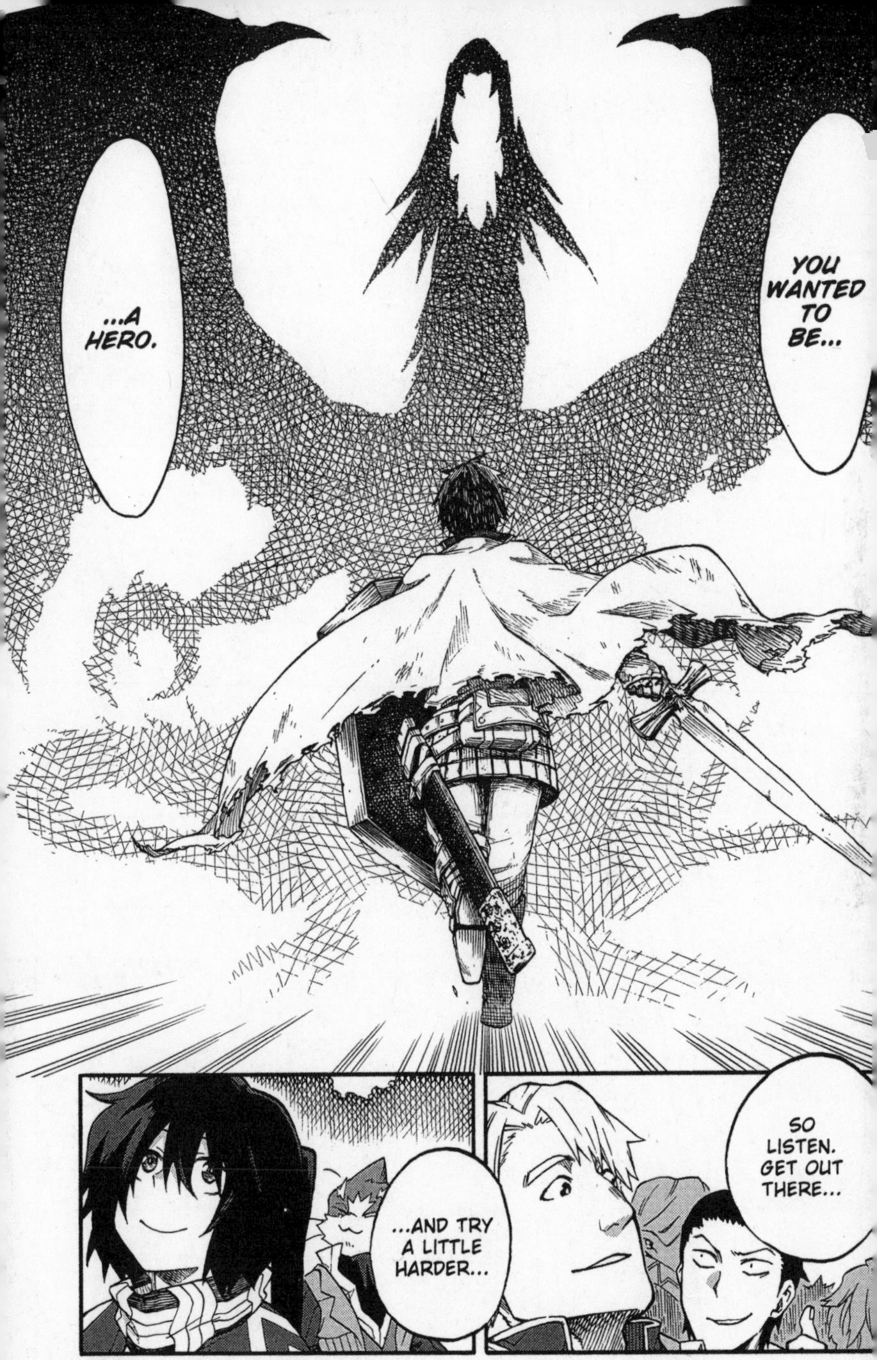
YOU WANTED TO BE...
...A HERO.
SO LISTEN. GET OUT THERE...
...AND TRY A LITTLE HARDER...

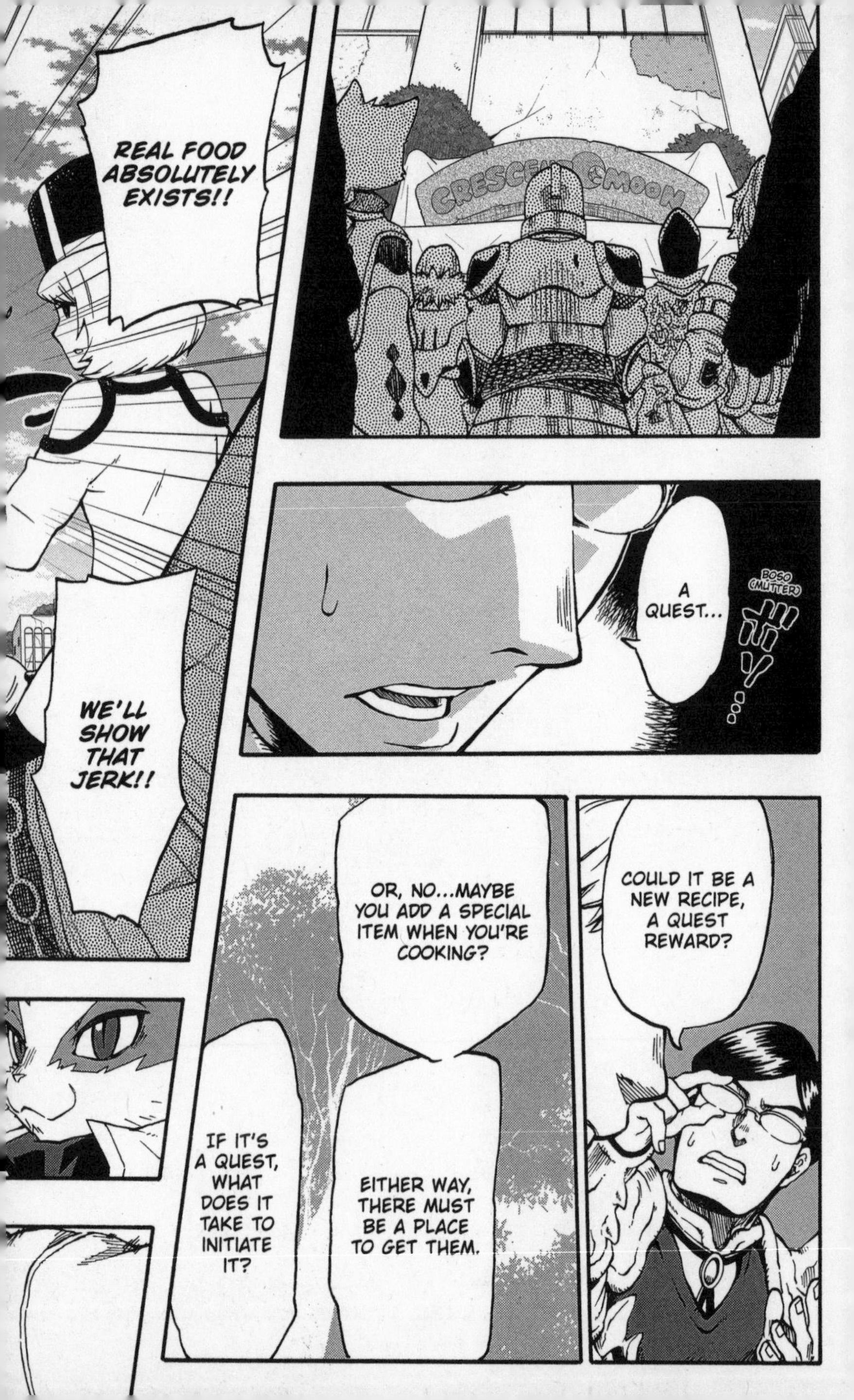

A QUEST...
BOSO (MUTTER)
REAL FOOD ABSOLUTELY EXISTS!!
WE'LL SHOW THAT JERK!!
COULD IT BE A NEW RECIPE, A QUEST REWARD?
IF IT'S A QUEST, WHAT DOES IT TAKE TO INITIATE IT?
OR, NO...MAYBE YOU ADD A SPECIAL ITEM WHEN YOU'RE COOKING?
EITHER WAY, THERE MUST BE A PLACE TO GET THEM.

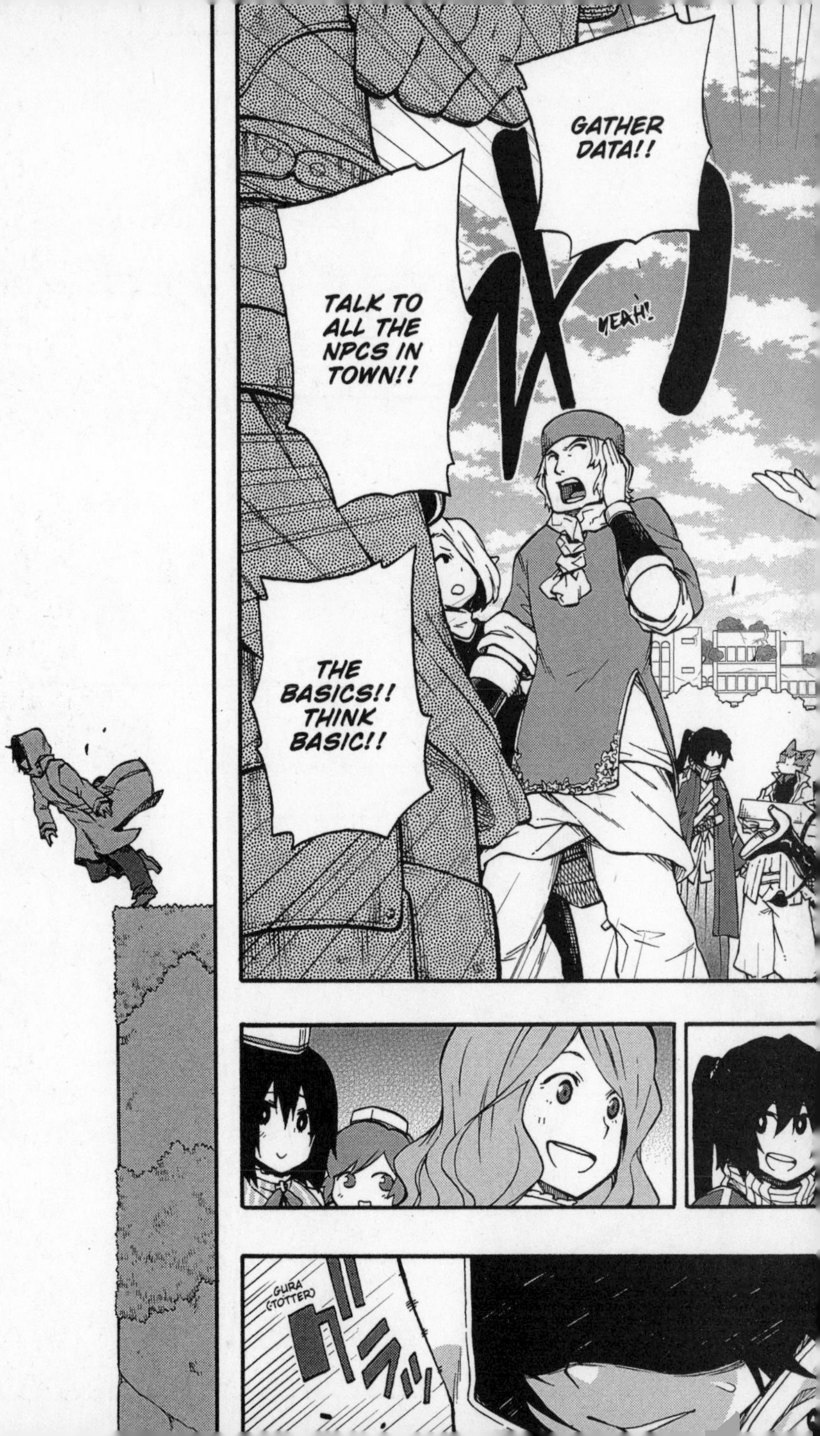
GATHER DATA!!
YEAH!
TALK TO ALL THE NPCS IN TOWN!!
THE BASICS!! THINK BASIC!!
GURA (TOTTER)

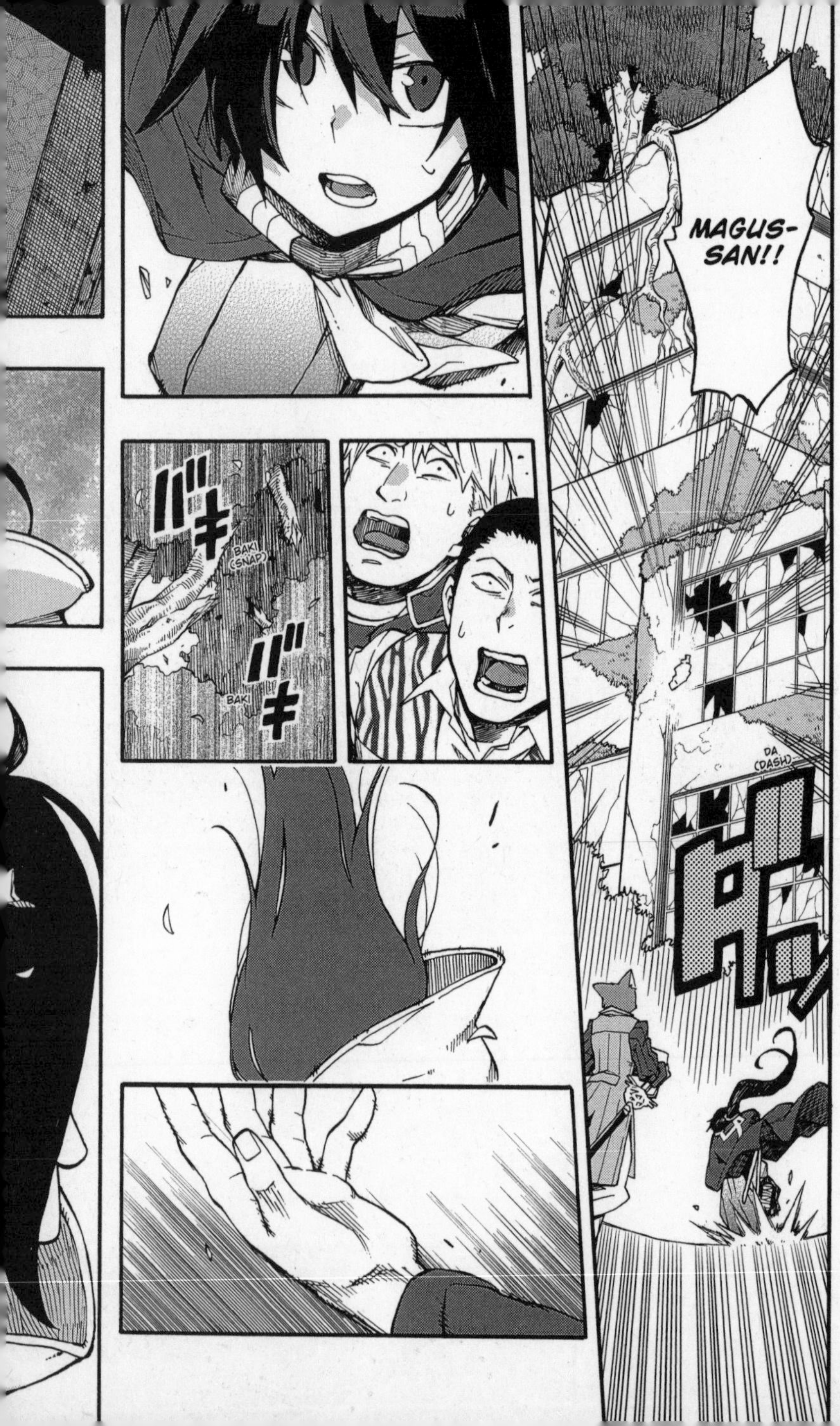
MAGUS-SAN!!
DA (DASH)
ダッ
バキ
BAKI (SNAP)
バキ
BAKI

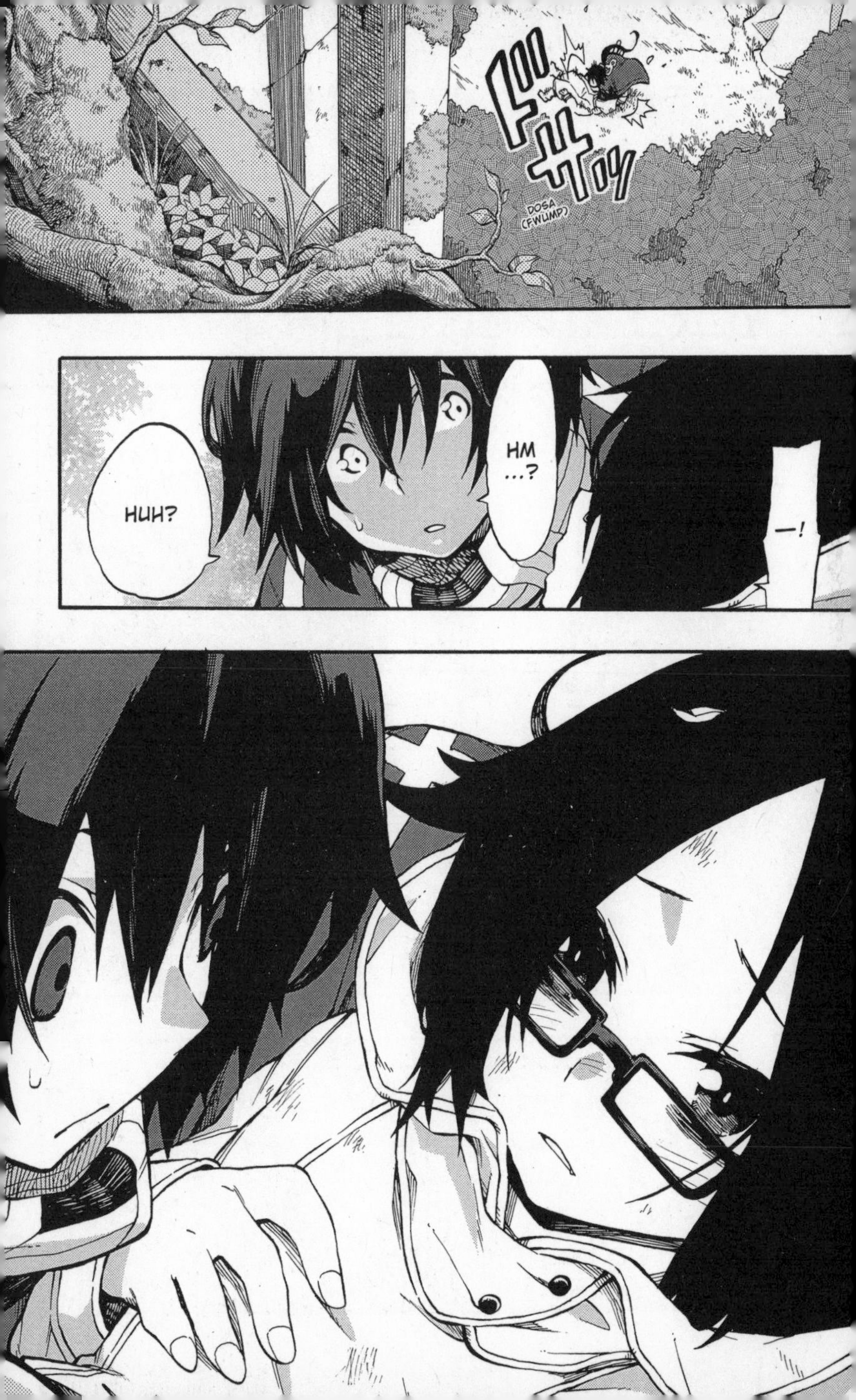
DOSA
(FWUMP)
—!
HM ...?
HUH?

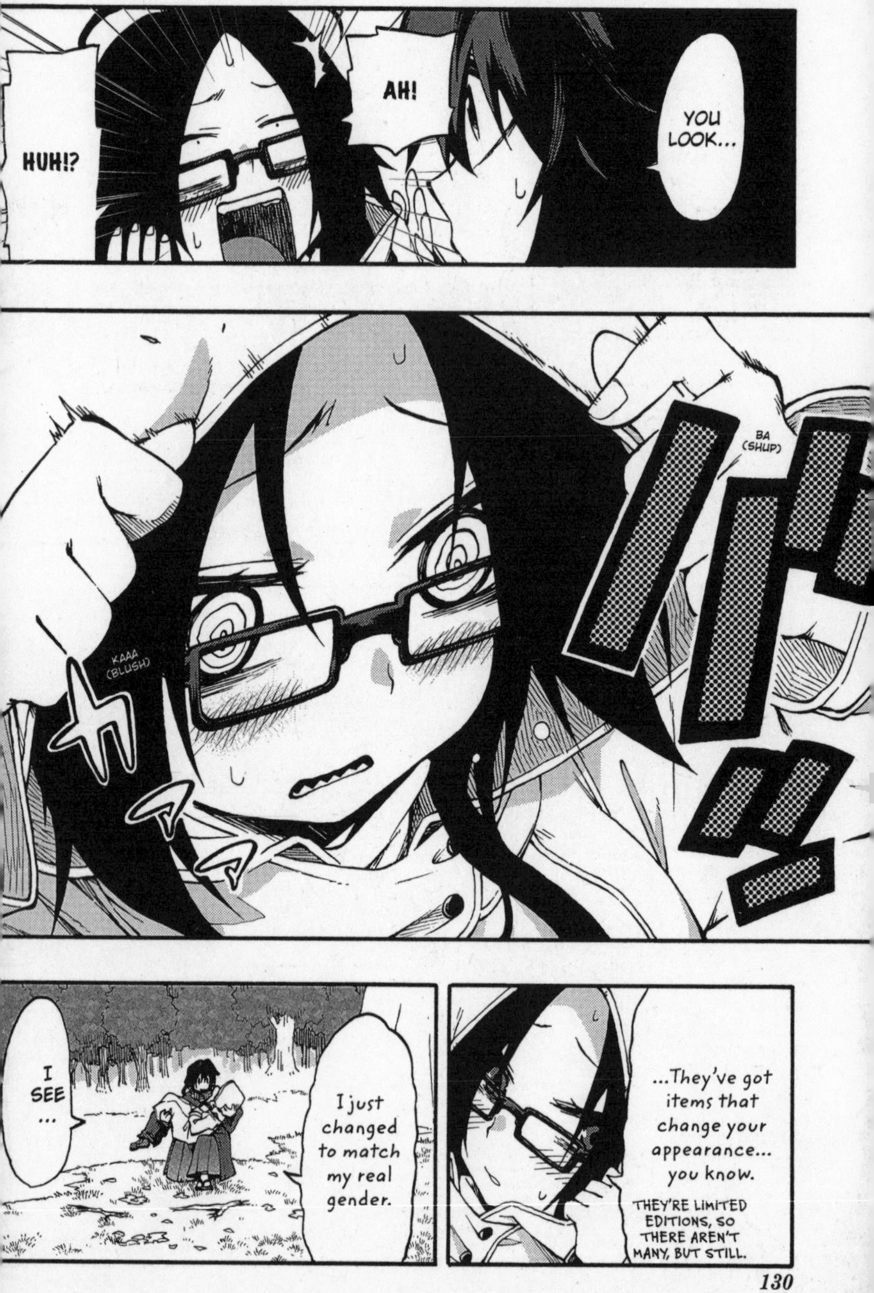
YOU LOOK...
AH!
HUH!?
BA (SHUP)
KAAA (BLUSH)
...They've got items that change your appearance... you know.
THEY'RE LIMITED EDITIONS, SO THERE AREN'T MANY, BUT STILL.
I just changed to match my real gender.
I SEE ...

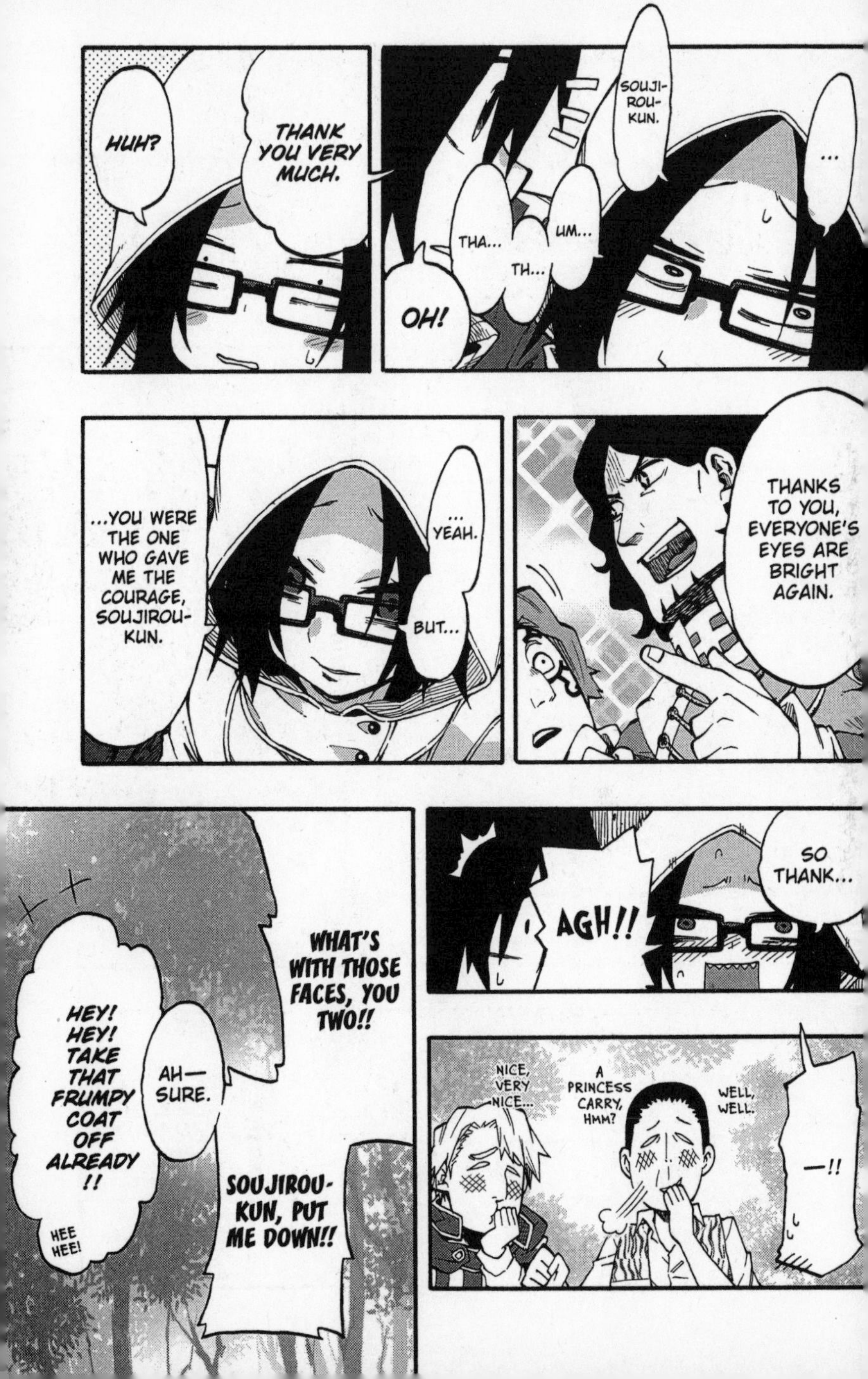
...
SOUJIROU-KUN.
UM...
TH...
THA...
OH!
THANK YOU VERY MUCH.
HUH?
THANKS TO YOU, EVERYONE'S EYES ARE BRIGHT AGAIN.
... YEAH.
BUT...
...YOU WERE THE ONE WHO GAVE ME THE COURAGE, SOUJIROU-KUN.
SO THANK...
AGH!!
—!!
WELL, WELL.
A PRINCESS CARRY, HMM?
NICE, VERY NICE...
WHAT'S WITH THOSE FACES, YOU TWO!!
SOUJIROU-KUN, PUT ME DOWN!!
AH— SURE.
HEY! HEY! TAKE THAT FRUMPY COAT OFF ALREADY!!
HEE HEE!

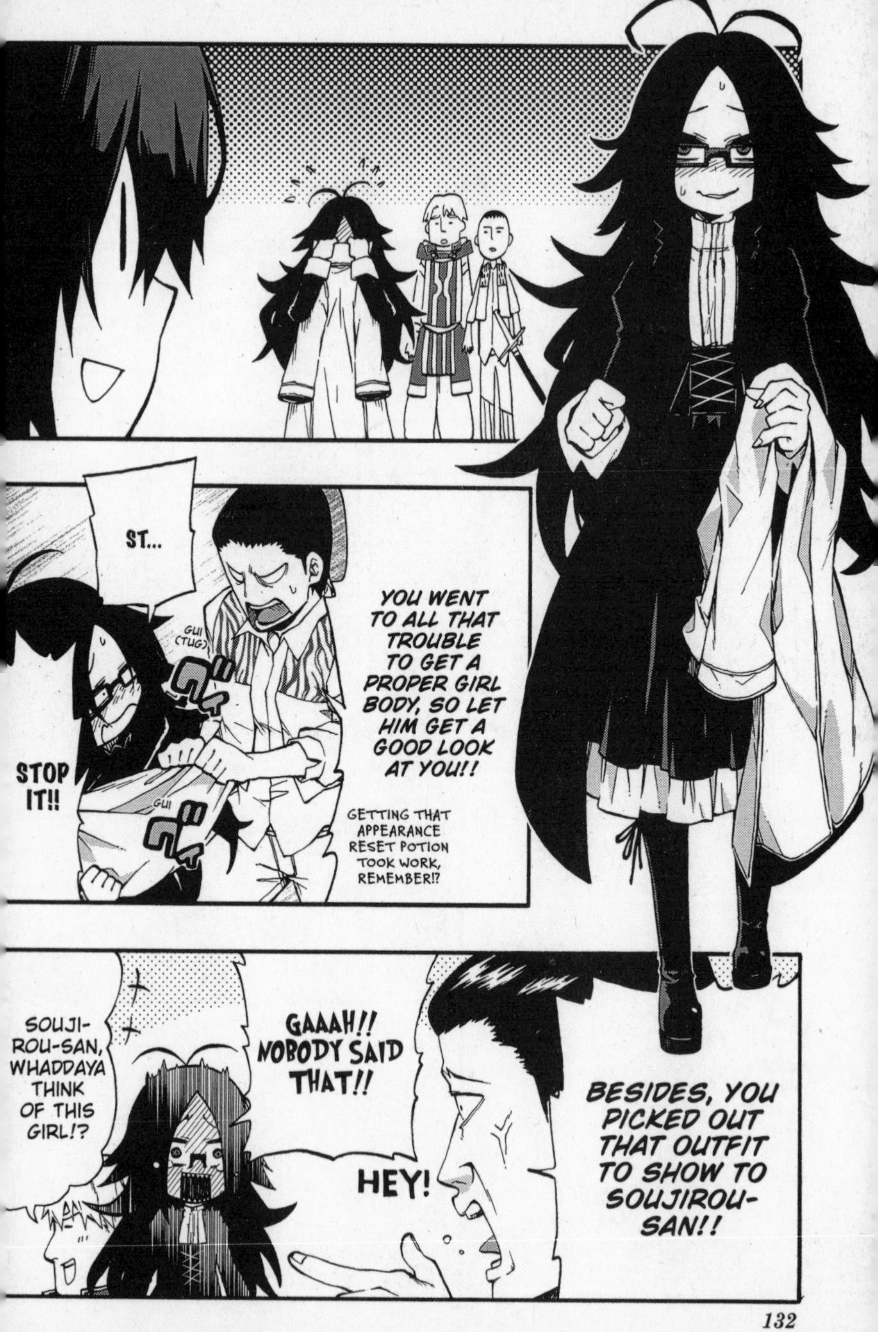
YOU WENT TO ALL THAT TROUBLE TO GET A PROPER GIRL BODY, SO LET HIM GET A GOOD LOOK AT YOU!!
ST...
GUI (TUG)
GETTING THAT APPEARANCE RESET POTION TOOK WORK, REMEMBER!?
STOP IT!!
GUI
BESIDES, YOU PICKED OUT THAT OUTFIT TO SHOW TO SOUJIROU-SAN!!
HEY!
GAAAH!! NOBODY SAID THAT!!
SOUJI-ROU-SAN, WHADDAYA THINK OF THIS GIRL!?

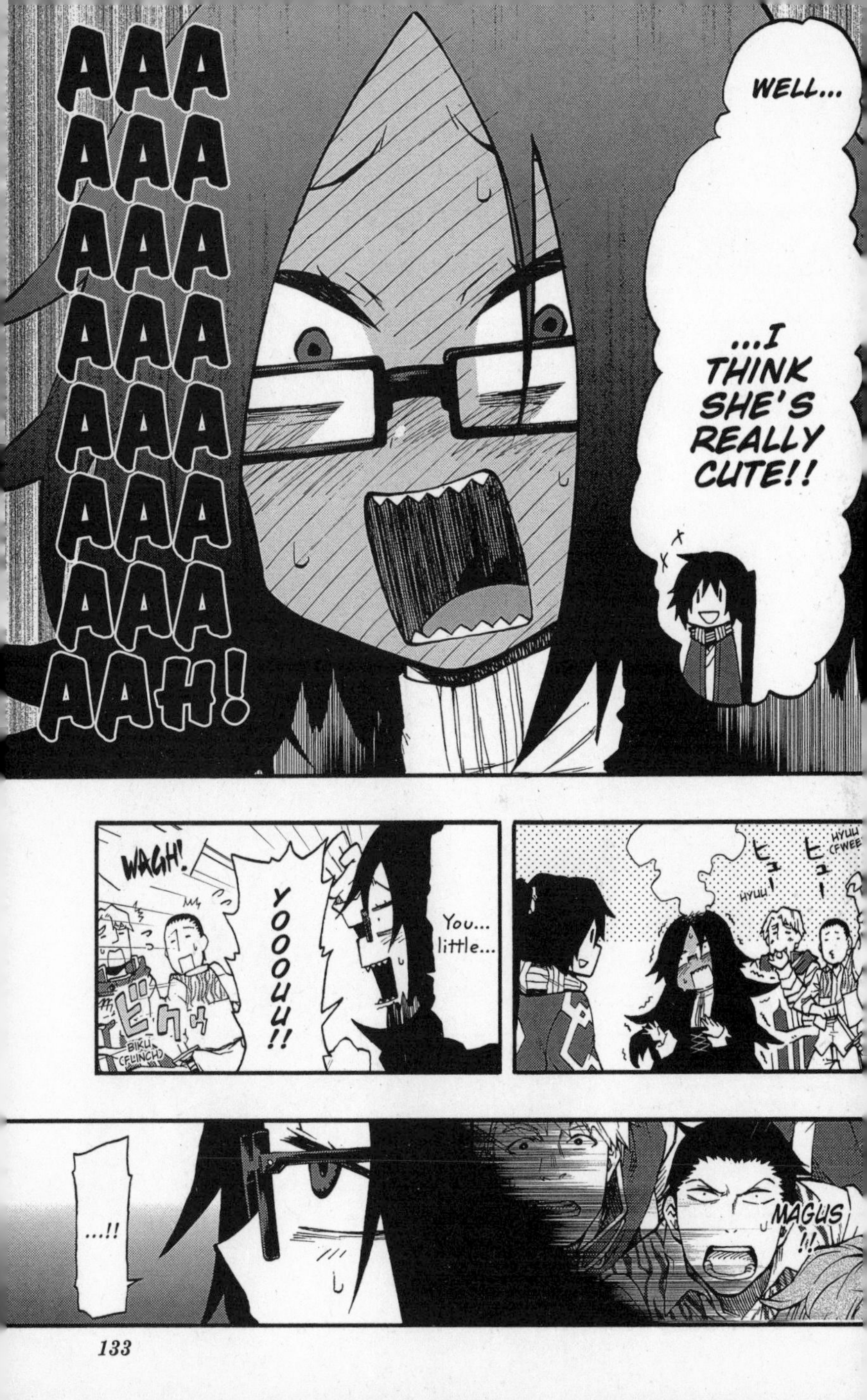

WELL...
...I THINK SHE'S REALLY CUTE!!
AAAAAAAAAAAAAAAAAAAAAAAAAAAAAH!
HYUU
HYUU
You... little...
YOOOUUU!!
WAGH!
BIKU (FLINCH)
MAGUS!!
...!!

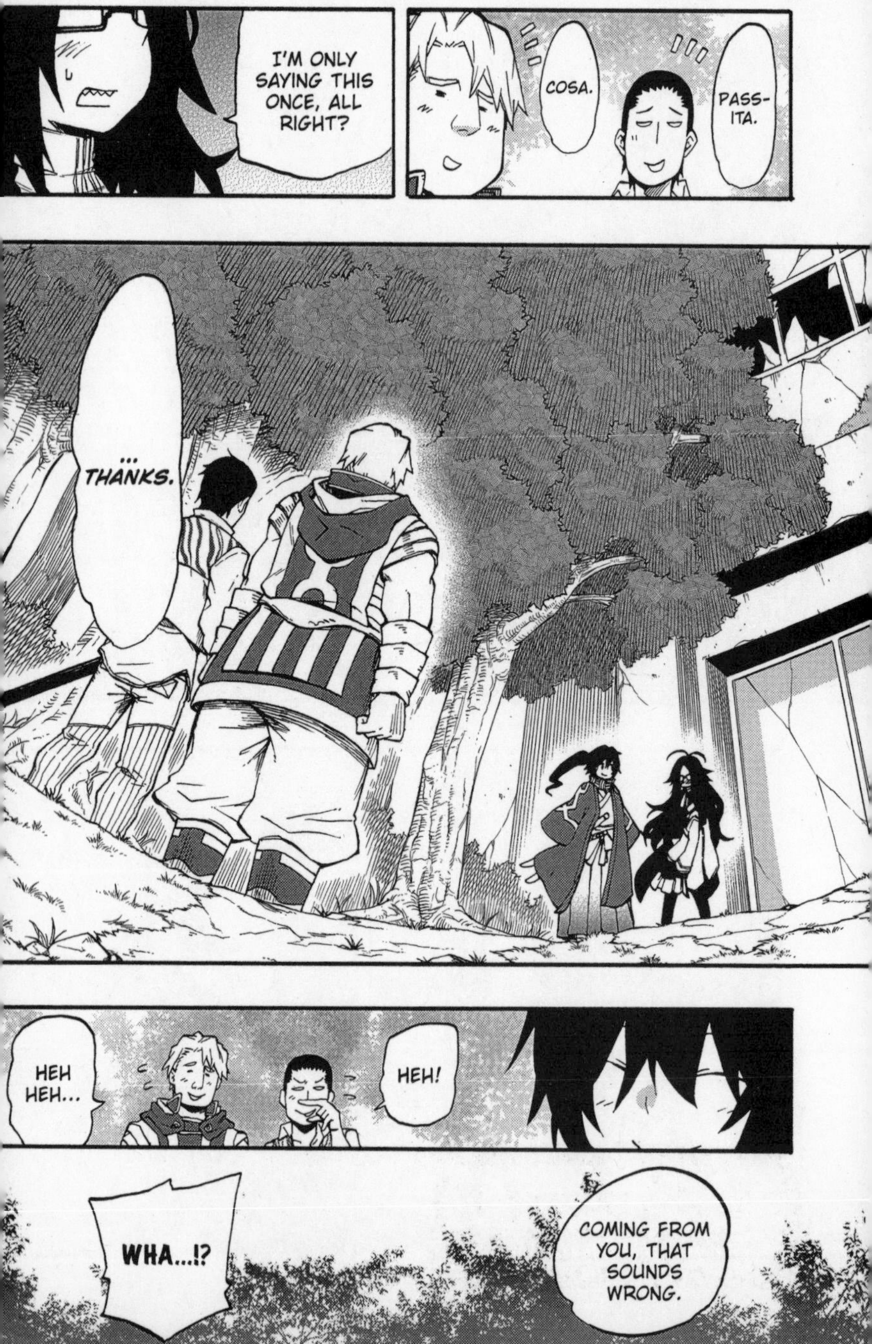
PASS-ITA.
COSA.
I'M ONLY SAYING THIS ONCE, ALL RIGHT?
... THANKS.
HEH!
HEH HEH...
COMING FROM YOU, THAT SOUNDS WRONG.
WHA...!?

LOG HORIZON

THE WEST WIND BRIGADE

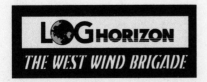

LOG HORIZON
THE WEST WIND BRIGADE

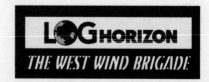

CHAPTER : 23 RE: THE TOWN OF AKIBA

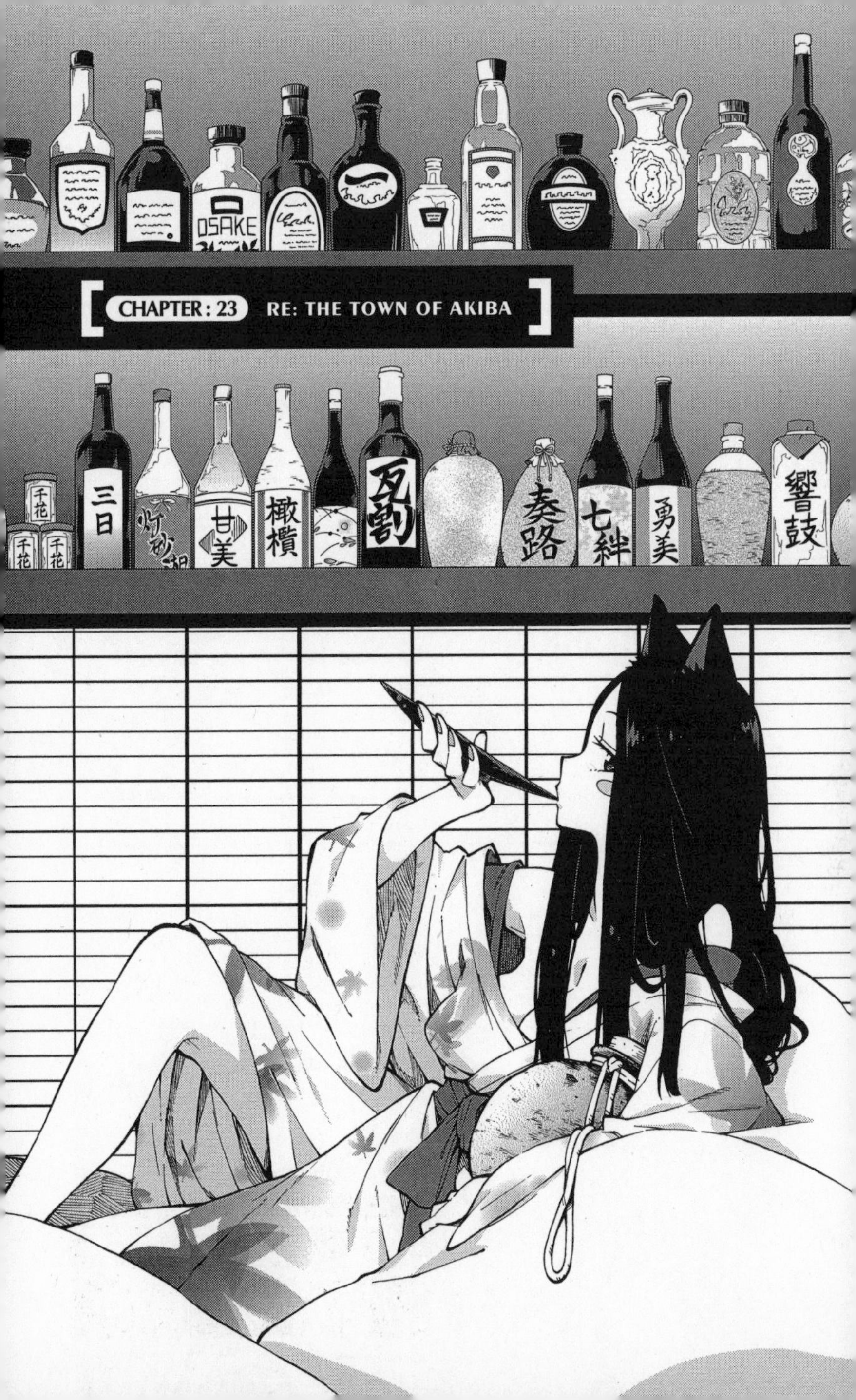
OSAKE
千花
三日
甘美
橄欖
奏路
七絆
勇美
響鼓

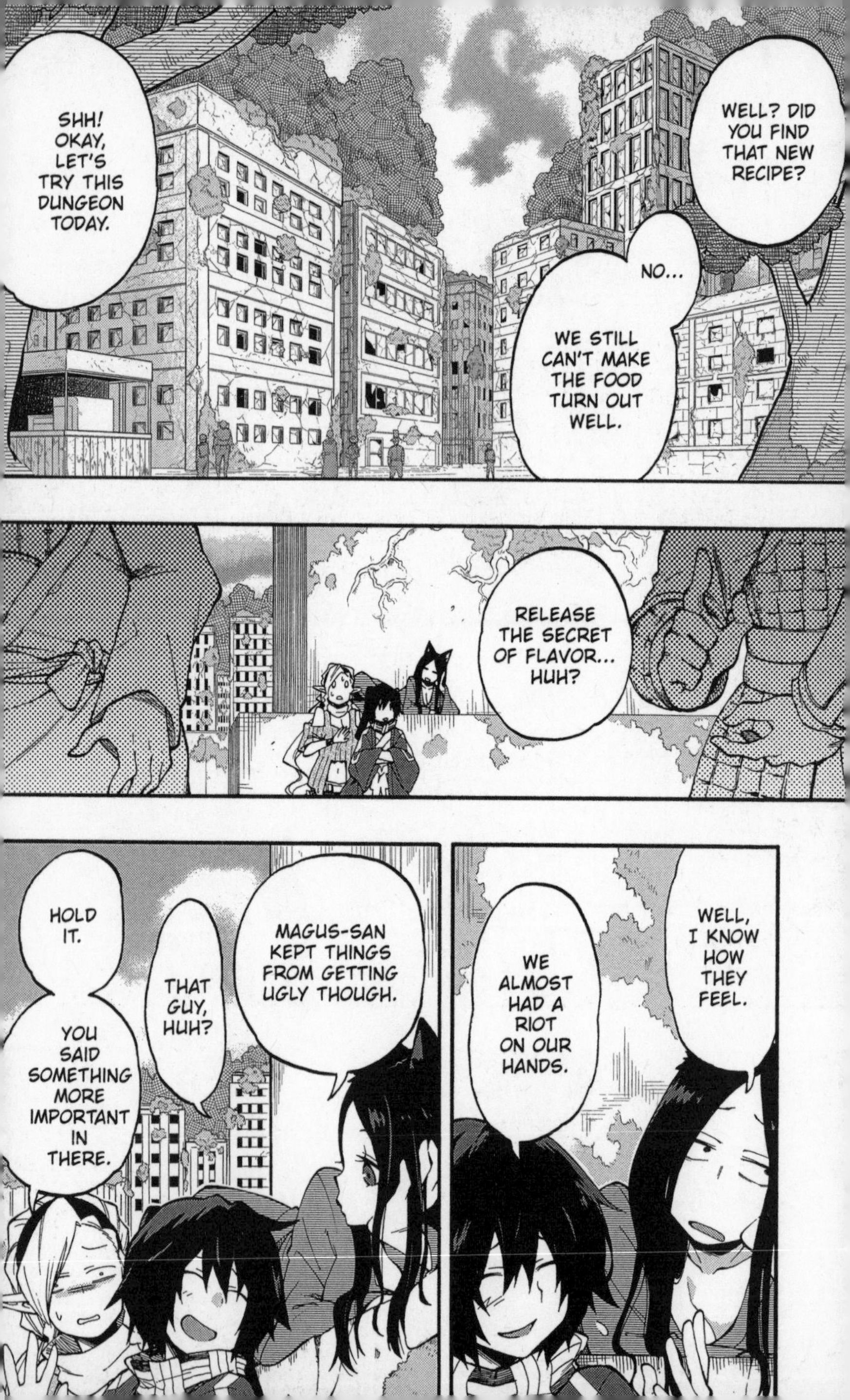
WELL? DID YOU FIND THAT NEW RECIPE?
NO...
WE STILL CAN'T MAKE THE FOOD TURN OUT WELL.
SHH! OKAY, LET'S TRY THIS DUNGEON TODAY.
RELEASE THE SECRET OF FLAVOR... HUH?
WELL, I KNOW HOW THEY FEEL.
WE ALMOST HAD A RIOT ON OUR HANDS.
MAGUS-SAN KEPT THINGS FROM GETTING UGLY THOUGH.
THAT GUY, HUH?
HOLD IT.
YOU SAID SOMETHING MORE IMPORTANT IN THERE.

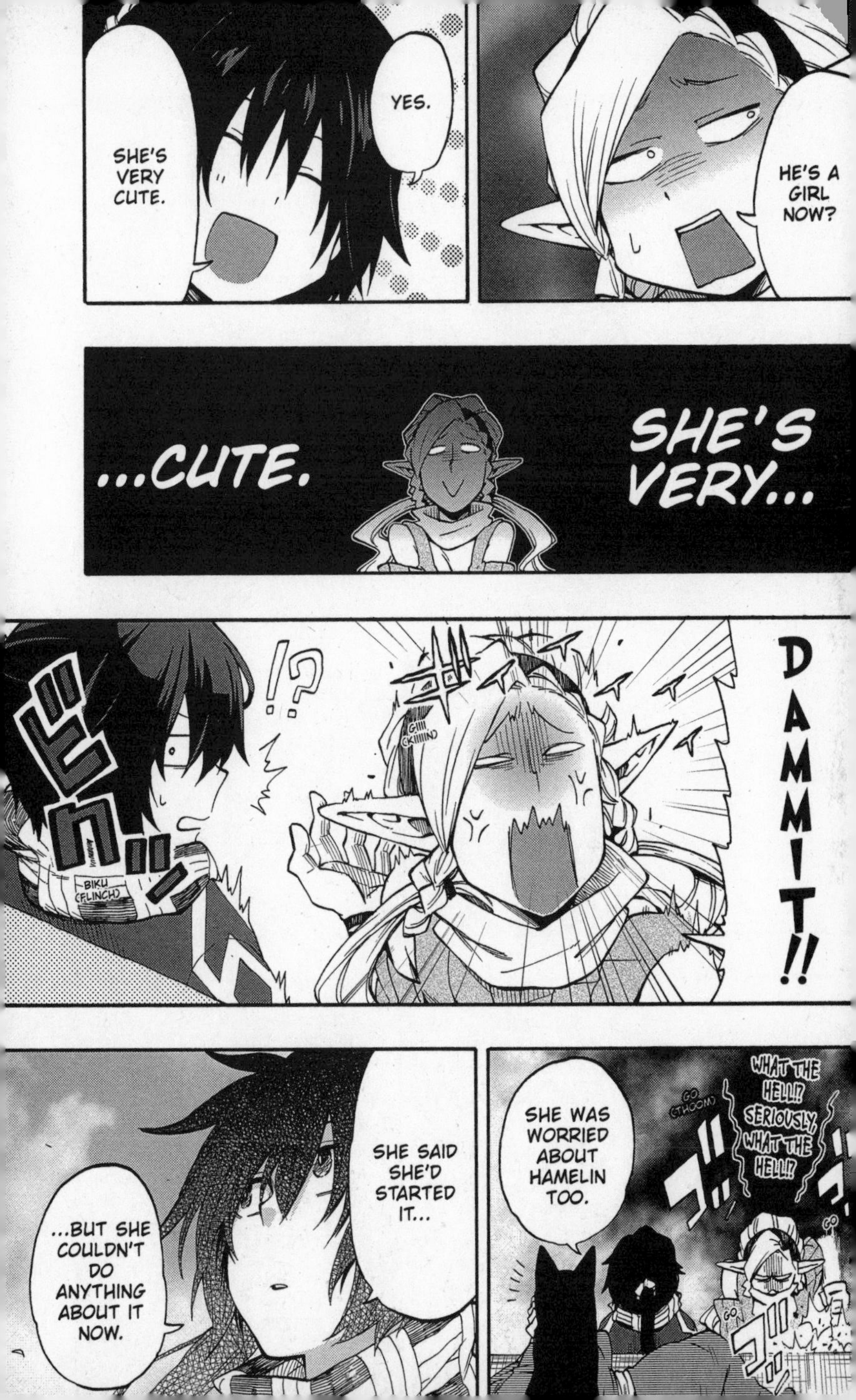
HE'S A GIRL NOW?
YES.
SHE'S VERY CUTE.
SHE'S VERY...
...CUTE.
DAMMIT!!
!?
BIKU (FLINCH)
WHAT THE HELL!? SERIOUSLY, WHAT THE HELL!?
GO (THOOM)
SHE WAS WORRIED ABOUT HAMELIN TOO.
SHE SAID SHE'D STARTED IT...
...BUT SHE COULDN'T DO ANYTHING ABOUT IT NOW.

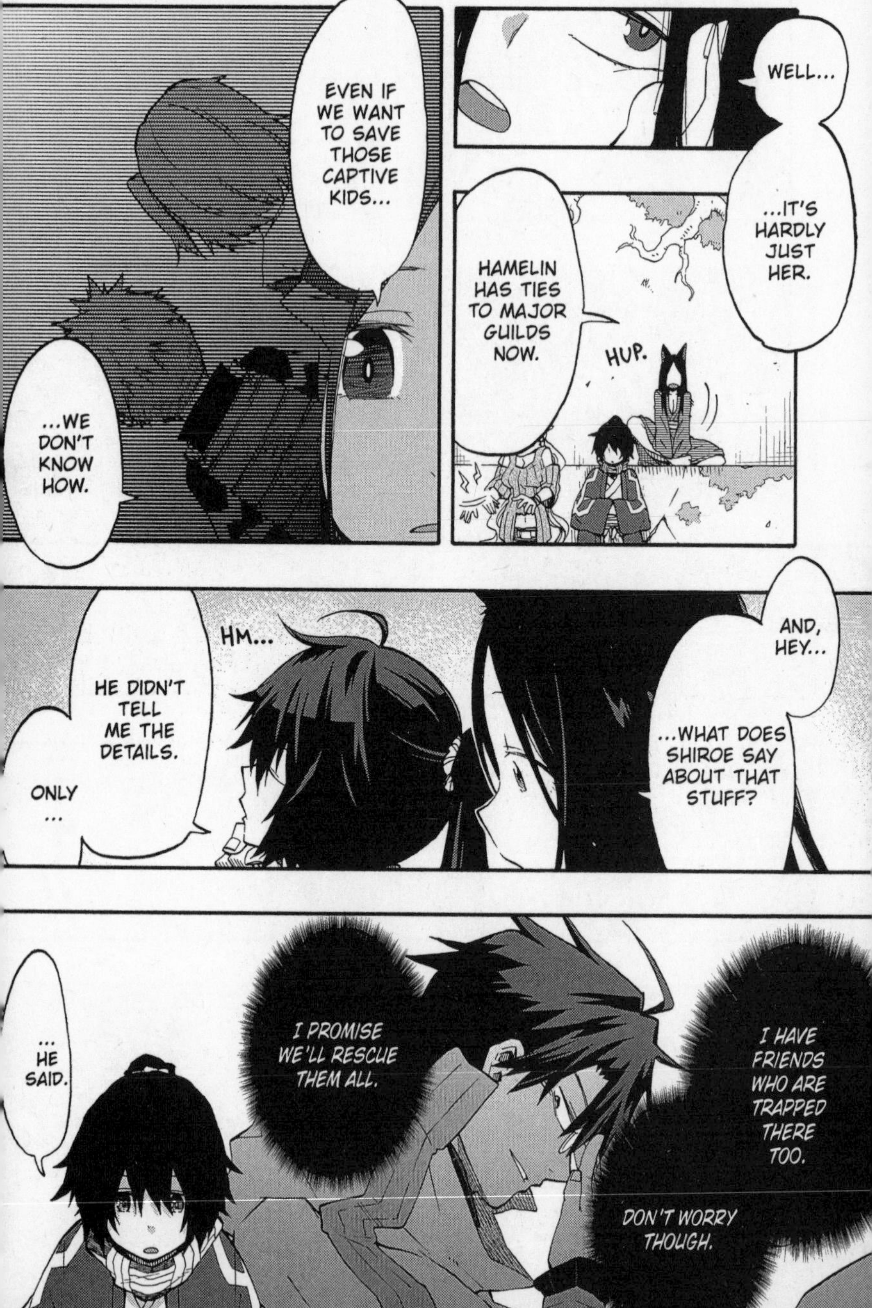
WELL...
...IT'S HARDLY JUST HER.
HAMELIN HAS TIES TO MAJOR GUILDS NOW.
HUP.
EVEN IF WE WANT TO SAVE THOSE CAPTIVE KIDS...
...WE DON'T KNOW HOW.
AND, HEY...
...WHAT DOES SHIROE SAY ABOUT THAT STUFF?
HM...
HE DIDN'T TELL ME THE DETAILS.
ONLY ...
I HAVE FRIENDS WHO ARE TRAPPED THERE TOO.
DON'T WORRY THOUGH.
I PROMISE WE'LL RESCUE THEM ALL.
... HE SAID.

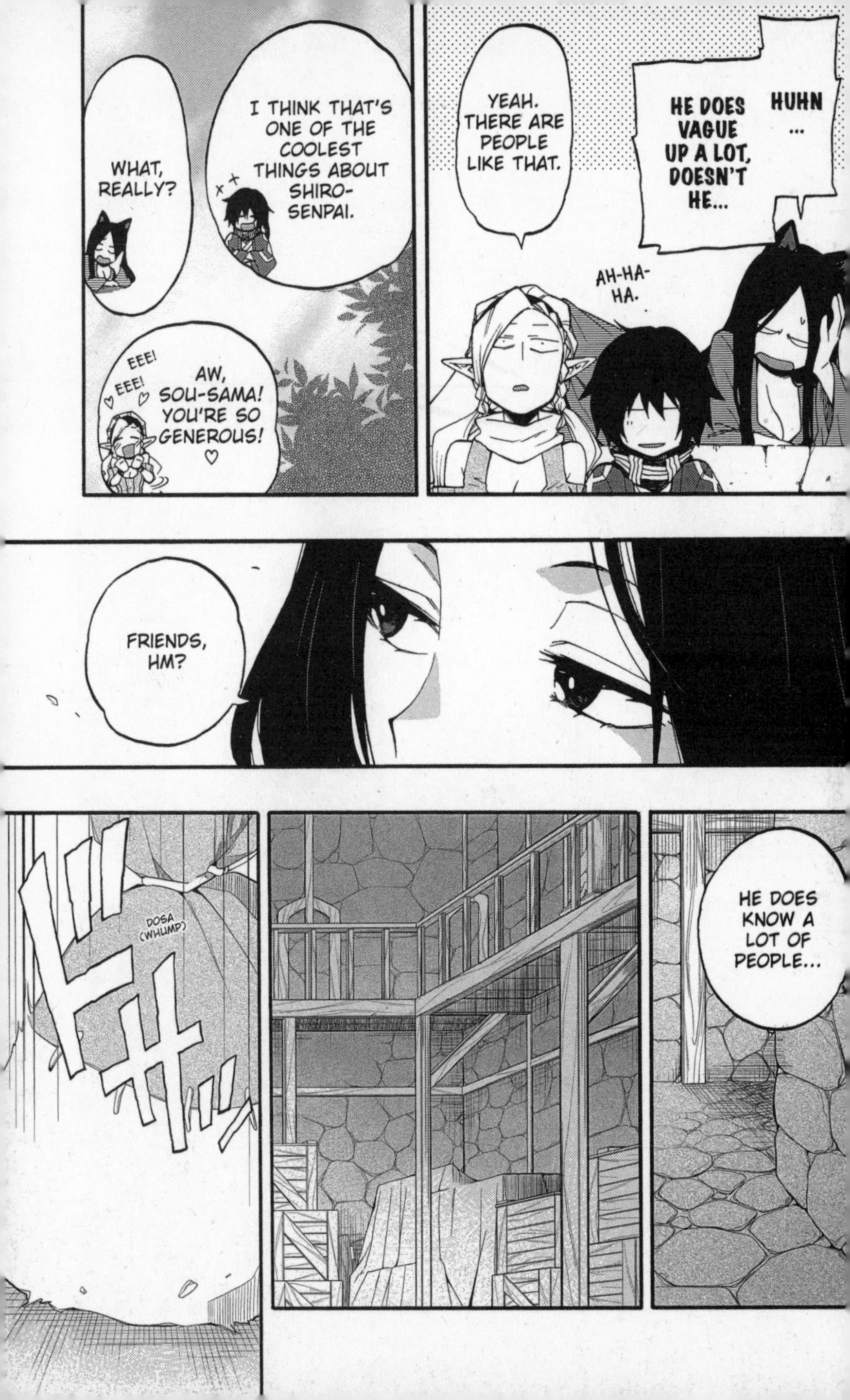
HUHN...
HE DOES VAGUE UP A LOT, DOESN'T HE...
YEAH. THERE ARE PEOPLE LIKE THAT.
AH-HA-HA.
I THINK THAT'S ONE OF THE COOLEST THINGS ABOUT SHIRO-SENPAI.
WHAT, REALLY?
AW, SOU-SAMA! YOU'RE SO GENEROUS!
EEE! EEE!
FRIENDS, HM?
HE DOES KNOW A LOT OF PEOPLE...
DOSA (WHUMP)

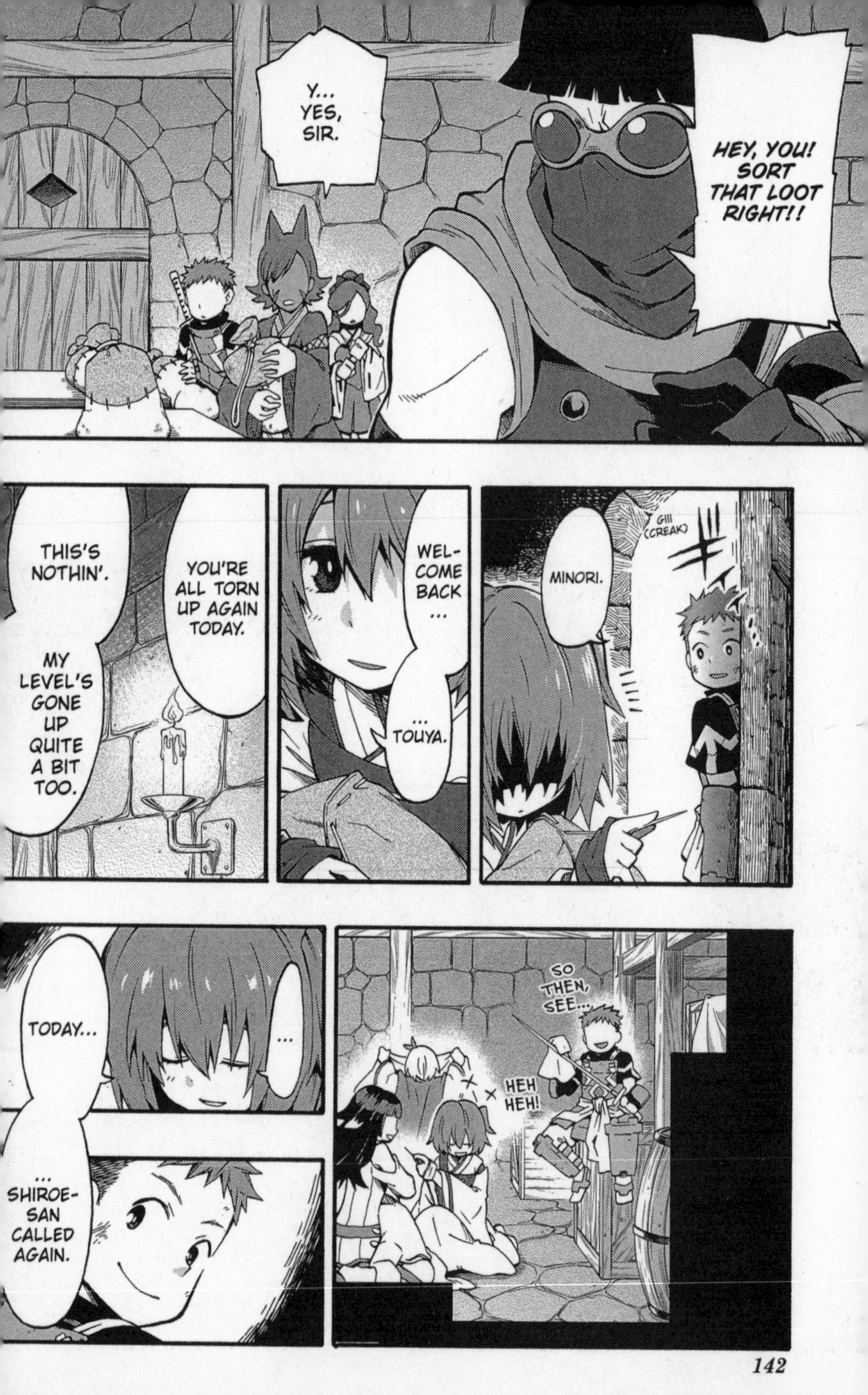
HEY, YOU! SORT THAT LOOT RIGHT!!
Y... YES, SIR.
GIII (CREAK)
MINORI.
WEL-COME BACK ...
... TOUYA.
YOU'RE ALL TORN UP AGAIN TODAY.
THIS'S NOTHIN'.
MY LEVEL'S GONE UP QUITE A BIT TOO.
SO THEN, SEE...
HEH HEH!
...
TODAY...
... SHIROE-SAN CALLED AGAIN.

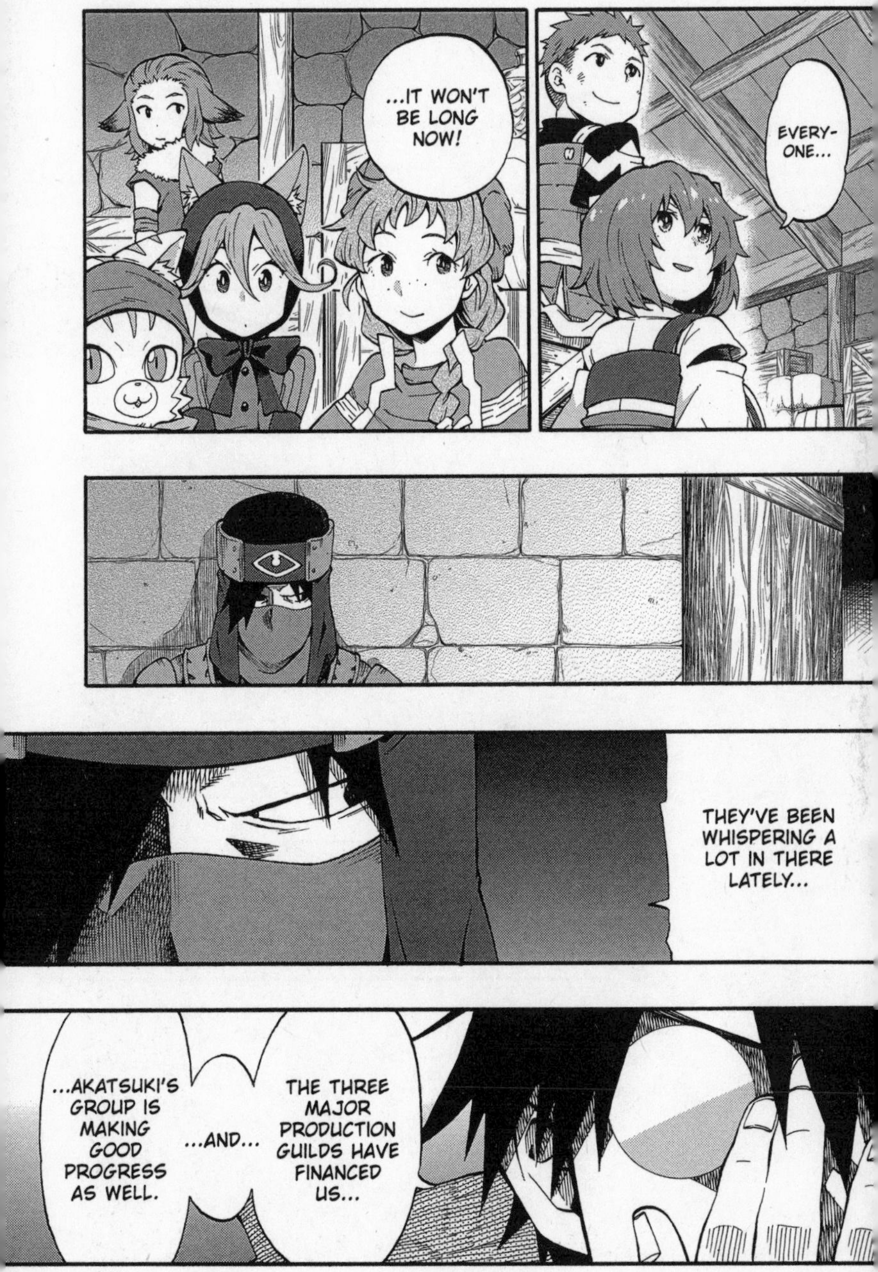
EVERY-ONE...
...IT WON'T BE LONG NOW!
THEY'VE BEEN WHISPERING A LOT IN THERE LATELY...
THE THREE MAJOR PRODUCTION GUILDS HAVE FINANCED US...
...AND...
...AKATSUKI'S GROUP IS MAKING GOOD PROGRESS AS WELL.

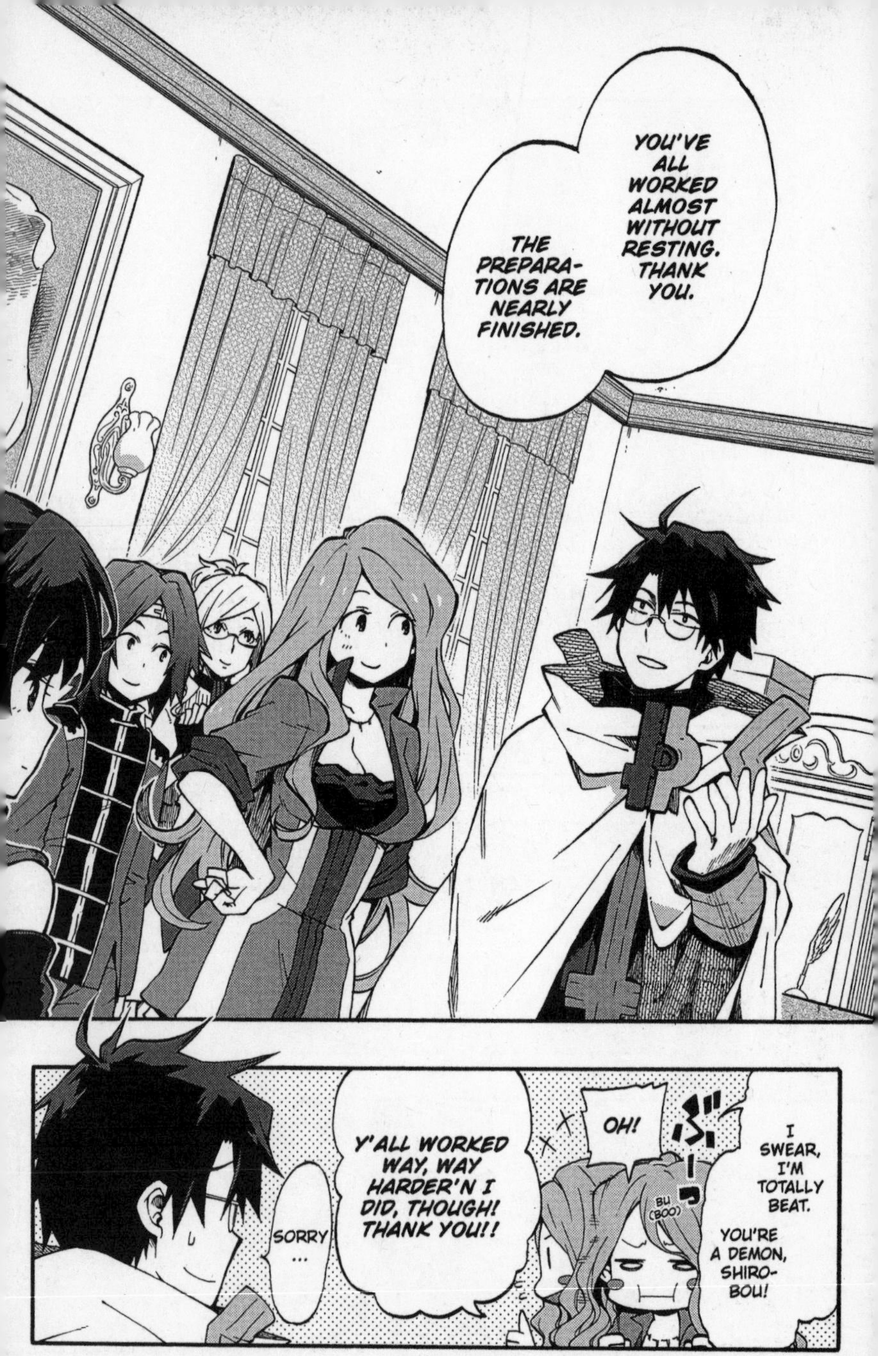
YOU'VE ALL WORKED ALMOST WITHOUT RESTING. THANK YOU.
THE PREPARA-TIONS ARE NEARLY FINISHED.
I SWEAR, I'M TOTALLY BEAT.
YOU'RE A DEMON, SHIRO-BOU!
BU (BOO)
OH!
Y'ALL WORKED WAY, WAY HARDER'N I DID, THOUGH! THANK YOU!!
SORRY...

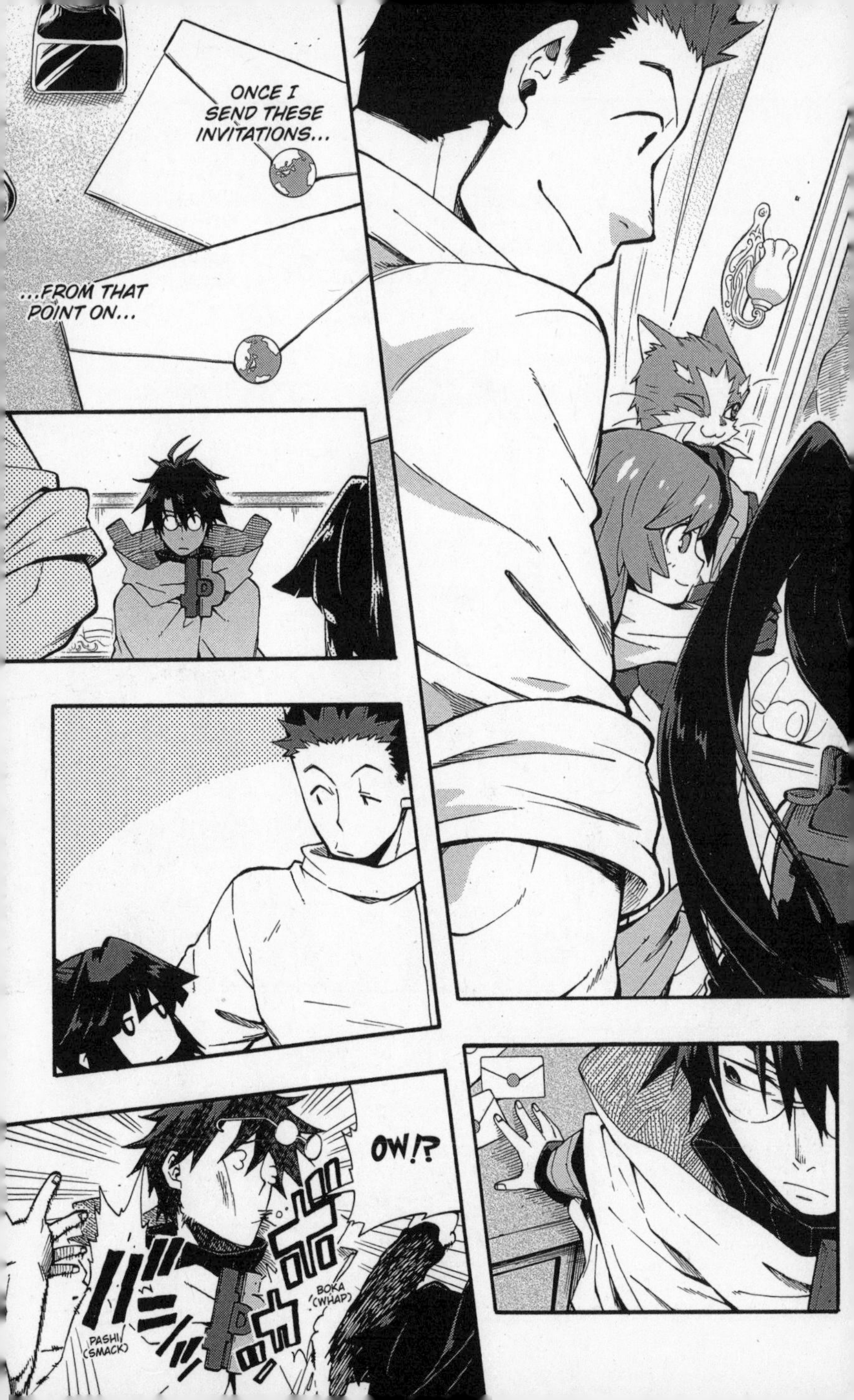
ONCE I SEND THESE INVITATIONS...
...FROM THAT POINT ON...
OW!?
BOKA (WHAP)
PASHI (SMACK)

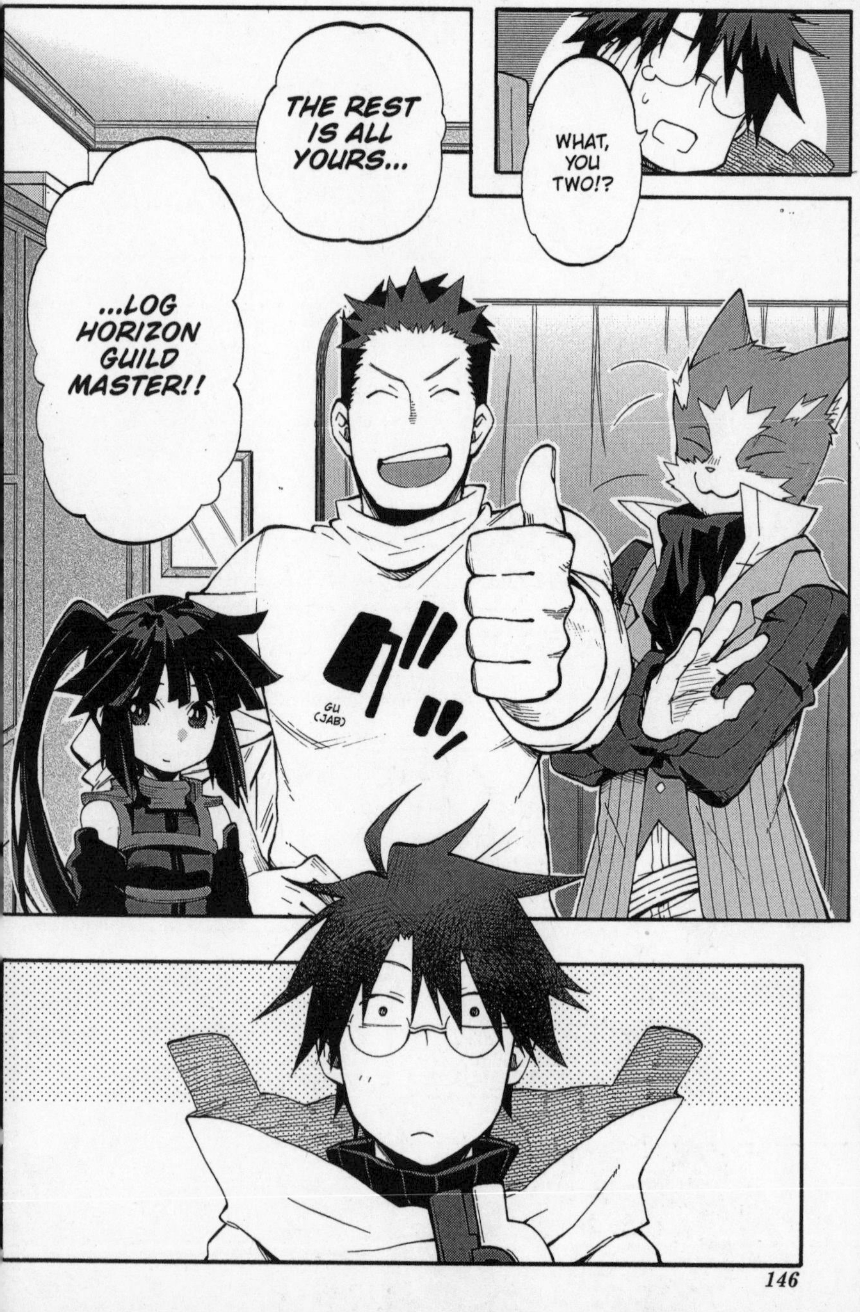
WHAT, YOU TWO!?
THE REST IS ALL YOURS...
...LOG HORIZON GUILD MASTER!!
GU (JAB)

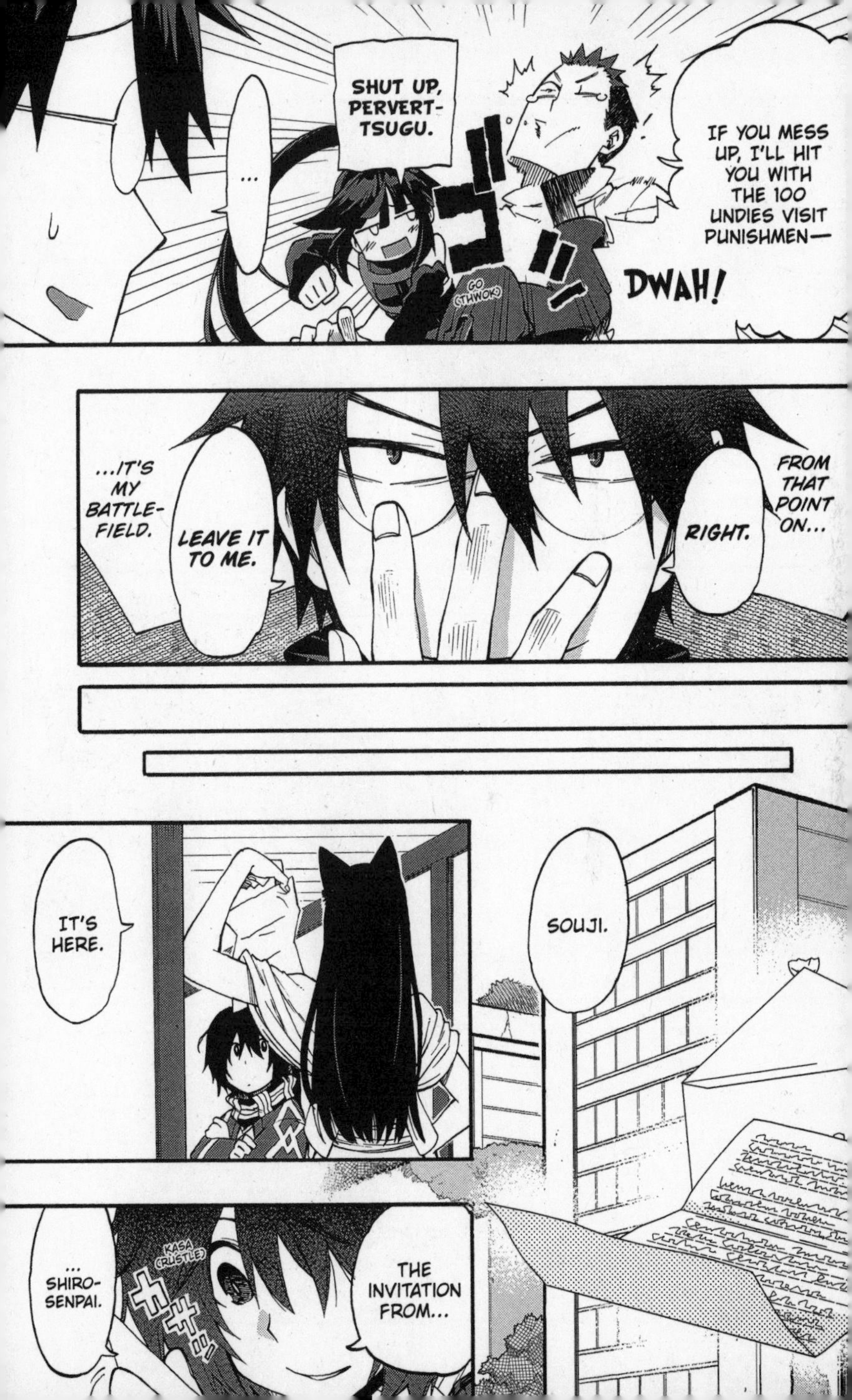
IF YOU MESS UP, I'LL HIT YOU WITH THE 100 UNDIES VISIT PUNISHMEN—
DWAH!
GO (THWOK)
SHUT UP, PERVERT-TSUGU.
...
FROM THAT POINT ON...
RIGHT.
LEAVE IT TO ME.
...IT'S MY BATTLE-FIELD.
SOUJI.
IT'S HERE.
THE INVITATION FROM...
KASA (RUSTLE)
... SHIRO-SENPAI.

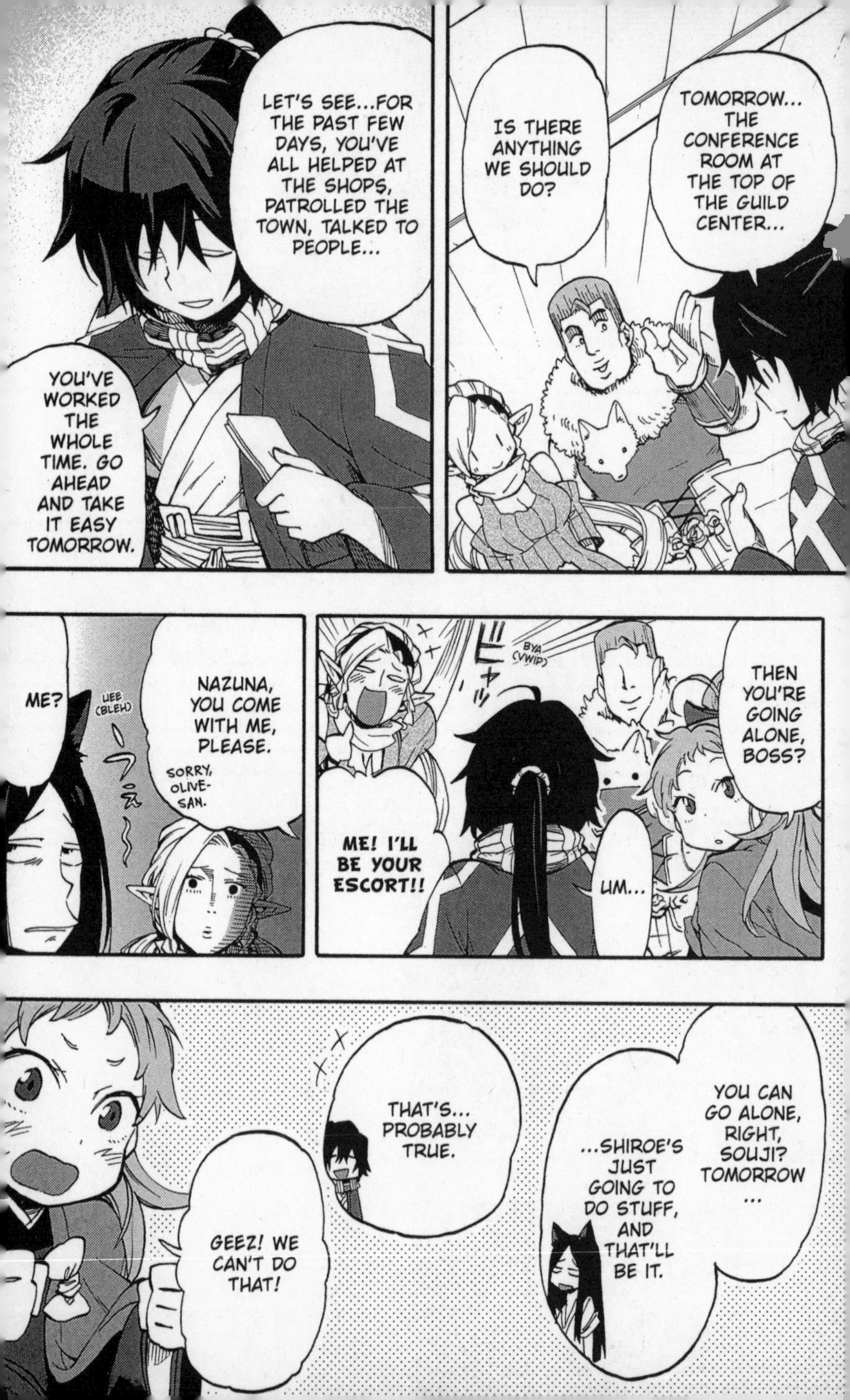
TOMORROW... THE CONFERENCE ROOM AT THE TOP OF THE GUILD CENTER...
IS THERE ANYTHING WE SHOULD DO?
LET'S SEE...FOR THE PAST FEW DAYS, YOU'VE ALL HELPED AT THE SHOPS, PATROLLED THE TOWN, TALKED TO PEOPLE...
YOU'VE WORKED THE WHOLE TIME. GO AHEAD AND TAKE IT EASY TOMORROW.
THEN YOU'RE GOING ALONE, BOSS?
BYA (VWIP)
UM...
ME! I'LL BE YOUR ESCORT!!
NAZUNA, YOU COME WITH ME, PLEASE.
SORRY, OLIVE-SAN.
UEE (BLEH)
ME?
YOU CAN GO ALONE, RIGHT, SOUJI? TOMORROW ...
...SHIROE'S JUST GOING TO DO STUFF, AND THAT'LL BE IT.
THAT'S... PROBABLY TRUE.
GEEZ! WE CAN'T DO THAT!

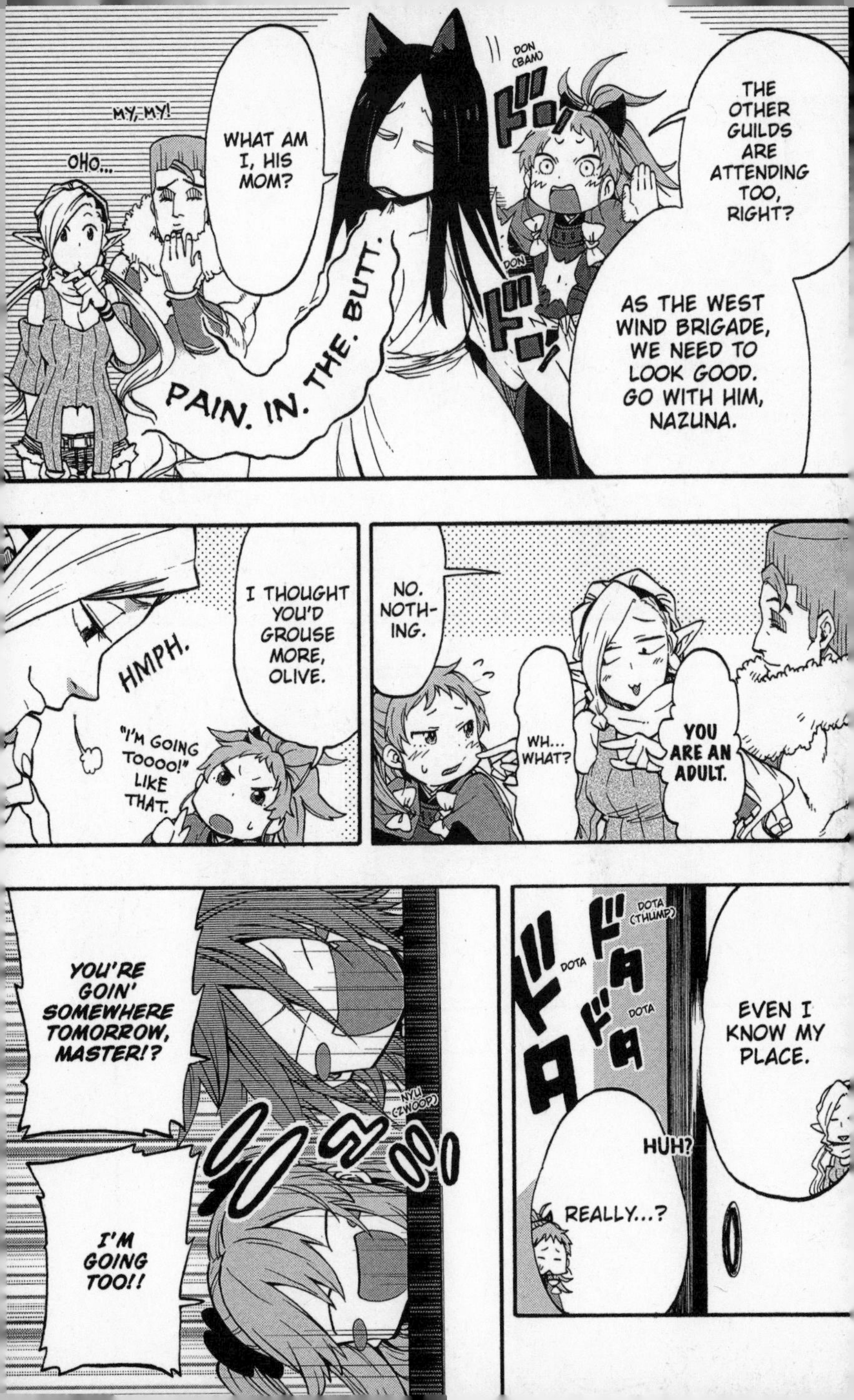
THE OTHER GUILDS ARE ATTENDING TOO, RIGHT?
DON (BAM)
DON
AS THE WEST WIND BRIGADE, WE NEED TO LOOK GOOD. GO WITH HIM, NAZUNA.
WHAT AM I, HIS MOM?
PAIN. IN. THE. BUTT.
MY, MY!
OHO...
YOU ARE AN ADULT.
WH... WHAT?
NO. NOTH-ING.
I THOUGHT YOU'D GROUSE MORE, OLIVE.
HMPH.
"I'M GOING TOOOO!" LIKE THAT.
EVEN I KNOW MY PLACE.
DOTA (THUMP)
DOTA
DOTA
HUH?
REALLY...?
YOU'RE GOIN' SOMEWHERE TOMORROW, MASTER!?
NYU (ZWOOP)
I'M GOING TOO!!

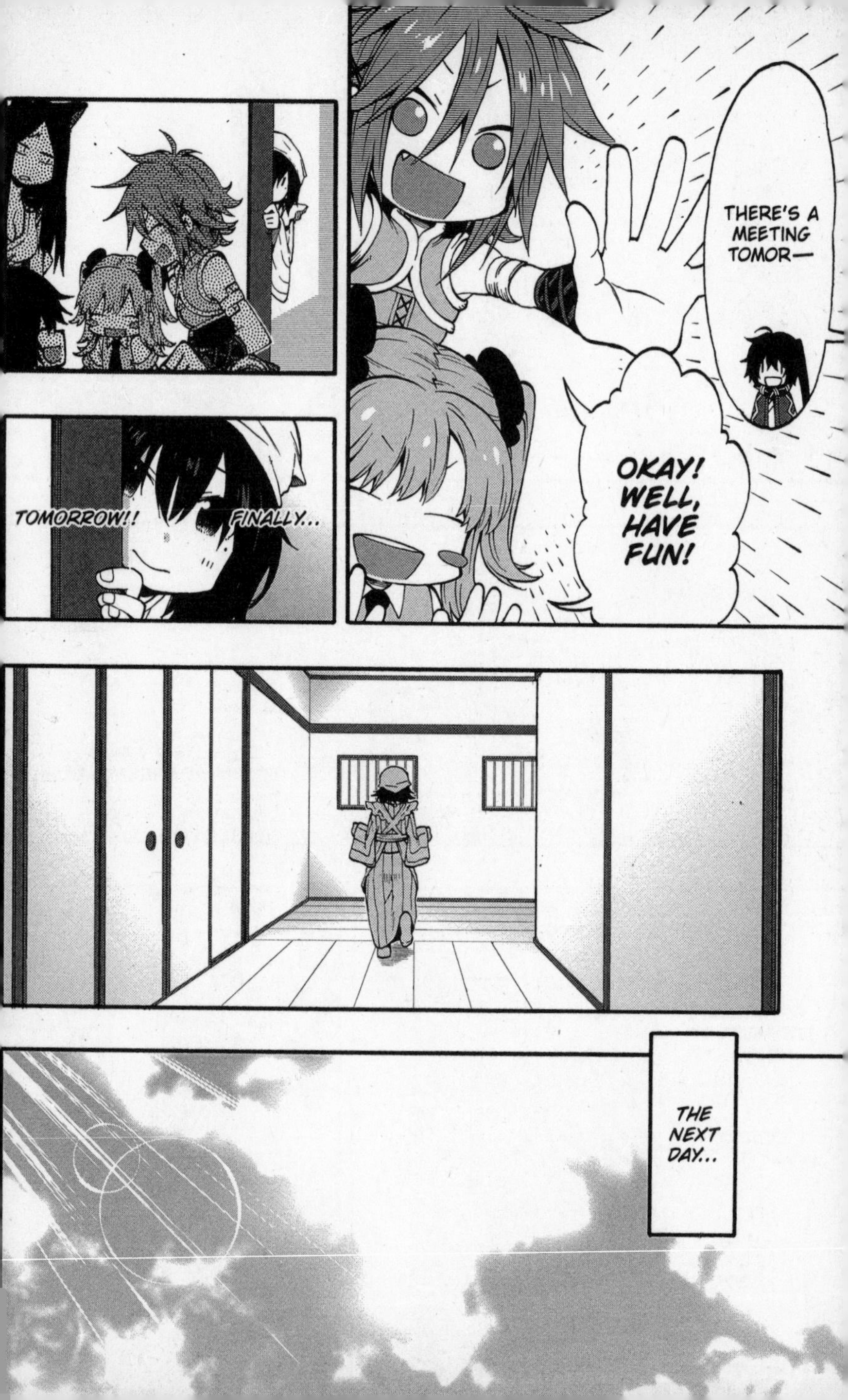
THERE'S A MEETING TOMOR—
OKAY! WELL, HAVE FUN!
FINALLY...
TOMORROW!!
THE NEXT DAY...

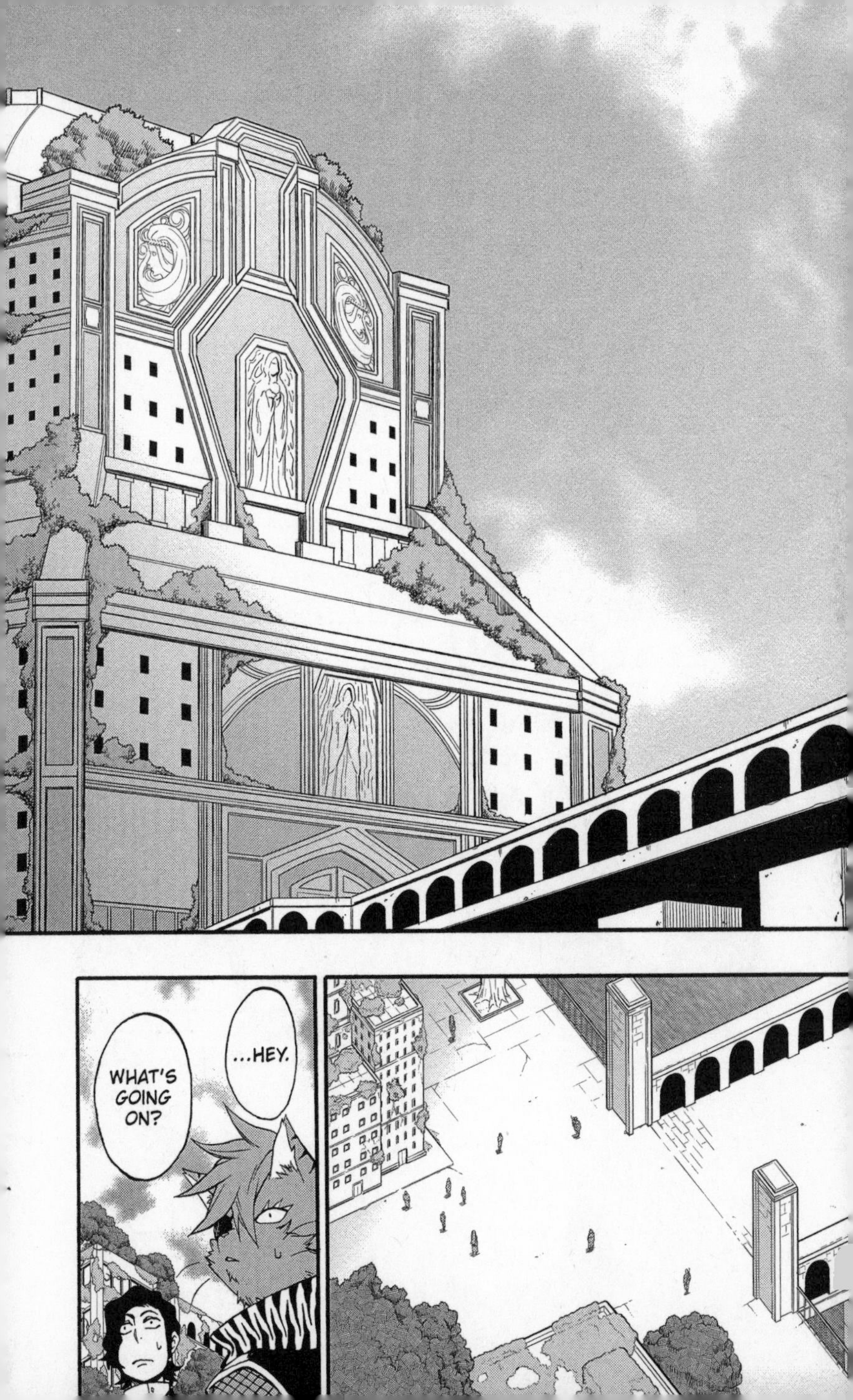
...HEY.
WHAT'S GOING ON?

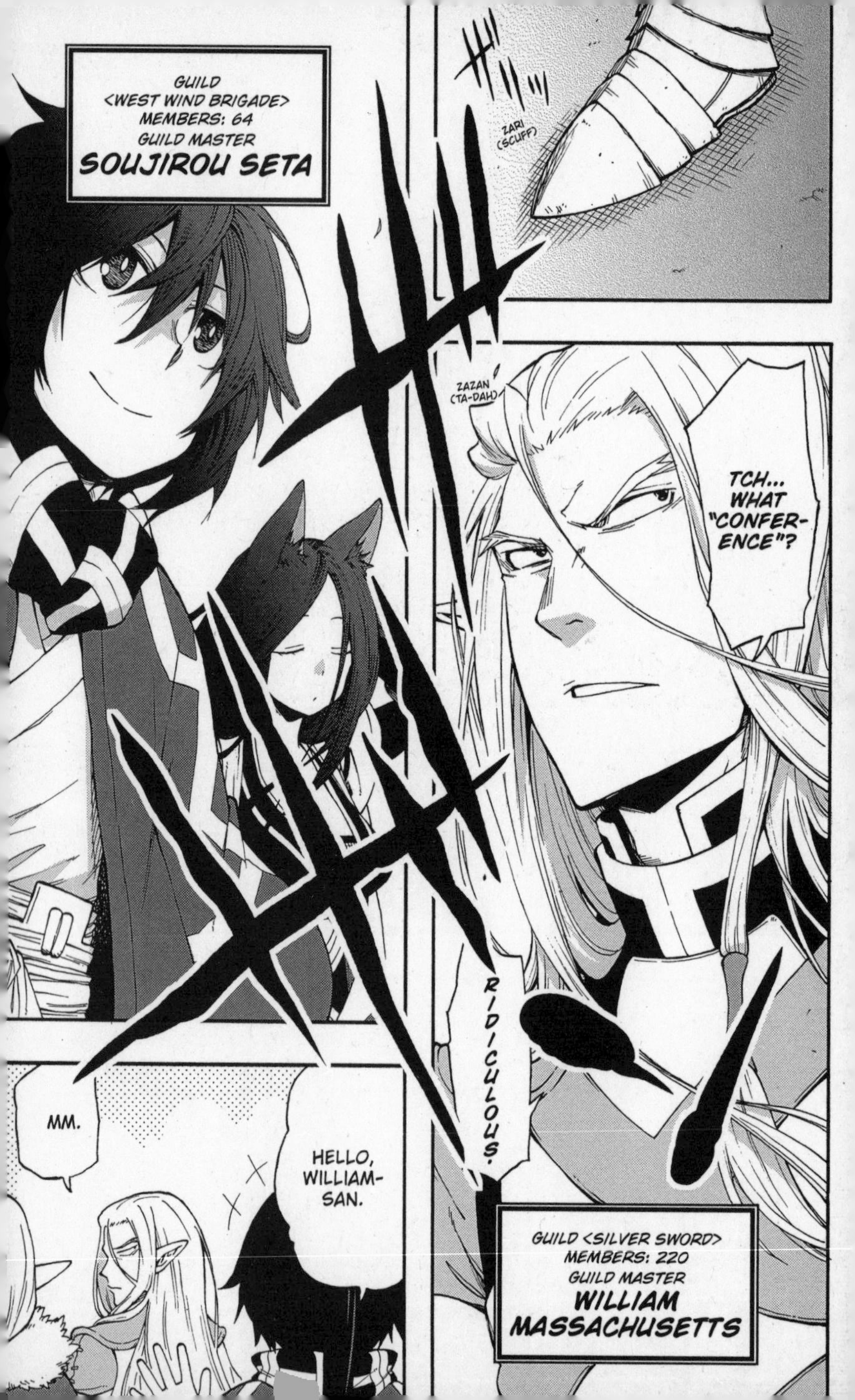
ZARI (SCUFF)
ZAZAN (TA-DAH)
TCH... WHAT "CONFERENCE"?
RIDICULOUS!
GUILD <SILVER SWORD> MEMBERS: 220 GUILD MASTER WILLIAM MASSACHUSETTS
GUILD <WEST WIND BRIGADE> MEMBERS: 64 GUILD MASTER SOUJIROU SETA
HELLO, WILLIAM-SAN.
MM.

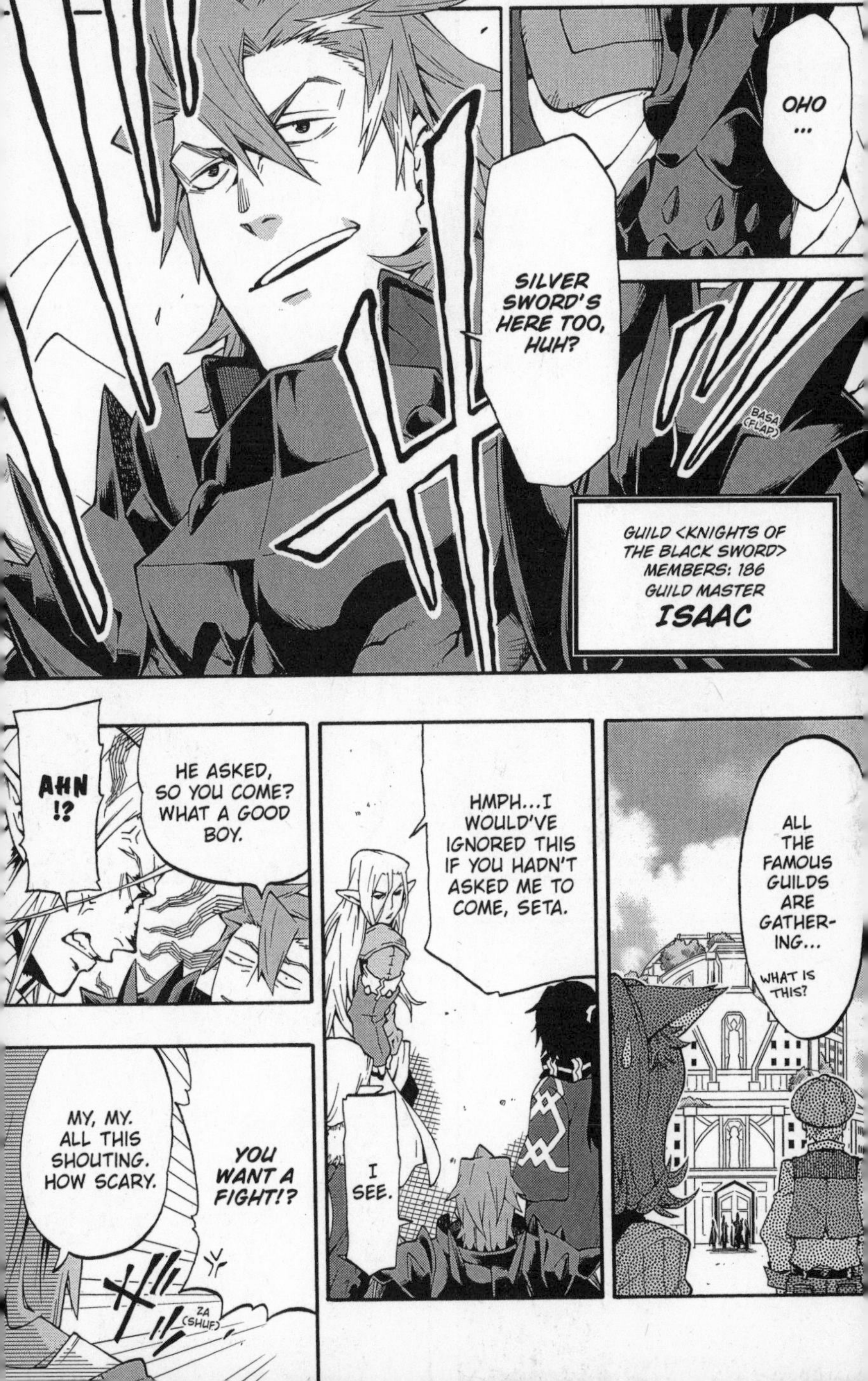
OHO ...
SILVER SWORD'S HERE TOO, HUH?
BASA (FLAP)
GUILD <KNIGHTS OF THE BLACK SWORD> MEMBERS: 186 GUILD MASTER ISAAC
ALL THE FAMOUS GUILDS ARE GATHERING...
WHAT IS THIS?
HMPH...I WOULD'VE IGNORED THIS IF YOU HADN'T ASKED ME TO COME, SETA.
I SEE.
HE ASKED, SO YOU COME? WHAT A GOOD BOY.
AHN !?
YOU WANT A FIGHT!?
MY, MY. ALL THIS SHOUTING. HOW SCARY.
ZA (SHUF)

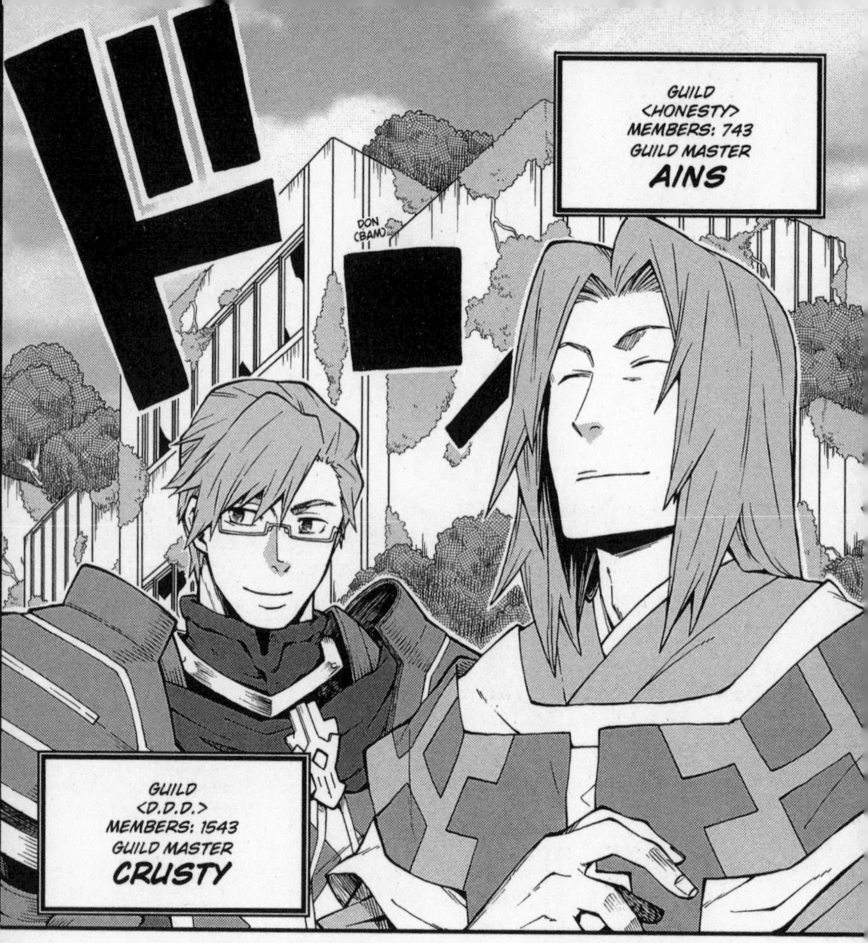
GUILD
<HONESTY>
MEMBERS: 743
GUILD MASTER
AINS
DON (BAM)
GUILD
<D.D.D.>
MEMBERS: 1543
GUILD MASTER
CRUSTY

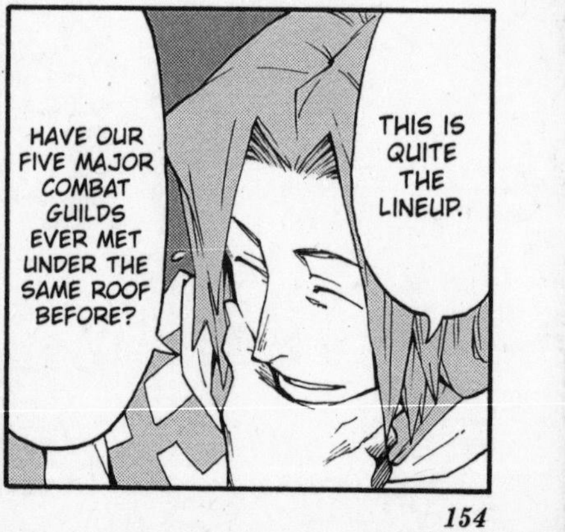
THIS IS QUITE THE LINEUP.
HAVE OUR FIVE MAJOR COMBAT GUILDS EVER MET UNDER THE SAME ROOF BEFORE?

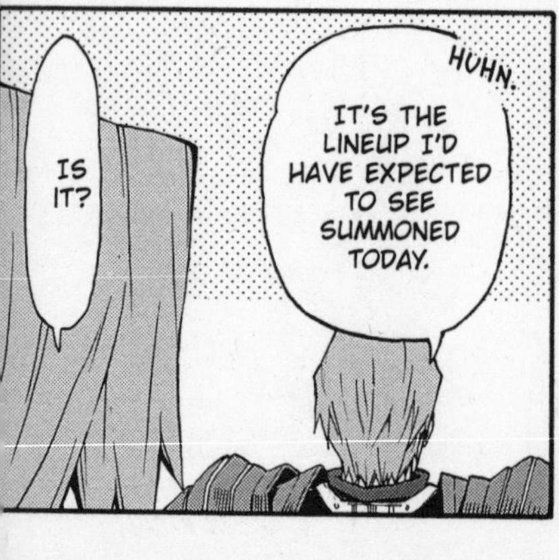
HUHN.
IT'S THE LINEUP I'D HAVE EXPECTED TO SEE SUMMONED TODAY.
IS IT?

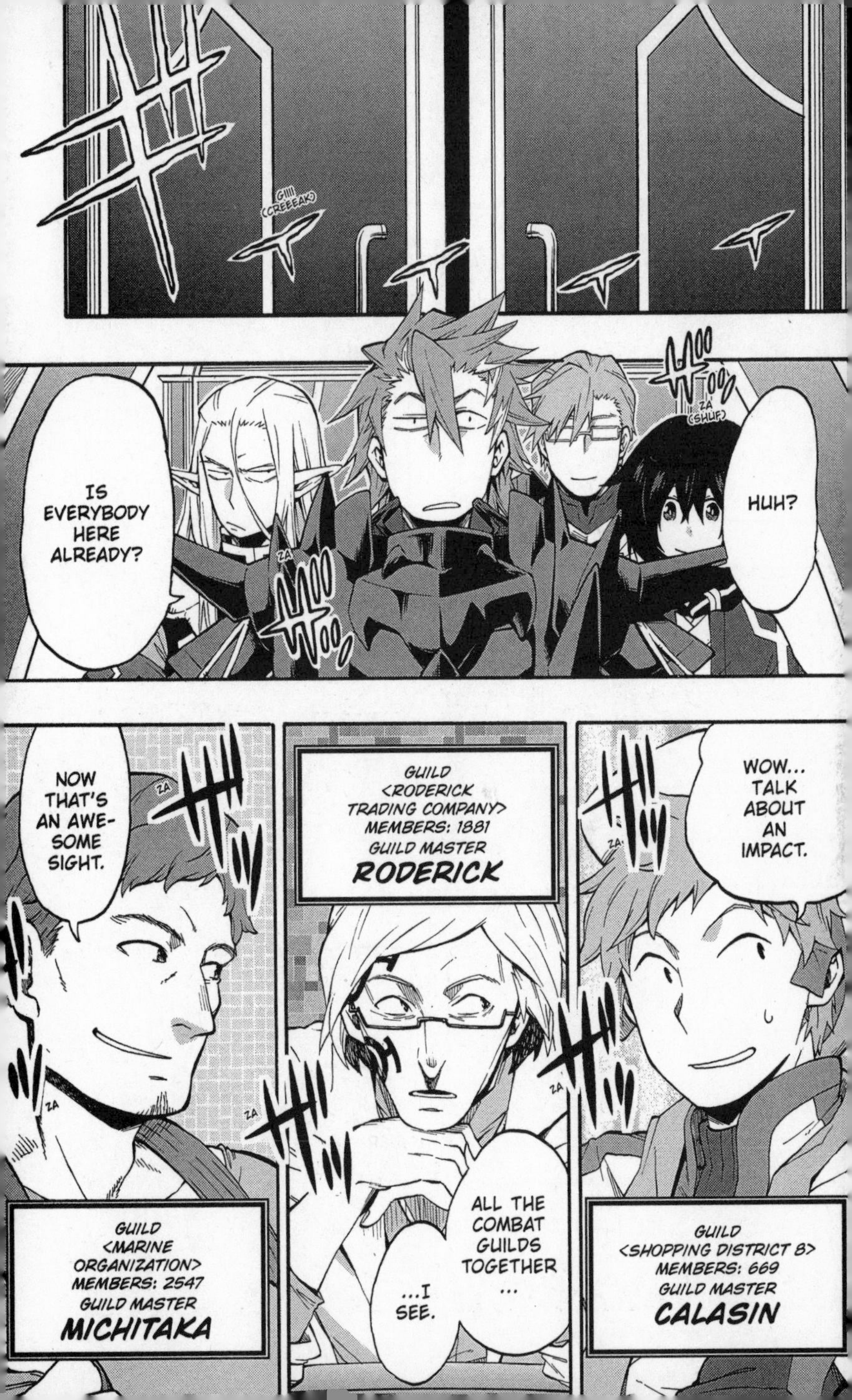
GIIII (CREEEAK)
HUH?
ZA (SHUF)
IS EVERYBODY HERE ALREADY?
ZA
WOW... TALK ABOUT AN IMPACT.
ZA
ZA
GUILD <SHOPPING DISTRICT 8> MEMBERS: 669 GUILD MASTER CALASIN
GUILD <RODERICK TRADING COMPANY> MEMBERS: 1881 GUILD MASTER RODERICK
ALL THE COMBAT GUILDS TOGETHER ...
...I SEE.
ZA
NOW THAT'S AN AWE-SOME SIGHT.
ZA
ZA
GUILD <MARINE ORGANIZATION> MEMBERS: 2547 GUILD MASTER MICHITAKA

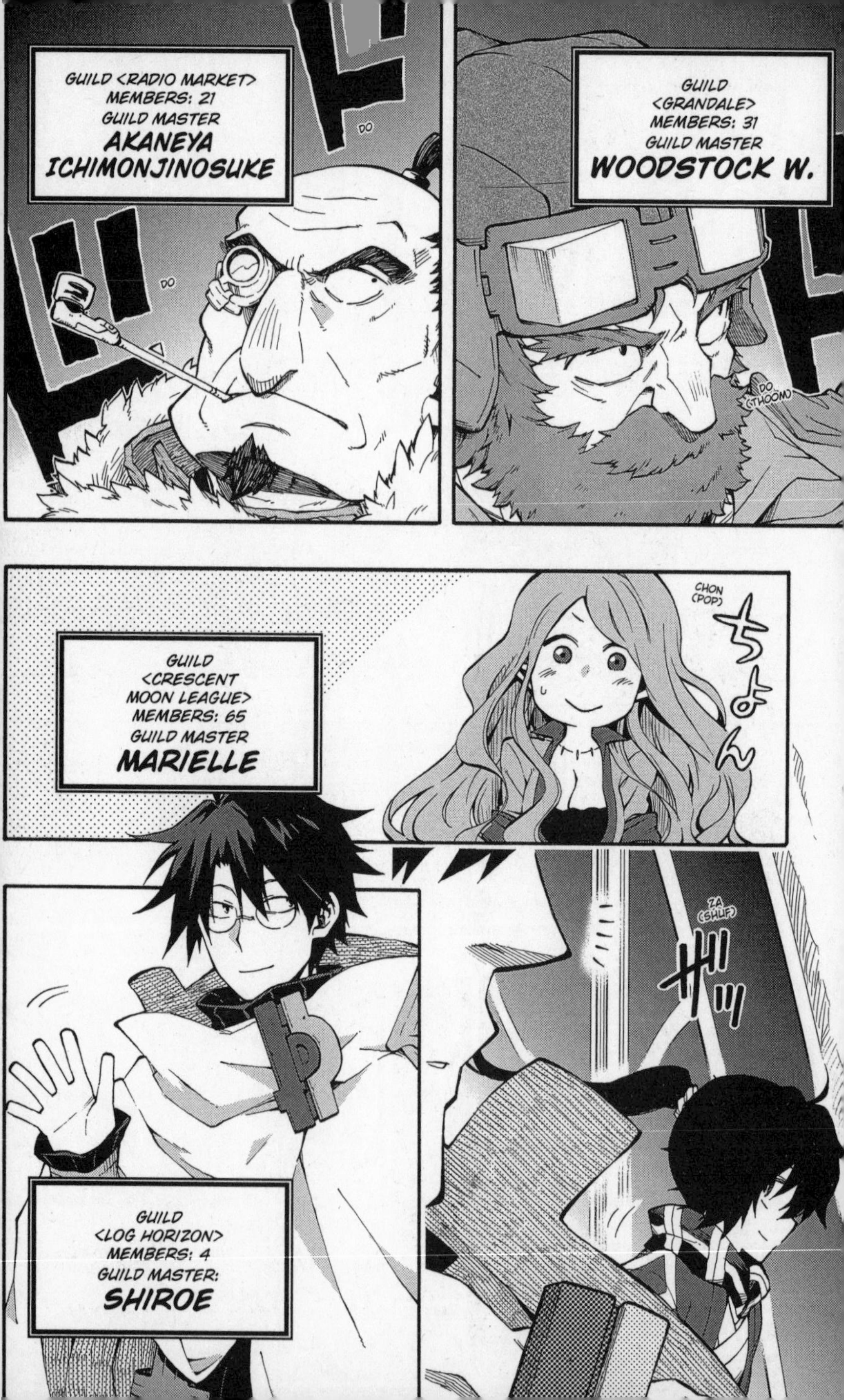
GUILD
<GRANDALE>
MEMBERS: 31
GUILD MASTER
WOODSTOCK W.
DO (THOOM)
GUILD <RADIO MARKET>
MEMBERS: 21
GUILD MASTER
AKANEYA ICHIMONJINOSUKE
DO
DO
CHON (POP)
ちょん
GUILD
<CRESCENT MOON LEAGUE>
MEMBERS: 65
GUILD MASTER
MARIELLE
ZA (SHUF)
ザッ
GUILD
<LOG HORIZON>
MEMBERS: 4
GUILD MASTER:
SHIROE

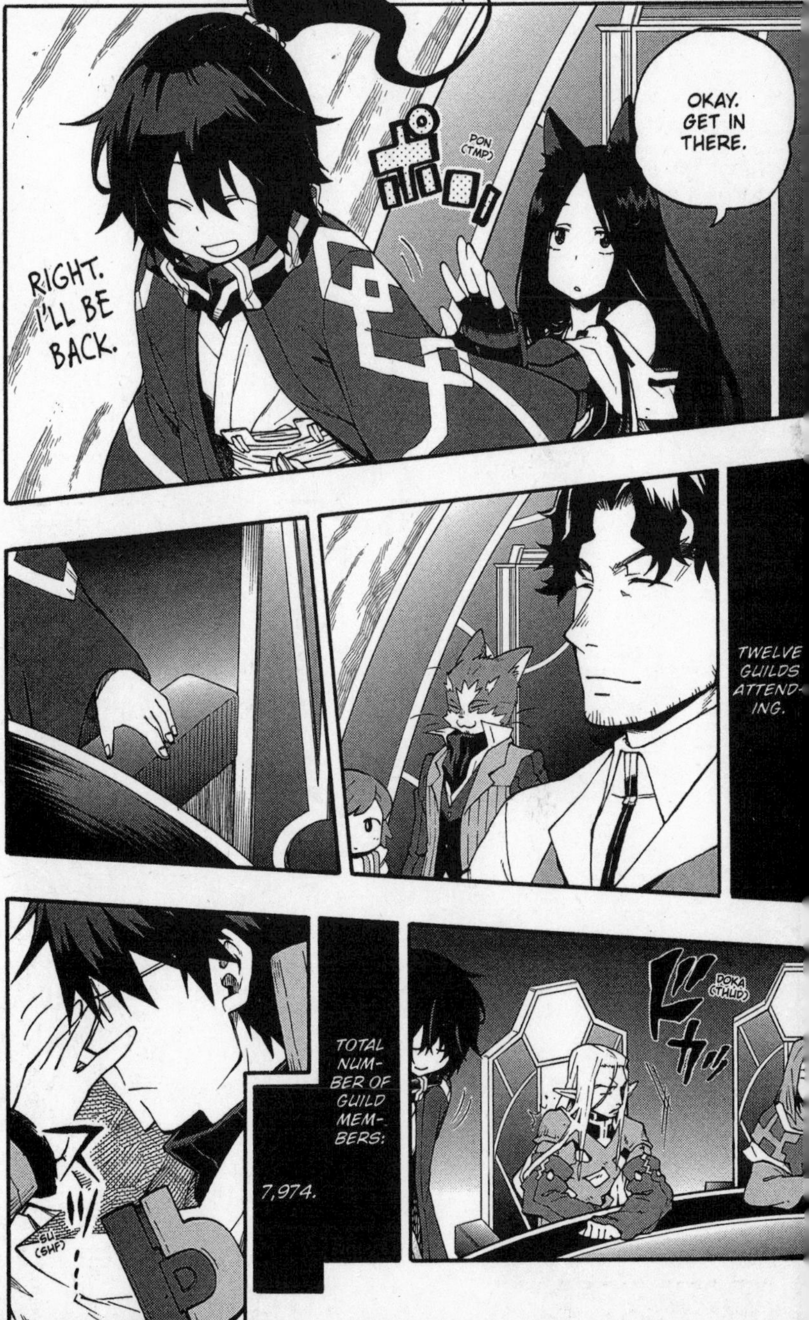
OKAY. GET IN THERE.
PON (TMP)
RIGHT. I'LL BE BACK.
TWELVE GUILDS ATTEND-ING.
DOKA (THUD)
TOTAL NUM-BER OF GUILD MEM-BERS:
7,974.
SU (SHF)

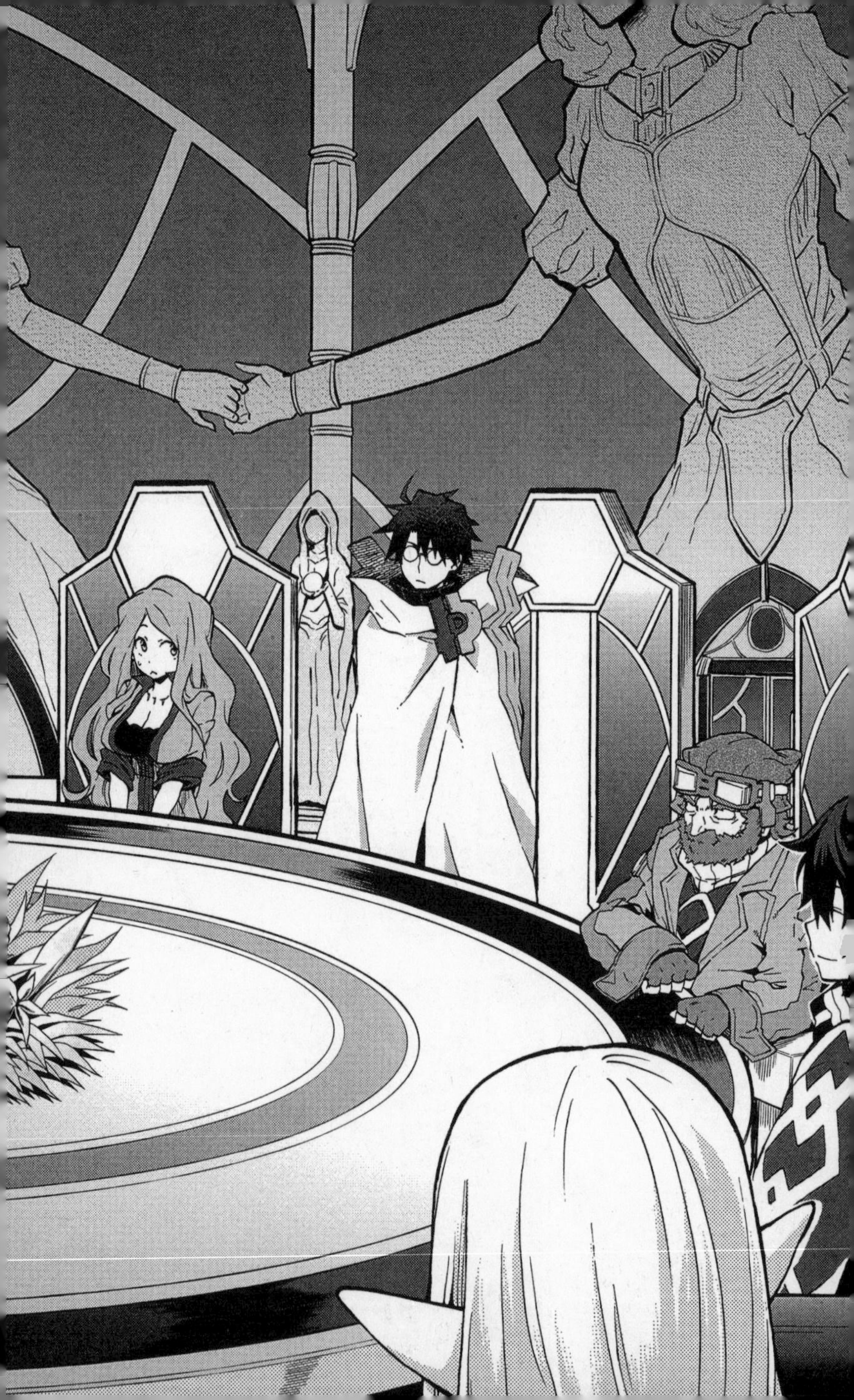

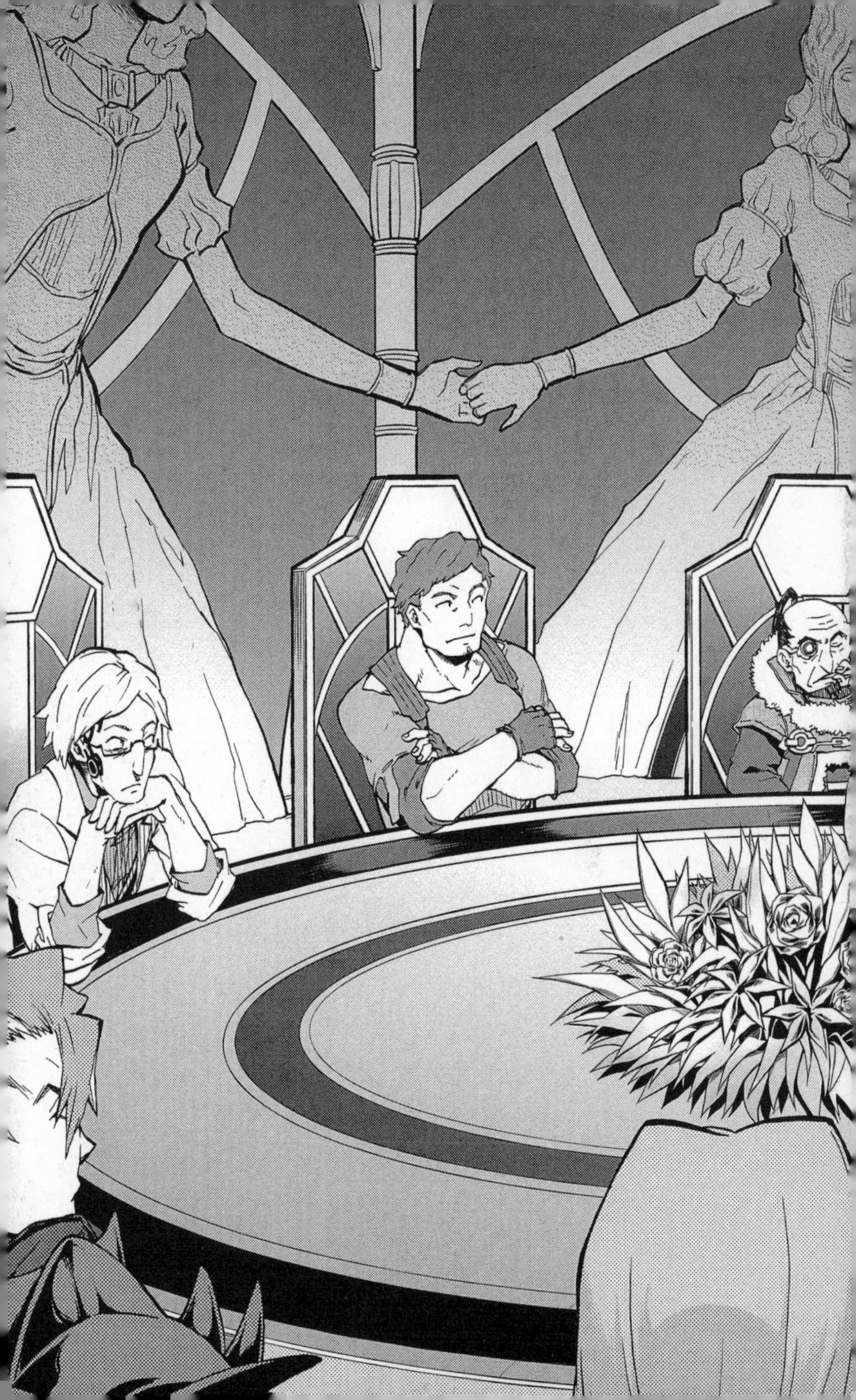

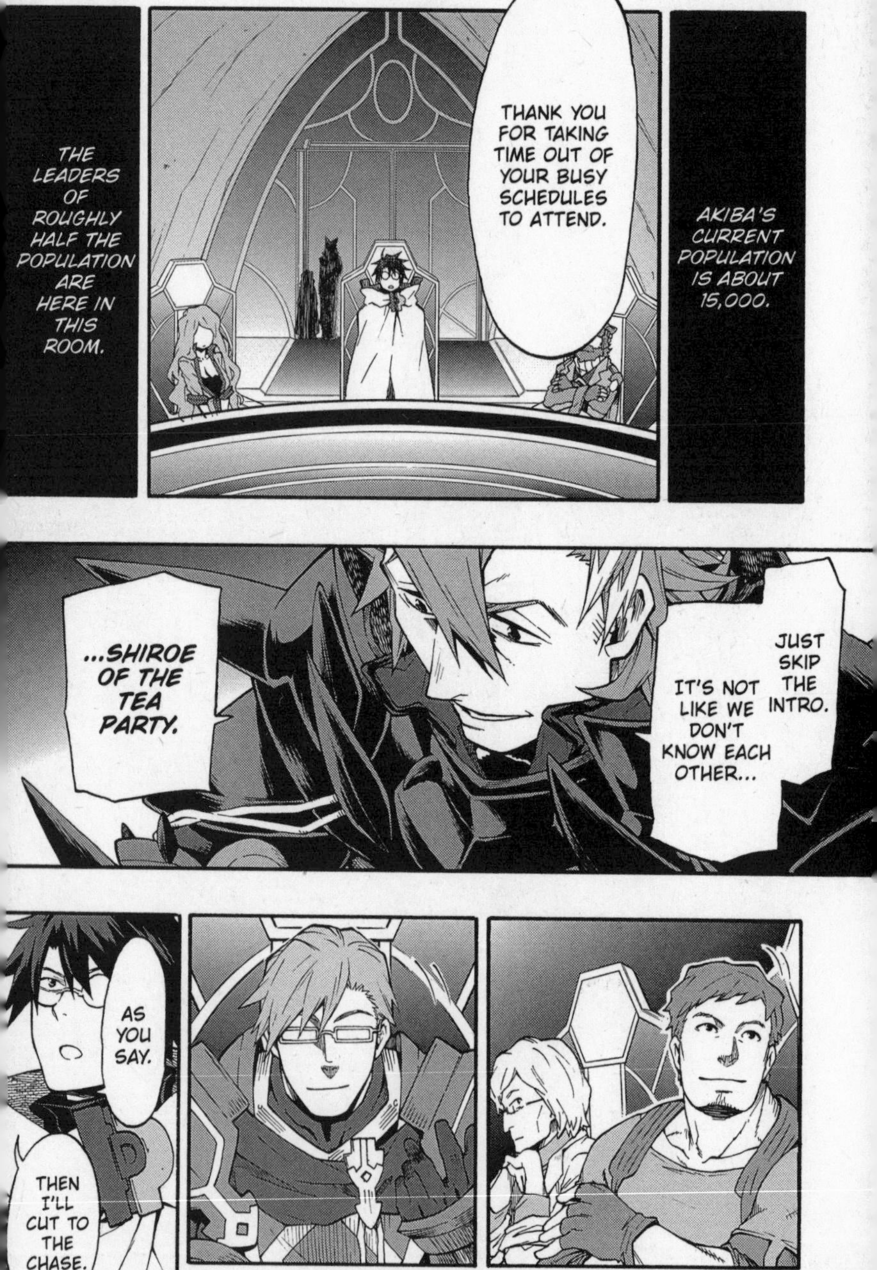
AKIBA'S CURRENT POPULATION IS ABOUT 15,000.
THANK YOU FOR TAKING TIME OUT OF YOUR BUSY SCHEDULES TO ATTEND.
THE LEADERS OF ROUGHLY HALF THE POPULATION ARE HERE IN THIS ROOM.
JUST SKIP THE INTRO.
IT'S NOT LIKE WE DON'T KNOW EACH OTHER...
...SHIROE OF THE TEA PARTY.
AS YOU SAY.
THEN I'LL CUT TO THE CHASE.

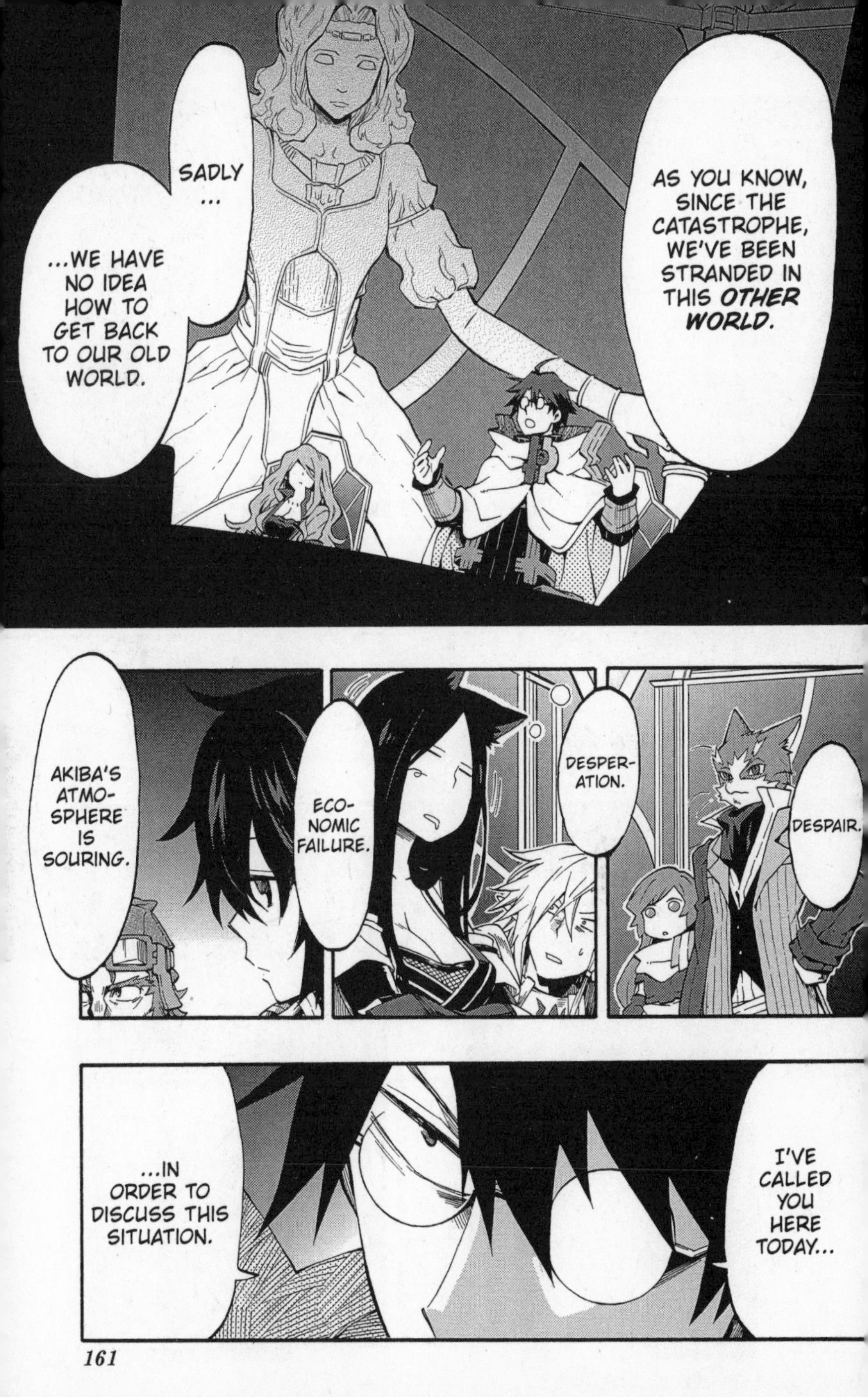
AS YOU KNOW, SINCE THE CATASTROPHE, WE'VE BEEN STRANDED IN THIS ***OTHER WORLD.***
SADLY ...
...WE HAVE NO IDEA HOW TO GET BACK TO OUR OLD WORLD.
DESPAIR.
DESPER-ATION.
ECO-NOMIC FAILURE.
AKIBA'S ATMO-SPHERE IS SOURING.
I'VE CALLED YOU HERE TODAY...
...IN ORDER TO DISCUSS THIS SITUATION.

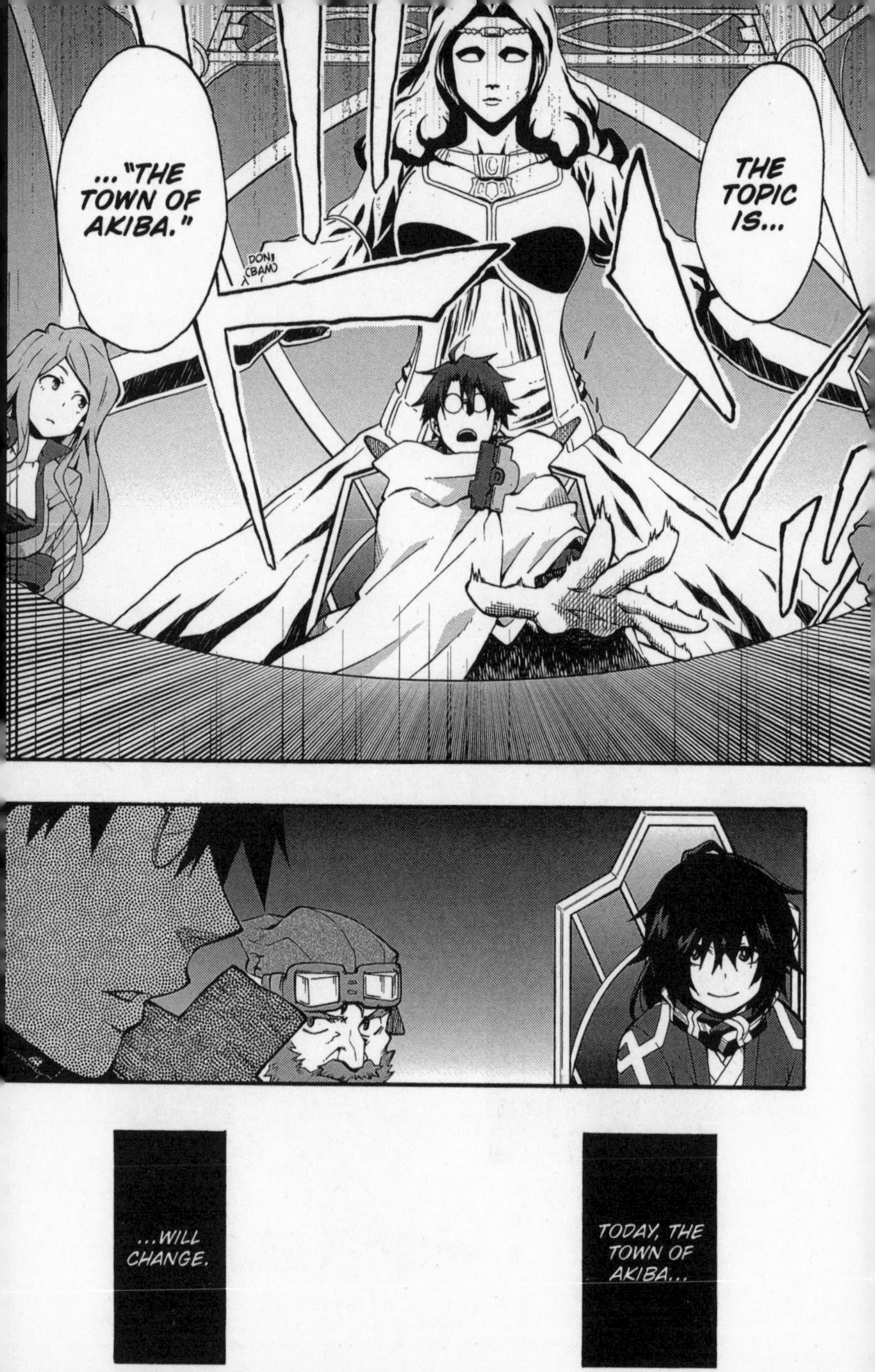
THE TOPIC IS...
..."THE TOWN OF AKIBA."
DON (BAM)
TODAY, THE TOWN OF AKIBA...
...WILL CHANGE.

TO BE CONTINUED IN VOLUME 5

LOG HORIZON
THE WEST WIND
BRIGADE 4

SPECIAL THANKS

ZAKI-SAN

AOKI-SAN

SAASHI-SAN

SONODA-SAN

ITSUKA-SAN

LOG HORIZON
THE WEST WIND BRIGADE ❹

ART: KOYUKI
ORIGINAL STORY: MAMARE TOUNO
CHARACTER DESIGN: KAZUHIRO HARA

Translation: Taylor Engel
Lettering: Brndn Blakeslee

LOG HORIZON NISHIKAZE NO RYODAN volume 4
© KOYUKI 2014
© TOUNO MAMARE, KAZUHIRO HARA 2014
First published in Japan in 2014 by KADOKAWA CORPORATION, Tokyo.
English translation rights arranged with KADOKAWA CORPORATION,
Tokyo, through Tuttle-Mori Agency, Inc., Tokyo.

Yen Press
1290 Avenue of the Americas
New York, NY 10104

Visit us at yenpress.com
facebook.com/yenpress
twitter.com/yenpress
yenpress.tumblr.com
instagram.com/yenpress

First Yen Press Edition: October 2016

Yen Press is an imprint of Yen Press, LLC.
The Yen Press name and logo are trademarks of Yen Press, LLC.

Library of Congress Control Number: 2015952586

ISBNs: 978-0-316-30910-3 (paperback)
        978-0-316-30911-0 (ebook)
        978-0-316-39516-8 (app)

10 9 8 7 6 5 4 3 2 1

BVG

Printed in the United States of America